HEALING THE EXPOSED BEING

HEALING THE EXPOSED BEING

A South African *Ngoma* Tradition

ROBERT J THORNTON

WITS UNIVERSITY PRESS

Wits University Press
1 Jan Smuts Avenue
Johannesburg 2001
www.witspress.co.za

First published in South Africa in 2017

ISBN 978-1-77614-018-3 (Print)
ISBN 978-1-77614-019-0 (PDF)
ISBN 978-1-77614-020-6 (EPUB N & S America, China)
ISBN 978-1-77614-021-3 (EPUB Rest of World)

Project managed by Hazel Cuthbertson
Edited by Pat Tucker
Proofread by Alison Lockhart
Indexed by Marlene Burger
Cover designed by Hothouse South Africa
Typeset by Newgen

Contents

List of figures

All images copyright the author unless otherwise specified.

---

*   The British Museum permits Wits University Press to use this image
        under a Creative Commons Attribution-NonCommercial-ShareAlike 4.0
        International (CC BY-NC-SA 4.0) licence.

Acknowledgements and dedication

I am grateful for the assistance of many individuals – sangomas, healers, colleagues in anthropology, botany, ethnobotany, archaeology, history, curators and other specialists.

I especially wish to acknowledge the close friendship with my collaborators during my work in Barberton: my teacher of *bungoma*, Magodweni (Fani Nkosi), my friend and assistant in many endeavours, Zelda Gama, my former student, Shado Dludlu, who became a sangoma and led me to Barberton, and guide and mentor, Joel Mnisi, in particular. Most of these friends have now passed away, as have most of the participants with whom I began my research in Barberton in 2000. They are deeply missed.

There were many others whom I do not name, but I am deeply grateful to them all.

In particular, I honour Sophie Jardim and the family of HIV orphans she raised together with her own children. I learned much from her and enjoyed her company and the meals she prepared from donated food for her large family. One member of her family, Catherine Mabila, helped me a great deal with the transcription and translation of material from videos that I shot with Zelda Gama, Joel Mnisi and Magodweni.

James G Harrison (Animal, Plant and Environmental Sciences, University of the Witwatersrand (Wits), Johannesburg) identified the beetle discussed in Chapter 9 as *B. ornatus*. He provided significant original research on the distribution of *B. ornatus* and supplied specimens from the university's collection for photography.

Jana Jiroušková (Naprstek Museum, Prague) gave me access to the Naprstek Museum archives and storerooms to enable me to examine the beetle amulet and associated materials in the Emil Holub Collection. Helena Gaudekova assisted me in exploring the collections. Gaudekova and Jiroušková also provided a forum for the first presentation of some of these ideas by inviting me to present a talk at the conference 'Museum and Cultural Identity' of the Réseau Internationale des Musées Ethnographique in Prague, 8–10 October 2012.

Catherine Elliott (Museum Assistant, Africa Collections, Department of Africa, Oceania and the Americas, British Museum) provided information relating to the British Museum examples of *B. ornatus* strung with beads.

Mark McGranaghan (Rock Art Research Unit, University of the Witwatersrand) steered me towards the Bleek-Lloyd online archive and pointed out that a beetle was referenced there. Sam Challis also provided guidance.

David Morris (Kimberley Museum, Kimberley, South Africa) provided invaluable assistance in understanding the Driekopseiland site where the rock engraving of *B. ornatus* was found (although the image is also part of the Bleek-Lloyd online archive).

Professors Anitra Nettleton (Wits Art Museum) and Kevin Balkwill (Botany, University of the Witwatersrand) had important discussions with me and supplied information that I have used in this book.

I profited greatly, too, from the comments and support of my readers and the conference attendees and seminar participants who listened to much of what is assembled here. Professor Richard Werbner and the members of the Satterthwaite Colloquium on African Religion and Ritual, held annually in Grasmere, England, were especially helpful.

The chapter on markets was significantly improved by discussions with Rijk van Dijk and Marliese Dekker at the seminar in Leiden out of which that chapter emerged.

Sarah A Bologne did an excellent job of editing the complete manuscript, suggesting many substantive changes as well as making the text more readable. I am grateful, too, for the insightful and helpful comments and suggestions from the anonymous readers. I am immensely grateful to all of these friends and colleagues.

I have published parts of this book in earlier publications. I thank the publishers for permission to reuse this material, and acknowledge its previous publication:

Chapter 4, 'The transmission of knowledge in *bungoma*', is based on an article, 'The transmission of knowledge in South African traditional healing', *Africa* 79(1): 17–34 (Special Issue edited by Trevor Marchand and Kai Kress. *Knowledge in practice: Expertise and the transmission of knowledge*, Edinburgh, UK: University of Edinburgh Press, 2009), and used with permission. Published online 19 May 2011 at: www.cambridge.org/core/journals/africa/article/div-classtitlethe-transmission-of-knowledge-in-south-african-traditional-healingdiv/AB7496C545C21C7A2045083D7DFC359B. DOI: 10.3366/E0001972008000582.

Chapter 5, 'Healing conflict' is derived, in part, from 'Four principles of South African political culture at the local level', *Anthropology Southern Africa* 28: 22–30 (25 September 2015). Published by Taylor and Francis on behalf of Anthropology Southern Africa association, and used with permission.

Parts of Chapter 6, 'Marginal utilities and the "hidden hand" of zombies' were originally published as a comment on Jane Guyer's 'Prophecy and the near future: Thoughts on macroeconomic, evangelical, and punctuated time', *American Ethnologist* 34(3): 437–439 (August 2007). Stable URL: www.jstor.org/stable/4496823.

Chapter 7, 'The market for healing', is derived in part from a chapter entitled 'The market for healing and the elasticity of belief: Medical pluralism in Mpumalanga, South Africa' in Marlene Dekker and Rijk van Dijk (eds), *Markets of well-being: Navigating health and healing in Africa* (African Dynamics Series, African Studies Centre): 144–172. Leiden, Netherlands: Brill, and used with permission.

My own ancestry provided surprising access to *bungoma*, the southern African healing tradition that recognises 'ancestors' as persons with a continuing interest in and influence over one's life.

My mother was able to read the entire manuscript as I was working on the final edit. She made comments and corrections on almost every page while I helped her through her final illness and sat with her through the work of dying. She died a month after having carefully worked through the manuscript. Reading her comments is like talking to her again and again. This book, like so much else, is better for what she did with her life. An educator, a scientist and intellectual, and a daughter, wife and mother, she engaged with me through everything I did, or attempted to do. She was a deeply involved citizen of the world in the many places where we lived and where I grew up: in Colorado, Iowa, Hawai'i, and Pennsylvania in the USA, in India and Uganda and later in many other parts of the world. She understood healing as she understood so much else.

Her father, Henry, was a Cornishman from a village on Bodmin Moor that lies in the midst of sacred wells, dolmens and stone structures of the most ancient Celtic traditions. I never heard him say that he was British, or from the UK. No, he was Cornish, clear and simple. He started his career as a miner at age 13 when his father was killed in a mining accident in the Keweenaw Peninsula that juts into Lake Superior on the USA and Canadian border.

My father, Givens, who grew up in Detroit, Michigan, the son of Appalachian economic refugees, taught me to watch and to listen. He supported his parents as a child soprano, singing on one of the first religious radio programmes, the controversial but extremely influential 'Father Coughlin's Radio Hour' at the Shrine of the Little Flower, Royal Oak, Michigan. My father taught us the central importance of music as cultural knowledge and taught me to sing and play the guitar. This background in southern USA and Appalachian rhythms, the music of Paul Robeson, George Gershwin (*Porgy and Bess*) and the Swing Bands, contained a kind of anthropological knowledge of pain, conflict, healing and transcendence that has always been with me. Though apparently far removed from southern African contexts of conflict and healing, the way in which deep humanism was encoded in the rhythms, melodies and lyrics of this music helped me to understand *ngoma* in its own terms.

My own ancestors, *emadloti*, also provided access to the deep knowledge of *ngoma*. The sangomas with whom I at first sought to work were deeply sceptical of whether I had the 'spirit', *umoya*, to understand their own understanding of the world. Was I just another white man seeking to capture their secrets? I explained my Celtic and Native American ancestry to Magodweni, a master healer who eventually became my teacher. All healers in Barberton had some knowledge of Native American and Celtic spiritualism from popular media, and perhaps especially from their white and coloured (to use the South African 'customary', canonical categories) clients who often also revered these traditions – what little they knew of them – from popular healing literature, media and practice.

Magodweni told me that he had consulted his ancestors. They were able, he said, to contact my ancestors through their shared spiritual connections. The connection between healers was 'like the Internet', he said, but did not, as far as he knew, include white people. In his dream, he said, he saw his ancestors speaking with mine on one side of a room, and me, 'the Prof', on the other side. His ancestors told him, 'you may teach Manyeva (my siSwati name) our knowledge'. This was a pivotal moment of entry.

I must acknowledge, therefore, my great-grandmother (my father's father's mother), Cornelia Alice Slone Thornton, a Kentucky Appalachian healer who preserved both Celtic-Appalachian and Cherokee healing traditions. She was a descendant of Aaron (Tsulagi'ugwiyuhi Totsu'hwa), known as Chief Red Bird, of Clay and Harlan Counties, Kentucky. Healing knowledge in this cultural tradition was 'women's knowledge' in the matrilineal societies of the mountains, and since she only had sons, this family tradition was lost, especially when she was forced to follow her sons to the northern city of Detroit.

My brother, Jonathan, found a letter in our family archive praising Alice's healing gift. Lizzie McNeil, Alice Slone's neighbour in Kentucky, wrote:

> She was one woman who lived just to do good – first for God, and then all others. No difference who it was, class creed or race if they were in trouble or suffering she was right on the scene. So many remember and love her as a ministering angel, bringing brightness and comfort into a dark room of gloom and suffering. Old Aunt May Ann Warren said it just seemed Alice Slone had magic in her touch. Since she was a girl people would send for her, such soft tender hands could move a sick person so gentle and easy and charm the pain away.

I dedicate this book to the memory of the healing traditions of Magodweni, my teacher of *bungoma*, and to my own ancestors, who, in one way or another, provided access to this marvellous African philosophy and practice of healing.

I received funding from the National Research Foundation (South Africa) and from the University of the Witwatersrand during the research and writing of this project, for which I am extremely grateful.

FIGURE 1: Alice Slone Thornton, my great-grandmother, a true healer in the Appalachian and Eastern Cherokee traditions.

CHAPTER 1

Bungoma or 'philosophy of the drum' in the South African Lowveld

There are many 'traditional healers' in South Africa. There are many healing traditions and indeed many different names and epithets for them, such as 'witchdoctor', 'shaman' or 'rainmaker'. The term 'sangoma' is used here to refer to a specific set of healers who have undergone strict training, initiation and induction into a guild, college or lodge of such healers. *Bungoma* is the term used for the general practice and 'philosophy' or knowledge and expertise associated with this practice. Jo Wreford (2005, 2008), who, as an anthropologist, has not only studied the life and practices of the sangoma but has been initiated as a practising sangoma, also uses the South African English term 'sangomas' or the isiZulu form *izangoma sinyanga*. Here the focus is specifically on sangomas, or what John Janzen (1992) has called practitioners of the art and philosophy of *ngoma*, itself fairly pervasive in the Bantu-speaking areas of Africa south of the equator (Janzen 1992; Van Dijk, Reis and Spierenburg 2000). This book is based, as explained more fully below, on research in eastern Mpumalanga province, just north of Swaziland and near South Africa's border with Mozambique.

The sangomas' public rituals of dancing and drumming, their peculiar dress styles, hairstyles and reliance on 'magic' or 'medicine' (*muti*) are generally well known (Hammond-Tooke 1989, 1994; Hammond-Tooke and Schapera 1974), especially in rural villages and the townships of small and rural towns in southern Africa. Most South Africans know at least this much about sangomas. But what I have called 'healing' is more than curing illness, even though illness is one of the primary concerns of healing.

When the sangomas I talk about here 'heal' (*kwelapha*), they think of this as 'making life' or 'making to live' (*kuphila*). The word for 'life', *imphilo*, also means 'health'. The root word, *-phil-* or 'life'/'health', connotes not so much a state of being as *being* itself. When one greets another in South African Nguni languages (isiZulu, siSwati, isiXhosa), one asks, '*Uphila njane?*' ('How are you living?'). The standard response is '*Ngisaphila*' ('I am alive') or '*Ngikhona*' ('I am here'). Without reading too much into these ordinary words, the greeting means that to be 'here' is to be alive and, more simply, to be. According to Van Dijk, Reis and Spierenburg:

> *Bungoma* denominates a southern African discourse whose subject is the coming to fruition of life and whose object is to ensure this fruition and to remove obstacles to it ... [for us] it has become clear that *ngoma* may pertain to all spheres of life – the personal, the social, the political, the economic and the ecological (2000: 6; Engelke 2001: 148).

In other words, *bungoma*, in the sense that it is understood by the people and expresses the ideas written about here, encompasses the economic, political and ecological. Despite its scope, however, it remains a marginal activity practised by a small minority. Each of these social fields is examined in turn and throughout the work.

Most of these healing traditions accomplish nothing like a 'cure'; most leave cures to biomedicine. The healing that these healers accomplish, then, is best understood as a response to life rather than – as is the case with biomedicine – a response to illness or disease. The individual person, caught in complex nets of relationships with other persons, is the focus of the philosophy and practice of *bungoma*. It is not simply the person – as 'body', 'spirit', or 'soul' – that the healer attempts to 'work on' (*kusebenta*) and thus to heal, but rather the network of influences that affect the life of the person.

The southern African philosophy of 'life' has been called ubuntu. The word means, most simply, 'humanness'. Much has been written and said about how southern Africans understand the person to be the product of other persons. It has been positioned, for instance, by Archbishop Emeritus Desmond

Tutu and President Nelson Mandela, as defining a South African character and is based on a common South African saying, '*umuntu ngumuntu ngabantu* (a person is a person through other people)', in which the root word *-ntu* means 'person'/'human' (Tutu 1999: 31; Van Binsbergen 2005). This approximates the meaning of the Kiswahili phrase *mtu ni watu* (Kresse 2007: 169), 'a person is people', and similar maxims in most other Bantu languages.

This mutuality of self-creation is very much the province of the healer, but primarily with respect to its darker, less talked about aspects. As people create other people they also retain lasting influence over each other. The ancestors (*emadloti*) are necessarily part of 'humanity', that is, ubuntu. Because of their humanity – and not withstanding their immateriality – they are both the source of misfortune and disease and the source of the power to heal these. This is because the ancestors have suffered and experienced violence and death and can therefore transcend them (Thornton 2008: 204–210; Ngubane 1977: 47–55). In other words, all persons stand not merely in relation to others – as friends, enemies, kin, spouses, colleagues and even strangers – but are also inescapably exposed to each other. It is this exposure or vulnerability to others that can ultimately weaken life itself and lead to illness, disease, misfortune and death. Each person is therefore an 'exposed being'.

Few healers in southern Africa are in any standard sense 'traditional', if by this term we mean rooted in the past, or deriving their knowledge and practices from long-established usage and custom. The healers written about here, however, say that they are 'traditional' and are mostly content with the label 'traditional healers' (Wreford 2008: xii). One of the most popular organisations for 'traditional healers' holds this precise name: the Traditional Healers Organisation (THO). But they are also not 'modern'. It could be said that they mitigate the failures of the modern and fill the aporia of medicine's and modernity's grand narratives with *local knowledge* or "local frames of awareness" (Geertz 1983: 6) and their own personal histories of seeking out what appears to be the closest thing to 'tradition' that can be found in their and our cultural environments (Thornton 1987). They mix and mingle ideas and practices, they innovate and change. The healers I have worked with and known as friends and collaborators travel long distances around the southern African region – they share knowledge, test treatments and collaborate with each other.

Surprisingly, the knowledge and practices of each healer are distinctively individual. Southern African traditional healers are less concerned with categories of disease and illness than they are with the intricacy of personal relations in the particular contexts of the patients they treat. Just as each patient is unique, so is each healer, and so is each intervention. It is not possible, therefore, to speak of healing – *bungoma* – as 'culture' or a 'worldview'. While the practice and philosophy is not entirely coherent, there is what we might call a 'grammar' that structures action; however, each healing episode, like each utterance of a language, is different.

It has been common in previous literature about healers to associate them with a 'culture', thus Zulu healers are Zulu, Xhosa healers are Xhosa, and so on. This association presumes that traditional healers constitute a homogeneous cultural block that can be characterised in ethnic terms. This is neither accurate nor useful, since healers, their clients, patients and students come from across the breadth of southern Africa, and even outside of it. In southern Africa, at least, healers deserve to be understood on their own terms – as semi-autonomous cultural brokers, organic philosophers and creative agents.

These healing traditions *parallel* each other through people's lives, apparently without one dominating or excluding the other. In fact, several parallel medical systems are understood as supporting each other (Wreford 2005: 1). Rather than being alternative or complementary, healing systems in this case appear to be understood as *additive* and *parallel* (Fadlon 2004; Pedersen and Baarts 2010). In the words of Judith Fadlon (2004), what was once 'alternative' or even opposed to biomedicine has now become 'domesticated'. It is part of the same 'market' for healing.

Inge Pedersen and Charlotte Baarts (2010: 1068) describe clients of multiple complementary and alternative medicine (CAM) and biomedical health providers in Copenhagen, Denmark, as searching for healing options and healers based on their notion of *expertise*:

> Expertise is: (i) embodied and produced by means other than those used in evidence-based knowledge or abstract expert systems; (ii) constructed by making a clear-cut division between the roles and responsibilities of the practitioner and the user; and (iii) constructed on the basis of specific training or education that practitioners have achieved.

The expertise that the users seek and construct is not necessarily available, and users therefore consult many different kinds of experts.

In general, three main forms of healing are practised by African traditional healers and their clients, all of which involve specific forms of expertise: (1) the healing practised by sangomas who have 'graduated' after a period of tuition and self-healing and passed through initiation; (2) the more general 'doctoring' practised by inyangas who (mostly) use or sell herbal remedies; and (3) the *amaprofeti* (from the English 'prophets') who practise faith healing in terms of one or other form of African syncretic Christianity. All these forms of healing make a 'clear-cut division between the roles and responsibilities of the practitioner and the user' (Pedersen and Baarts 2010: 1068), whether or not the services offered are in fact efficacious.

None of these categories is exclusive, however. Sangomas typically belong to Christian churches, and may also practise faith healing; some herbalists do too, and faith healers occasionally dispense herbs. Specific to sangomas, however, is their ritual incorporation into a particular profession in whose practices and beliefs they are trained. They undergo a rigorous and exhausting period of apprenticeship (*ukuthwasa*) and perform a 'graduation ceremony' – known as 'eating the *intwaso*' – often lasting several days and nights. Thereafter, as long as they have fulfilled a range of strict conditions they may pass into the full status of a sangoma and membership of their teacher's school (Chapter 3). The process of teaching and learning the profession of the sangoma, then, distinguishes it from the many other forms of healing with which it runs in parallel and competes.

Each type of healing augments the person in different ways. Healers can be described as participating in a market for healing, which allows for the operation of parallel healing traditions as though they existed in a market. For instance, the role of zombies – persons who are magically captured by their controllers in order to work for them – can be understood in terms of marginal utility and the 'hidden hand' in classical economics (Chapter 6). The participation of healers and their patients in complex exchanges of 'energy' can also be presented as a kind of market for healing (Chapter 7).

Some might attribute the apparent efficacy of parallel healing methods to what could be called 'belief' (Good 1994: 40) and the 'placebo effect', but it is now known that these effects are physiologically real, genetically and culturally variable and contribute substantially to overall health and perception of pain in biomedical practice (Bishop, Jacobson, Shaw and Kaptchuk 2012; Finniss, Kaptchuk, Miller and Benedetti 2010; Hall, Loscalzo and Kaptchuk 2015; Kirsch 2011; Wiley and Allen 2013: 69–70). The placebo (Latin, 'I shall be acceptable or pleasing', from *placer*, 'to please') effect refers to the fact that if a patient believes a medication might or should be effective it will have some effect, despite the fact that there is no active ingredient, or nothing, that is, that will have any measurable physiological, chemical or medicinal effect on the body.

But I have also seen as much scepticism as belief in my years of interaction with the southern African tradition of *bungoma*. There are no grounds to conclude that the success of traditional healers in the context described is due to a generalised *cultural* acceptance of the practice simply because it is 'traditional'. Rather, belief in the healing power of *bungoma* is a pragmatic choice in a multi-therapeutic environment (Flint 2008).

During my experience with healers and with healing in one part of South Africa it was difficult to identify a single structural theme, or even an identifiable and stable social or cultural *structure*. Accordingly, a number of the standard categories of social analysis are discussed, including religion (Chapter 2), politics (Chapters 4, 5), economy (Chapters 6, 7) and science (Chapters 9, 10) in an effort to approach *bungoma* through a multi-modal analysis that exposes its essential kaleidoscopic quality.

As an 'economy' it exhibits a number of market-like qualities that allow clients and patients to select one type of healer, or even many at the same time. Notions of the zombie, as the occult capture of persons in a way that deprives the zombie of agency – that is, of personhood – in order to secure profits or to 'bring money', rest on obvious business metaphors. The capture of zombies is even discussed as a form of 'outsourcing' (Chapter 6). But *bungoma* is also political because people have power over one another and are vulnerable or *exposed to others*. This notion of mutual exposure of persons to each other, and to other forces, is fundamental to the way in which *bungoma* is conceived and how it works. However, this also implies a play of social power in a way that demands a kind of political analysis. But, since this 'political' analysis is limited to the local scale of person-to-person networks, it is not political in the standard sense of having to do with negotiation and the distribution of state resources. Alternatively, 'scale is an effect of power' (Dilger,

Kane and Langewick 2012: 16) and the limitation of traditional healing to the local is inevitably bound up with its struggle in the general economy and politics of healing. 'Healing and medicine in Africa reveals a great deal about politics and power, social organisation and economic conditions', Dilger, Kane and Langewick (2012: 1) argue, as well as about 'global regimes of value and local practices of valuing bodies, kin, and community'.

Many have argued that traditional healing in Africa should qualify as 'religion', that is, as a proto-religion that anticipates Christianity in some way, especially the belief in a 'high god'. The first missionaries, such as Robert Moffat (1846) and David Livingstone (1857), soundly rejected this idea (see Chapter 2), but later missionaries and Christians have wanted to bring 'African' religion into the fold of world religions (Chidester 1996; Chidester, Kwenda and Petty 1997). Indeed, African traditional rituals and practices have made a deep impact on the practice of Christianity in southern Africa.

It is argued here, however, that African healing practices do not constitute a deficient or proto-religion any more than they are a deficient or proto-medicine, or a deficient science (Chapter 10). Instead, it seems that they are a radically material logic (Chapter 2), a magic of objects constituting a distinctive southern African ontology that deserves to be understood in its own right. Traditional healers experiment and develop their knowledge accordingly. They hold a rich fund of knowledge about plants, animals and minerals. In this sense they do possess a science. But it is also possible to see them as hunters and gatherers when they set off to 'dig', as they say, in the bush for healing plants, animal parts and substances and minerals.

In examining traditional healing through the lenses of our 'standard' epistemological categories – economy, markets, politics, religion, science and medicine – the aim is to show the ways in which these categories fit the realities of southern African traditional healing practices, but also to demonstrate the ways in which they do not.

My preference is not to tell '*that* story' (Wainaina 2005), or the 'one story' (Mkhwanazi 2015: 194) about a deficient Africa that lurches from one failure to another. This work does not attempt to fit into the narrative of colonialism in which the African 'pre-colonial' period seems just to have been waiting for the colonial to happen to it and, in the 'post-colonial' period, appears just to fall gracelessly away from 'civilisation'. To treat an element of African culture such as *bungoma* as a reaction to 'the West', the colonial, the neoliberal, or some external '-ism' is also to treat it as less than these grand historical moments. Here I say what I can about my limited contact with a rich cultural tradition, and treat it as much as possible on its own merits.

Bungoma and the work of the sangoma

Bungoma is the word used here to label, in general, the knowledge and practice of the sangoma, otherwise known as 'traditional healer'. The *bu-* prefix indicates that the word refers to the general quality, content or practice of *-ngoma*, while the *isa-* prefix indicates a person who practises this. The practitioners of *bungoma* are called *isangoma*. I use sangoma, the South African English version of this term, throughout.

The words *bungoma* and *isangoma* derive from an ancient Bantu root word that is still current across most languages from the Bantu family of languages in southern Africa. The same is true for the ancient Bantu root word *ganga* or *nganga* for a 'spiritual healer', for instance, *inyanga* (isi-Zulu), *n'anga* (chiShona) and *nganga* (Kiswahili). Wreford uses '*izangoma sinyanga*', that is, 'healers who heal'. The root, *-ngoma*, refers broadly to 'drum', 'song', 'music' and 'dance' or, rather, to the social institutions and practices that include all these methods as modes of *knowledge practice*, that is, the ways in which knowledge is acquired, assessed, validated, legitimated and used.

Janzen, in *Ngoma: Discourses of Healing in Central and Southern Africa* (1992), gauges the sweep of similarity and difference among the many practices that seem to fall under the general label of *-ngoma*, a 'dominant trope' in the Bantu language family that extends across most of the southern half of the African continent (Engelke 2001: 147; Janzen 1991: 291). Victor Turner called them 'cults of affliction' (Turner 1968: 15; 1995). These different orders provide for

> ...the interpretation of adversity, paradox, and change within the framework of specialized communities, cells, and networks [and through] their use of drumming and rhythmic song-dancing, and the colloquial designation in many societies of the region of the whole gamut of expressive dimensions by the term *ngoma* (drum). The

drumming is considered to be the voice or influence of the ancestral shades or other spirits that visit the sufferer and offer the treatment (Janzen 1992: 1).

Janzen (1992: 2) identifies several common key features, including

> specialisation of healers within this institution and their organisa-tion into 'communities, cells and networks',…the interpretation of 'affliction', illness, disease and misfortune as the result of specific non-human agents; the specification of an appropriate response to this through joining of a cult of the afflicted, under the guidance of a specialist 'doctor' or healer; and the use of drums (*ngoma*) in healing rituals that involve specific dance styles and songs in which the drums are considered to be the 'voice' of the ancestral shades of spirits.

While these features are also true of southern African healing 'cults' of *ngoma*, Janzen (1992: 37) also correctly notes that in South Africa there is a

> shift, from south to north, of increasingly elaborate technique and demonstrative trance in divining-healing. Among the Xhosa, undra-matic meditative and counselling techniques are used between healers and their clients.…Among Zulu diviners, mechanistic bone-throwing techniques prevail. The Swazi, however, although the same holds true for a part of their work, have recourse regularly to far more demonstrative possession trance behaviour.

This work is concerned with the 'demonstrative Swazi practices', although the ethnic–linguistic is more accurately regional rather than tribal.

Similar regional shifts in the focus, use and meaning of *ngoma* occur across the entire subcontinent, and even out to the African diaspora in India and, more recently, around the world. *Ngoma*, or *goma* as it is pro-nounced in western India among the Sidi, accompanied African sailors, servants and slaves to India from as early as the sixteenth century and remains a potent symbol of their identity, even though they have entirely lost their previous African languages (Basu 2008). North of South Africa in Zimbabwe and northern Botswana, *ngoma* cults become 'tributary to the region's dominant territorial cult of Mali or Ngwali',' according to Wim van Binsbergen (1991). In the Democratic Republic of Congo *ngoma* is often assimilated into royal and ordinary rituals, although it also simply means dance and entertainment in many contexts. Among the Kongo, for instance:

> Music itself was and is thought to enable communication with the dead, often inducing spirit possession, 'causing the spirit to descend'. The presence of the strict is recognised when everybody is carried away, having a good time. Parties and ritual events, which are often much the same thing, are enlivened by music, dancing, alcohol, ululation, and explosions of gunpowder...Drumming adds greatly to the excitement attendant on divination, and in so doing makes the result more convincing (MacGaffey 2002: 12, 14).

On the Swahili coast of Kenya, *ngoma* is associated with a number of musical and poetic styles that are performed during a range of religious and secular occasions (Askew 2003; Campbell and Eastman 1984). John Blacking, in a discussion of what he calls Venda 'possession music', shows that 'musical performance is a way of knowing...[and is] an important means of reflection, of sensing order and ordering experience, and relating inner sensations to the life of feeling of one's society' (Blacking 1985: 66). Elisabeth Meintjes (2004) argues that in contemporary, post-apartheid South Africa *ngoma* permits 'individualised expression' and is 'a critical means of attaining responsible [Zulu] manhood' in KwaZulu-Natal. For Peter Pels, writing about the rapid mass conversion to Christianity among the Luguru of eastern Tanzania in the 1930s, '*ngoma*, in all its senses, means the embodied – danced, drummed, or otherwise performed – change in the rhythm of life that metonymically connects different states of being within Luguru society and beyond it...a moving pattern that can include alternatives and counterpoints' (Pels 1996: 163). *Ngoma*, in the case of the Luguru, allowed them to incorporate Christianity as a new 'rhythm', which they called *ngoma kizungu* ('white rhythm'), even though it eventually overwhelmed the indigenous forms.

Ngoma cannot be assigned to any ethnic or linguistic label, as is commonly done. In the context of Kenya and Tanzania, for instance, Kelly

Askew (2003: 613) warns against the 'all too common alignment of *ngoma* with tradition/stasis/community…the purportedly frozen-in-time *ngoma*'. Throughout its range, *ngoma* is not owned by any culture, chief or institution and is as flexible and subject to social change, cultural syncretism and hybridity as all other aspects of African culture.

Thus, *bungoma* is what might be called a philosophy of the drum (-*ngoma*), or the embodied knowledge both symbolised and enacted through drumming and dance (Janzen and Feierman 1992; Janzen 1991, 1992; Van Binsbergen 1991; Van Dijk, Reis and Spierenburg 2000). The connection between drums and drumming, song and dancing is not merely 'entertainment' – although it may also serve this purpose – but reflects a kind of poetic construction of language, music, knowledge and, above all, altered consciousness.

When sangomas drum, however, they often attract audiences who view the performance as little more than entertainment. Various sangomas ruefully assert that some are present in their ranks just for the dancing and singing, or just for the money. Rhythm is a central organising motif for both knowledge and practice, since dancing and rhythmic verbal interactions are pervasive and knowledge is considered to be a kind of pulsed flow across bodies and disembodied persons (often called 'spirits').

While the 'discipline' of the drum-and-song, or *ngoma*, is a central unifying motif throughout *bungoma*, it can be further divided into six – more or less – different disciplines. These have been described in different contexts by different authors and are emphasised differently and to different degrees by different healers. There are regional, historical and other differences in how and whether these disciplines are practised, related to the different aspects of their practice, learning and teaching and their link to the local ecologies of healing plants, animal and mineral substances. The disciplines are: 1. **Divination** – *ukupengula* (Cumes 2004; Hammond-Tooke 1986, 1989; Werbner 2015); 2. Knowledge of **medicinal substances** and their relation to local ecologies and landscapes (Hirst 1997); 3. Knowledge of *Nguni* **ancestors** (*emadloti*) and the methods used to communicate with them, known as *kupahla*; 4. Knowledge of **'foreign' and water spirits**, together with the ritual used to heal through their agency known as *kufemba*; 5. Experience and **knowledge of *ngoma***, 'deep' embodied knowledge expressed through singing, dancing, drumming and the 'trance' or 'enchantment' of the dancers (Janzen 1992: 1; Ngubane 1977); 6. The **teaching relationship** between the *gobela*, the teacher of the arts and knowledge of *bungoma*, the student (*lithwasana*) and the school (*mpandze*), together with systems of knowledge transfer and criticism (see Chapters 3, 4).

There are other disciplines that are more peripheral but nonetheless important, such as crafts involved in the design and tailoring of costumes, the making of beads and amulets, carving or forming dancing implements such as sticks, axes and knives (often made of wood), so-called fly-whisks (*lishoba*), the construction of drums and other articles and objects that are essential to the practice. Some sangomas specialise in the collection and drying of plant substances. Some sell or trade in *muti*, as these substances are called. This set of practices structures the daily practice of all sangomas in one way or another and in varying combinations.

Across the Bantu-speaking region the complex of *ngoma* refers to – and evokes in sensory and emotional terms as well – a kind of gnosis that can be termed 'trance' or trance knowledge, that is, knowledge that can be acquired as much through dreams as through being taught by teachers. This knowledge often has what might be called the 'shape' of dreams; the knowledge of dreams contributes especially to deep social and personal insight. Trance and dreams are more or less equivalent since this is know-ledge experienced while in a dissociated cognitive state. The sangoma in southern Africa, then, is a practitioner of a specialised knowledge practice, a technician of ritual, objects and language, and one who is initiated into a guild, 'college' or 'secret society' of other healers.

The legal definition of healing

In 2004 the South African government attempted to formalise and regu-late the teaching and therapeutic practices of sangomas by means of the Traditional Health Practitioners Act (No. 35 of 2004), signed into law on 11 February 2005 by President Thabo Mbeki. The Act specifies that 'tra-ditional health practitioners' must have achieved the status of recognised practitioner through specific 'traditional' educational and training pro-cesses. It explicitly defines the 'traditional health practitioner' and the 'tra-ditional tutor' (*gobela*). In the Act, 'traditional health practice' is defined as the performance of a function, activity, process or service based on a traditional philosophy that includes the utilisation of traditional medicine or traditional practice and which has as its object –

(a) the maintenance or restoration or prevention of a physical or mental health function; or

(b) the diagnosis, treatment, or prevention of a physical or mental illness; or

(c) the rehabilitation of a person to enable that person to resume normal functioning within the family or community; or

(d) the physical or mental preparation of an individual for puberty, adulthood, pregnancy, childbirth, and death,

...[but] excludes the professional activities of a person practising any of the professions contemplated in the Pharmacy Act, 1974...the Nursing Act, 1974,...the Health Professions Act, 1974,...the Allied Health Professions Act, 1982, or the Dental Technicians Act, 1979,...and any other activity not based on *traditional philosophy* (Traditional Health Practitioners Act No. 35 of 2004: Chapter 1.1 Definitions; emphasis added).

Surprisingly, the Act does not mention religion or cult, initiation, spirits, mediums, possession or trance states, all of which are associated with traditional healing in popular and academic literature. It does not specifically exclude them from religious office or practice and therefore implies that they cannot be considered elements of 'religion', even of 'traditional African religion'.

The Act also implicitly recognises that 'traditional health practitioners' are professionals by stipulating that they are *not included* among the *other* professions contemplated under the Health Professions Act of 1974. Instead, the central criterion of the definition is the subscription to a 'traditional philosophy'.

The legal definition fails, however, to locate a specific central practice. It does include virtually anything that might have a 'traditional' component and is broadly related to health, illness or death and to any performance that can be said to be involved in the 'preparation' for puberty, adulthood, pregnancy or childbirth. The definition of 'traditional philosophy' is even more peculiar:

> ...indigenous African techniques, principles, theories, ideologies, beliefs, opinions, and customs and uses of traditional medicines communicated from ancestors to descendants or from generations to generations, with or without written documentation, whether supported by science or not, and which are generally used in traditional health practice (Traditional Health Practitioners Act, No. 35 of 2004: Chapter 1.1 Definitions).

In addition, the Act defines 'traditional medicine' – what many South Africans refer to colloquially as *muti* – as:

> an object or substance used in traditional health practice for –
> (a) the diagnosis, treatment or prevention of a physical or mental illness; or
> (b) any curative or therapeutic purpose, including the maintenance or restoration of physical or mental health or well-being in human beings, but does not include a dependence-producing or dangerous substance or drug... (Traditional Health Practitioners Act, No. 35 of 2004: Chapter 1.1 Definitions).

Apart from these 'definitions', as they are called in the Act, most of the text of the Act is concerned with the establishment and function of a regulatory body under the Department of Health to which all traditional healers are required to belong. In fact, no more than about 30% of all healers in South Africa today belong to voluntary associations. They see themselves as professionals, but their mode of organisation is far from bureaucratic.

According to the Act, the education of the healer and the judgement of the adequacy of his or her knowledge are to be taken over by the state through the agency of a council that will 'accredit' healers in a bureaucratic fashion. It appears that the government's intention, then, is to regulate the practice of traditional healing in all its forms and to take control of the knowledge practices associated with the transmission of healing knowledge in order to standardise its practice and modes of knowledge transmission. As of mid-2016, however, none of the Act's provisions had been implemented.

The legislation sets retrogressive standards – reminiscent of apartheid-era legislation and misunderstandings – by which traditional healing can be judged. Perhaps for the first time in the history of law, the existence of the occult category of 'ancestors' is explicitly recognised as a *source* rather than an object of knowledge. It legislates the existence of 'tradition' as something that is passed on 'from generation to generation' rather than as a category of critical and dynamic knowledge that is as much part of modernity as any other field of knowledge. Johannes Fabian (2014) has called this type of error the 'denial of coevalness', forcing sangoma tradition into an imagined pre-colonial past.

The legislation denies the possibility of empirical observation and verification, relegating the knowledge of the sangoma tradition to the category of 'indigenous African philosophy', understood as a mysterious, explicitly secret cult informed only by the past. Instead, the legislation restricts its vision of these practices to a weak version of medicine and social work.

Contrary to this position, most healers seem to understand themselves as belonging to an intellectual tradition of which healing is just one part. They believe it to be a kind of science that possesses its own standards of empirical evaluation and criticism. Few sangomas today see their knowledge as the unmodified product of the past. No two sangomas appear to believe or act in precisely the same way. This form of science is constantly in circulation, producing a diversity of regional, local and personal variants. Its essence is defined by the *process* of its transmission *as knowledge*. This confers the status of *expert* on the sangoma.

Writing *bungoma*

I write as an anthropologist and as a student of traditional healing in a specific southern African context. When I act as an anthropologist in the context of the academy I teach Anthropology. In this book, I teach about the knowledge of traditional healers. In my view, traditional healers are a kind of anthropologist of the local world, even as they are embedded in a global discourse of healing and a regional market for healing. I studied traditional healing with an extremely able teacher, Magodweni, in Barberton, South Africa. I never had the courage or – as a fully employed academic anthropologist, householder and parent of three children – the time to fully qualify as a healer, or to undergo the rites that I describe. However, I believe I was a good student and I present my knowledge in the fairly equivalent role of a 'junior lecturer' in the academy of African knowledge systems that healing represents.

My ethnographic approach has been to eschew the style of ethnography practised mostly outside the discipline of anthropology, which consists of a pastiche of relatively unfiltered 'quotes' from focus groups, questionnaire 'feedback', or so-called 'grounded research/theory'(Glaser and Strauss 1999). It is not a 'critical ethnography' since I neither promote a political or humanitarian perspective with respect to healers, nor attempt to advocate traditional healing vis à vis biomedicine. Nor do I seek to explore, as I and others have done elsewhere (Green 1999; Langwick 2011, 2015; Thornton 2003; World Health Organization 2002; Wreford 2005), whether and how sangomas can or should seek to integrate with biomedical systems. I prefer to treat these as parallel systems in a multi-therapeutic environment.

I conducted research and writing periodically over sixteen years from 1998 to 2014. My data is multi-modal and multi-sited, spanning the 'rural' chiefdom, the formal town and townships and informal settlements. I had no direct access to mines or farms, but I talked to those who worked there. I have hiked through the mountains to contact people who prefer to live in the bush, and walked the streets of towns and townships to work with the vast majority who prefer their limited urbanism and opportunities. I have worked intensively with chiefs, indunas and members of the tribal council, with sangomas and herbalists, doctors and healers; I have talked with members of the municipal government and civil service, with business people of all kinds and with ordinary labourers and local 'captains of industry'. I have formed close relationships over many years of interaction with leading business people and politicians as well as with those engaged in the informal or unobserved economy, including some criminals. I have based research on interviews, ethnographic participant observation and questionnaires. For instance, one questionnaire on chiefship, municipal politics and service delivery was administered twice, once in 2000 and once in 2009, giving a temporal dimension of ten years to the results (Thornton 2012b).

I use my own photographs throughout this book. I also have video records of various sangoma consultations with their clients and of traditional court sessions in the 'tribal authority' area of Emjindini. I have recorded, transcribed and translated the healing performances of sangomas and some proceedings of the traditional court. I have consulted historical records and observed the archaeology of Barberton.

A good part of my attraction to what has been called 'traditional healing', and what I call *bungoma* in this context, does not come from my desire to describe *bungoma* ethnographically as the so-called *Other* (Fabian 2014) or as an 'alien' culture. I do not use the term 'culture' here at all. Instead, what I describe is a *discipline*, that is, a regulated and institutionalised cultivation and valuation of healing knowledge *in use*. The knowledge that sangomas attain and that shapes their practice cannot easily be described as *systematic*. In other words, I cannot call it an 'indigenous knowledge system' or IKS, as many other writers do. Each sangoma practises in a way that is almost unique to that person since each one has come to *bungoma* for different reasons, and each context, each teacher, each ecology and pharmacopoeia of organic and mineral substances is local.

In retrospect I feel that I have engaged with *bungoma* much as I engage with other disciplines that attract me – because of their intellectual appeal and the significance of the problems that they attempt to solve, such as medicine or archaeology.

As I began my encounter I realised that *bungoma* already appeared to me as familiar as if the practitioners of *bungoma* were already anthropologists and ethnographers. They possess a set of intellectual tools that allow them to ask pertinent questions of 'strangers' – that is, their patients and clients – in order to construct accounts of their clients' life ways. Sangomas are chronic outsiders in their own contexts. I won't say in 'their own societies' since they already constitute their own society, as they see it, with its own set of more or less coherent beliefs and practices. They are acutely aware of their difference from others. Others around them are acutely aware of the difference they perceive between them – the 'normal' or 'ordinary' people – and the sangomas who live among them, and to whom they sometimes turn.

As a consequence of this realisation, I take the authorial voice in most of this study. I regard *bungoma* as a theoretical system itself, not an unreflective transmission of tradition and I take the role of explaining, as a teacher and anthropologist, an approach to the world that also takes the transmission of critical knowledge seriously and attempts to understand the role of knowledge and its practices in other people's lives. In short, I see myself here as explaining not another 'culture', but rather another anthropology.

My anthropology, and the implicit 'anthropology' of the healers I have worked with, approach the human condition as something we need to understand critically, in order that we might intervene where possible – and with some effect. My anthropology, and the anthropology of the sangoma, both try to interpret the apparent disjuncture between what is obviously the case and what seems to be the 'something else' that lurks behind the obvious 'material' world that we all inhabit, rendering it never all that is the case. Moreover, our different anthropologies are concerned with the nature and structure of human relationships – with each other and with the environment. The 'ethnographic voice' I use here is predicated on this understanding of my role as a fellow investigator who is also attempting to explain our anthropologies to a global audience, some of whom are anthropologists too.

I use the first person, therefore, as interpreter and presenter. I write in the ethnographic present not because I wish to negate history but because the systems I work *from* (academic anthropology) and those I work *with* (*bungoma*) are relatively stable in the time scale of a couple of decades at the beginning of the twenty-first century.

The problem of the history of *bungoma*, however, is certainly a relevant concern. Sangomas and their clients are a 'people without history' (Wolf 1982), since there is no textual record of their practices, knowledge and beliefs. For the sangoma, 'history' as an account of the past and how it affects the present is irrelevant. All knowledge exists in a timeless present (we might even call this an ethnographic present) that is associated with 'ancestors'. I have never heard from sangomas that this knowledge comes from a clearly defined past or that it is understood as codified knowledge of the past. It is received from other contemporary sangomas (colleagues), from teachers and from dreams, but also from empirical explorations of what works, that is, from critical trial and error. My own interest in the history of healing – of great concern in the academic understanding of medical anthropology – and my queries about the history of *bungoma* have been met with indifference by my sangoma colleagues.

As I worked on this volume I also turned my attention to how I might write a history of this knowledge system and its practices, given that there are no written records. I turned to archaeology and to reading about the rich material culture and sciences (indigenous botany and zoology, as it were) of *bungoma*. This additional project, provisionally titled 'Metals, magic and *muti*', is based on a close examination of the rich evidence of beads, glass, metals, plant and animal materials (see Chapter 10) in southern African archaeology. In this current project I try to interpret the archaeological record as if through the eyes of a southern African healer, which leads to a fairly radical re-interpretation of southern African 'Iron Age' archaeology.

FIGURE 1.1: The mantis, symbol of deep knowledge and pre-carious wisdom in southern Africa.

Concepts

While rooted in medical anthropology and ethnography, I seek to develop theoretical perspectives on the continuing and growing popularity of traditional healing. However, as mentioned above, 'healing' is only one aspect of what sangomas do. Since most previous work has focused on this aspect I have sought to explore the larger field of the sangoma's knowledge and practice. Thus, with one exception (*Boophone disticha*, Chapter 9), I have neither described nor discussed the pharmacological effects (if any) of herbs that sangomas use to heal, nor have I taken any position on the question of efficacy, since this has been discussed elsewhere (Langdon 2007b; Langwick 2015; Waldram 2000). The one case of a powerful herb I discuss at great length, however, since its apparent pharmacological effects cannot be isolated from historical, ecological and cultural context or from its use across all the historical cultures and regions of southern Africa. This is generally true of all herbal agents, whether or not they have measurable pharmacological effects. To say more about this, however, is far beyond the scope of this volume.

I hope, in other words, to counter the mistaken and superficial notion that sangomas are simply deficient doctors primarily concerned with curing physical ailments. There is a constant desire among politicians and entrepreneurs to discover powerful *medicinal properties* in the southern African pharmacopoeia. This has generally met with little success, despite high hopes and massive funding. These hopes rest on the idea that 'real science' can discover hidden potential in what seems to be merely 'cultural' uses for plants. This notion of hidden wisdom waiting to be discovered by science, which will make someone buckets of money, is rooted in the idea that this 'tradition' is simply deficient in its ability to appreciate the value of its own resources.

Equally, I have chosen not to portray the knowledge and practices of the sangoma as a deficient or 'primitive' religion. By far the most cogent presentation of the opposite view is David Chidester's detailed and scholarly account of how Europeans reacted to the southern African philosophical cultures, including traditional healing, then called 'witchdoctoring' or worse. At first, missionaries, travellers and officials found no religion, or even anything that resembled religion. Later, according to Chidester, they 'discovered' that religion had been there all along. In *The Religious System of the AmaZulu* Henry Callaway (1868) is perhaps the first to make this 'discovery', although Chidester (1996: 242) credits Joseph Cox Warner, another missionary in the Eastern Cape, with having done so 'in the 1850s'.

According to Chidester, the southern Africans possessed what Europeans believed to be merely a mistaken or deficient religion. Their religion had not yet been 'discovered' as a real religion. Chidester accounts for this in the usual way, that is, as deliberate blindness to African indigenous religion on the part of 'colonialists' because the African lack of religion justified colonial control. Alternatively, colonialism provided a narrative of African religions as more primitive than Christianity, relegating Africans to a lower rung on the evolutionary ladder. While this argument has merit, the historical truth of the colonial impact still fails to approach African philosophical systems in their own right, seeing them only as reactions to (in this case) Christianity, or, more generally, to colonialism and global systems of domination. Here, instead, I present *bungoma* as an autonomous system of thought on its own terms. This accords with Chidester's insistence that ultimately we must 'avoid the mistakes of the past, to diminish the violence that has been committed under the aegis' of the category of 'religion' (Chidester 1996: 259).

Usefully, Chidester promotes a polytheistic definition of religion as a 'cluster concept' that 'signifies an open set of discursive, practical and social strategies of symbolic and material negotiation'. Herein, religion is 'not the object of analysis [but rather] an occasion for analysis' by providing a 'lens for reflecting on human identity and difference' (Chidester 1996: 259).

Sangomas act within and by means of networks of things, knowledge and persons, linking these in webs of narrative through divination and ritual practices that patients experience as 'healing'. Their knowledge of herbs, minerals and animal substances (for example, fats as salves and emollients) is neither a simple science nor a cookbook, any more than they are deficient doctors. And, I argue, they did not simply lack religion during the period of early significant cultural contact with Christianity. Instead, during the eighteenth and nineteenth centuries, when southern African practices were first recorded in a way that we can understand today, they reasoned in a way that clearly did not resemble Eur-Asian religion, even in the 'family resemblance' way of the polythetic category. I believe that some of this distinctive dif-ference in *bungoma* thought still exists today and I attempt to present this as clearly as possible. Ironically, this often means that I explicitly compare *bungoma* with Christianity (usually very early Christian ideas of, for instance, Saint Augustine or Thomas, the author of a non-canonical gospel).

What sangomas do, then, is neither a simpler or 'misguided' analogue of biomedical practice, nor an incomplete science, nor a not-quite religion. But it is also not fully consistent with the many other 'New Age' con-temporary practices that also offer 'healing'. Sangomas compete with and partially integrate what they glean from other healing practices in their environment, including the biomedical. Indeed, they are empiricists in a fairly radical sense in that they explore and test their own perceptions of the properties and efficacy of treatments and modify their practice accord-ingly. They practise what I call 'magical empiricism'.

As I learnt what *bungoma* was about and how it worked, I became increasingly uncomfortable with the standard vocabulary – both popular and social scientific – by which we have so far described this African school of thought. Some words, like 'spirit' and 'ancestor', risk being mistaken for the somewhat similar European concepts with the same names. The terms for much of this discourse were set by the many Christian missionaries who attempted to make sense of what they understood as paganism. For the most part, since they were trained in Latin and Greek, and often Hebrew, among other Mediterranean languages, their intellectual capacities relied on these resources. Saint Augustine, for instance, wrote in *City of God* (Augustine 1890 [ca. 410 CE]) that 'all the religion of the Pagans has reference to dead men' and that 'all dead men are thought by them to be gods' (Bk I, Ch. 26).

The discourse about *bungoma* has become so laden with Christian theology that it is difficult to present – as I try to do here – an interpretation of *bungoma* thought that is more faithful to the pre-Christian philosophies, or to explain the activities and practices these concepts motivate today. Throughout the book I seek to distinguish the distinctive regional cultural meanings of the vocabulary used within the community of practitioners and begin to develop a more useful, precise and considered vocabulary.

As I have sought to write about sangomas and their practices, several key concepts have formed in my mind which have provided the new vocabulary I was searching for. Most previous accounts of traditional healers have imposed what is essentially the ancient Mediterranean understanding of how bodies fall ill and how they may be healed. Hippocrates is the name we associate most strongly with this tradition and the Hippocratic oath is still mandatory for any biomedical practitioner to speak as a rite of passage. It is an ethical and intellectual commitment to a specific set of roles for the healer and the patient.

I argue here that southern African healers, while having a strong ethical commitment to their patients, and a commitment to 'first do no harm', occupy a radically different role-position with respect to patients. Through much of the relevant early ethnography of Callaway's *The Religious System of the Amazulu* (1868), or Wilhelm Immanuel Bleek's collections of Bushman oral literature (Bleek 1864, 1875; Bleek, Lloyd and Bleek 1923; Bleek, Lloyd and Theal 1911), it is clear that humans do not die: they are killed. Death is not natural, it is caused by other people and other things that eventually conspire to penetrate the person's protective resources.

While mortality and morbidity are caused by other persons and are not part of a natural process, it is not correct to call them a 'social causation' of death and illness. This is because the cause is not so much social as relational; that is, it is other specific persons, including persons who are no longer living as well as 'person-like' objects and forces, that can do harm. These persons act or have causal effect, not because of social roles or position – for example class, seniority, race or gender – but because they have a specific relationship to the 'victim' or target. Some of these relations between persons, tangible or intangible, are evil, and evil is real. Evil is directly experienced – we could say *empirically* experienced – by the fact of mortality and morbidity.

It is also not correct to call the target of evil a victim. The sufferer is not the victim of deliberate intentional harm – although this might be the case where sorcery is specifically used, but is simply exposed to harm of this sort as all people are. This state of being I call the 'exposed being', and healers attempt to heal by protecting their clients from this existential condition of exposure. But all protection, all *muti*, ritual, amulets or spells work only temporarily, and usually only conditionally. Eventually, the person is exposed again … and again. Ultimately, it is this condition of exposure that kills or leads to other misfortune.

My work with sangomas, together with early ethnographic records, has convinced me that it is not only actual people who are 'persons' in this world. By 'person' I mean an entity that has intentionality, agency, a felt (or real) presence, and a positionality or *relation* to another person. Of course, all living physical persons fulfil these criteria, but, in *bungoma*, the qualities are also attributed to witches (who may be physical persons), ancestors, spirits of other kinds, and physical objects such as beads, organic material (*muti*), tokoloshes, zombies and other more bizarre presences. However, not all these 'persons', so conceived, are tangible. Partly as a way of avoiding the usual vocabulary of 'spirits' that is so overloaded with meanings drawn from the Abrahamic religions I have chosen to call the non-material entities of this sort *intangible persons*.

In response to this, each person is insufficiently able to accomplish the task of preserving his or her own life. His or her being must be augmented. By augmenting the self through any number of acts and substances a person seeks to avoid the danger of inevitable exposure to other people and to sources of evil. In this way, the act of healing – as opposed to therapeutic *curing* – aims to achieve the augmented self as a healed person.

The concept of an 'exposed being', however, is also the condition for the possibility of the healing act. The healer must be exposed to patients in order to sense what is wrong with their lives, not just their bodies. The healer must be exposed to death and illness and must feel that exposure deeply as the condition for his or her success. This is why the healer is said to die in the process of becoming a healer. The healer lives 'under water' for a long time during training. As a metaphor, and occasionally as real immersion, the healer experiences the pain and suffering of others as if it is the pain and suffering of the self.

Accordingly, a good deal of what the healer does is not only intended to heal the client or patient, but to heal himself or herself. The self must be augmented, while simultaneously remaining exposed and being fully conscious of this exposure.

The concepts of 'exposed being', 'augmented self' and 'intangible persons' provide, I believe, a more sensitive and accurate conceptual vocabulary for describing *bungoma* as philosophy and as practice.

The research site: Barberton municipality, Umjindi district, Mpumalanga province

The approach and data presented here are based on long-term ethnographic fieldwork in and around the town and township of Barberton and the chiefdom or 'traditional authority' of Emjindini in Umjindi, a municipality established in 2001 in the Ehlanzeni district of Mpumalanga province, South Africa. The town of Barberton, the administrative and historical centre of Umjindi municipality, was established in 1884 as the principal mining centre of the old Zuid Afrikaansche Republiek (Transvaal Republic). The bulk of my research was conducted in Barberton town and the surrounding Umjindi municipality, which includes the traditional authority of Emjindini. I use the locators Barberton, Umjindi and Emjindini throughout the book without further specification.

In August 2016 Umjindi municipality was merged with Mbombela municipality to the north to create the City of Mbombela Local Municipality (MP326). Nelspruit – likewise called Mbombela – is its administrative centre and is also the capital of Mpumalanga province. However, I continue to use the now-historical term Umjindi in the rest of this text.

Today Umjindi is sustained by farming, gold mining, forestry and government services. Illegal gold mining and marijuana smuggling from Swaziland are also important, though illegal, sources of livelihood. Barberton lies just 40km from Nelspruit and therefore houses many civil servants, as well as a large population of employees of the two large government prisons in town. Ecologically, Barberton and its environs lie in what is called the Lowveld, the semi-tropical lowlands below the Great Escarpment that extends along the entire length of eastern Africa. Nelspruit and Barberton lie close to the 31st eastern longitude and just north of 26 degrees of latitude.

Social identities in Umjindi are complex, overlapping and diverse. Sangomas must deal with these facts in their practice. This social flux, as much as the high burden of disease and lifestyle morbidity coupled with poor biomedical care, creates pervasive and permanent anxiety and ill-health (Thornton 2008). Although the Swazi language (siSwati) predominates, English is the principal language of commerce, government and education, while Afrikaans and other South African languages are also spoken widely in the district. The complexity of multiple political regimes and loyalties, of the systems of land tenure and settlement with multiple ethnic, racial and class identities, and of the variety of economic institutions, kinship and family life defy any simple geographic, historical or structural account.

There is little historical depth that might create more stable social or cultural solidarities. Most of the ancestors of the current South African population, excluding the descendants of the San (Bushmen) and Khoikhoi peoples, have been resident here for approximately five centuries. There is ample evidence of much earlier but very sparse Late Stone Age peoples and Bushmen, although there is little historical continuity with these earlier peoples in today's population. The Swazi appear to have travelled and grazed across the land north of today's Swaziland, but the first permanent settlement in Umjindi dates to 1864 when armies returning from their defeat at Mariepskop established a settlement on the uMgwenyane or Queen's River (Myburgh 1949). Barberton town was just over 130 years old in 2016. Even though this is old in historical Lowveld terms, it is extremely young in comparison to virtually any other region in the rest of the world. The population has changed rapidly over these years, especially from the early days when Barberton was a frontier mining town. During the South African War of 1899–1902 British forces established concentration camps there for large numbers of Afrikaner prisoners, particularly women and children. Many died there, having been removed from their scattered farms during the conflict (Bornman 2006; Thornton 2012b). Barberton still hosts two large prisons.

Mpumalanga is one of nine provinces that were demarcated after the promulgation of the 1994 Constitution that signalled the end of apartheid. These nine provinces replaced the old four provinces of the Cape, Natal, Transvaal and Orange Free State that were the legacy of nineteenth-century migrations and wars, and eventual political consolidation as independent republics (Orange Free State and Transvaal Republic) and British colonies (Natal and Cape). After the South African War and the formation of the Union of South Africa in 1910 they became provinces of the Union and, in 1961, the Republic of South Africa. Mpumalanga occupies the southern and south-eastern portion of what used to be the old Transvaal. It has many cultural and historical similarities with Limpopo and North West provinces, together with the highly urbanised Gauteng province, which contains the Johannesburg and Pretoria megacities. Immediately to the south of eastern Mpumalanga lies the kingdom of Swaziland, an independent ethnically-homogeneous country entirely surrounded by South Africa. The Swaziland border is only 20km south of Barberton over the Makhonjwa mountains.

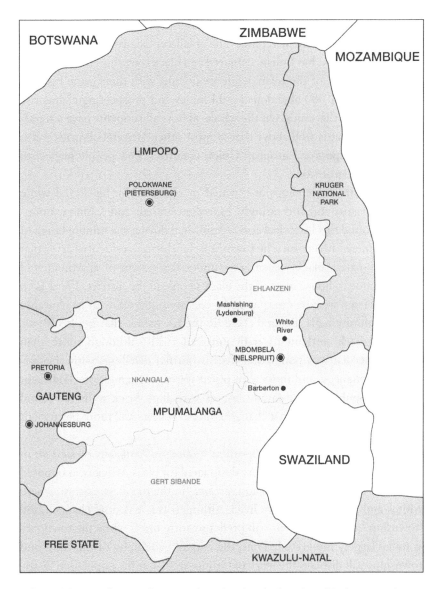

FIGURE 1.2: Map of Mpumalanga province showing the location of Barberton and surrounding districts. Emjindini is 8km to the west of Barberton.

Barberton today still looks like a well-regulated South African town, with a grid of paved streets edged with shops, banks, restaurants and hotels. Jacaranda trees line the streets of its small suburbs, which consist of typical

South African single-storey, tiled-roof, three-bedroom houses and fenced gardens on single residence plots. The small centre, dating from the late nineteenth century, has Indian, coloured and black townships to the north – the downhill side of the town, while mountains with their game reserves and more than 1 000 abandoned gold mines and prospecting claims rise immediately to the south. On the whole, almost all residents have a standard of living that is well above that in most other African countries and is comparable to poorer European Union countries. Few people neglect to dress well in Barberton.

The main street shops are owned or operated by black and white South Africans, and increasingly by recent Indian and Chinese immigrants. Around this historical core, established during the mining boom of the late nineteenth century, lie townships, less formal residential areas that were designated 'black' urban areas under the system of apartheid, and that continue to house most of the black people in the district. There is an Indian quarter, with its mosque, and a coloured quarter, with its churches and community halls. Beyond these lie the townships that grade off into informal shack settlements with unpaved roads, although more than 80% of the district's population lives in formal dwellings with electricity and appliances, and most with piped water and sanitation. Well-kept and even opulent single-family houses with high brick walls are found next to decrepit plots with a changing mix of renters and more permanent residents.

The terms 'township' or 'location' (*lokasie* in Afrikaans or *loksheni* in siSwati) applied to areas that were designated for black Africans, as opposed to the town (*dorp* in Afrikaans and *edropini*, 'in the town', in siSwati) where whites and Indians generally lived. Although this has now changed, the 'township'/*lokasie*/*loksheni* is still predominantly black, while the town/city is today largely integrated. Thus, the overall geography of the town and townships still displays the mark of Group Areas, but the population distribution within this residential infrastructure is determined today more by income or class than by race.

Outside the towns, cities and townships the social order and geography of South African life is structured by three distinctly South African social forms: the farm, the mine and the chiefdom. Each of these forms occupies its own demarcated territory, with boundaries that are surveyed and registered by the state. In practice, boundaries are often more custom-ary than cadastral. The farm, chiefdom and mine are structurally similar in their relative economic and political autonomy and geographic patterns and often house distinctive lifestyles, rules and local cultures. People – res-idents, migrants and citizens – may belong in or on one or several of these entities and derive a sense of identity from them.

The term 'farm' describes a registered and surveyed piece of land from hundreds to thousands of hectares in extent. These pieces of land were sur-veyed in the eighteenth and nineteenth centuries, and were initially granted mostly to white farmers (*boers*), but also to Christian missions and mining companies; occasionally they were purchased by black or Indian owners. Many farms today are state owned or have been transferred to 'communities' under the Restitution of Land Rights Act 22 of 1994, as amended. These are still the backbone of land ownership regimes outside of the towns and cities. Each farm develops its own social system, with the owner (usually white Afrikaans- or English-speaking, although this is changing) at the social apex in command of incorporated African settlements, villages and labour accom-modation, and including resident managers, labourers and tenants.

Mines are far more than industrial operations since they also have their own distinctive culture, languages and settlements of mine labour, management and other personnel, who are often resident within the mine compound and entirely dependent on the economic fortunes of the mine. The chiefdom (tribal area/reserve, traditional authority) is structurally similar to the farm and the mine, but with the hereditary chief in the apical position. The chief distributes land and adjudicates local disputes over land, property and family matters. Chiefs are mandated by the South African Constitution to oversee 'customary law and the customs of communities observing a system of customary law' (Sect. 211 of 1994 Constitution). Since 1994 the governing party, the African National Congress (ANC), has given increasing powers to 'traditional authorities'.

There are two chiefdoms in Umjindi – Emjindini lies to the west of Barberton town and Lomshiyo lies to the east. Emjindini tribal authority came into being as the result of a successful land claim over a portion of a farm. Lomshiyo belonged to the apartheid-era Swazi tribal 'homeland' of KaNgwane. There are five major gold mines in operation – Fairview, Consort, Agnes, Sheba and Lily – and numerous artisanal, but illegal, small-scale gold mines. The farms produce tropical fruits such as bananas, lychees and papaya, with some sugar cane and vegetables.

According to the 2011 Census, the population of Umjindi district was just over 67 000, with 10.4% in tribal areas, 17.3% on 'farms' and the rest mainly in Barberton town and townships. Mpumalanga had a population of 4.3 million in 2015, but the vast majority is concentrated in the western part of the province near Johannesburg and Pretoria (Statistics South Africa 2017).

Barberton town has a stable population of whites (10% of Umjindi), blacks (87%), and coloured and Indian people (3%) – roughly in proportion to South Africa as a whole – who live largely, but not exclusively, in their respective neighbourhoods, where their families have lived since Barberton's foundation. Only 18% of adults over the age of 18 are married.

In designating the 'racial' types of South Africans I use the canonical terms that are enshrined in daily usage, law and population censuses – 'black', 'coloured', 'Indian' and 'white'. I use these terms as formal but somewhat arbitrary, colloquial categories.

In Barberton there are also significant immigrant populations from China, Pakistan and surrounding African countries, especially Mozambique and Zimbabwe. Most white, Indian and coloured people speak Afrikaans (8.5%) and/or English (5.4%). The majority of black Africans (73%) have siSwati as their first language but most speak English and/or Afrikaans as well. Many also speak other Bantu languages such as Sepedi and/or Shangaan (or xiTsonga, 3%). Relative to the rest of South Africa, and despite its diversity, the municipality's political history has been remarkably peaceful, even during the apartheid period. With the exception of the predominantly Muslim Indian group, most of Barberton's population is at least nominally Christian.

The economy is only partly legal and formal. A large proportion of it comes from illegal gold mining, the smuggling of marijuana from Swaziland and cigarettes from Mozambique, and from the informal, cash-only trade in most other commodities and services. Indeed, the town is jokingly described as a small drinking town with a gold-mining problem.

The primary formal industries of Barberton – mining, forestry and timber and prisons – are violent but resilient. Despite its political quietness, there is a high level of violence, drinking and alcoholism in the town.

Many people carry visible scars, or other signs of trauma, on their faces and bodies, the result of interpersonal and domestic violence. Ten years of observation, and of stories and court cases heard at the tribal court, suggest that both men and women initiate and engage in violence.

HIV prevalence is among the highest in the world. Tuberculosis (TB), including multi-drug-resistant TB (MDR-TB), is also extremely widespread, with high levels of HIV and TB co-infection. Barberton hosts a specialised TB treatment facility. In addition, diabetes and obesity predominate, especially among black people and Afrikaans-speakers (mostly white and coloured). However, malaria and other common tropical diseases such as diarrhoea are largely absent. Witchcraft accusations are common, too, but almost never result in violence against suspected witches. Accusations are strongly downplayed and discouraged by the leaders of the traditional court where criminal cases are most commonly heard. Public life in the streets, shops and workplaces is generally congenial, with no obvious tension among people across all of these categories.

The context for *bungoma*

The *conceptual locale* of this study is the South African small town. While sangomas are increasingly located in urban centres, their centre of gravity lies in small towns, townships and more recent semi-urban conglomerations that lie outside of the major urban centres.

The distinction between 'small towns' and cities, or between the 'cultural heartland' (as the South African tourism authorities often call it) and cities can still be understood as a rural/urban dichotomy, but this holds the risk of confusing its dynamic with Euro-American concepts of 'rural' and 'urban'. The South African small town has its own dynamic and identity that is not rural and not yet 'urban'. It is often far more practically 'integrated' across race and class in day-to-day interactions than the urban areas, yet attitudes of racism and class distinction are often more pronounced. This anomaly alone creates its own cultural dynamic as residents and the local citizens of small towns struggle to come to terms with these dichotomies.

Outside South Africa's main cities – Johannesburg, Pretoria, Cape Town and Durban – and provincial capitals such as Nelspruit lies a fairly incoherent mix of peoples, settlement types and governing structures. The

South African state is often only remotely glimpsed by residents in these areas.

There is, of course, a flow of people between small towns and cities, as there once was between 'rural areas' and 'urban areas', but small towns today have acquired a new and distinctive identity. In small towns, especially, people explore the interactions between different forms of 'tradition' and 'the traditional' in the domains of medicine and healing, as they do in the politics of chiefs, traditional authorities and municipal government. The growing popularity of sangomas, together with herbalists, other types of healers and 'prophets', is especially noticeable in South African small towns where public performances of prophets, healers, herbalists, and an assortment of New Age and popular 'healers' and spiritualists compete for recognition and clientele. The music, drumming, colourful costuming, posters, crowds and marquees constitute a distinctive sonic landscape and visual environment. Barberton is typical in this respect.

Here 'tradition' is treated as neither 'from the past', that is, a static and unchanging 'heritage', nor as 'invented', that is, an inauthentic creation in response to nationalism, mass media, the state and/or capitalism. Despite their popularity I consider both these approaches to be incomplete, though not necessarily incorrect. Instead I see tradition or 'the traditional', as it currently exists in contemporary South Africa, as a genuinely creative process that uses elements of the South African past as well as elements of world culture (including dance, music, New Age healing and religion), popular culture and local political and cultural innovation, in assembling new life ways.

The practices and beliefs I discuss here are not simply elements of a 'national (or racial, or ethnic) consciousness' or responses to a collective experience. This point is important, since these practices – *bungoma* – neither create a 'congregation', nor belong to any coherent community, except the community of practice and knowledge that they themselves create. Esther Langdon (2007a: 43), writing about Brazilian shamanism, for instance, talks of 'a traditional shaman without necessarily a traditional community following'. Similarly, healers and other practitioners of various therapies do not necessarily have any 'traditional community' with shared cultural assumptions and beliefs that accepts or underwrites their practices. While each healer, prophet, priest or doctor evidently markets his or her therapies, practices and prayers, there is no such thing as a regulated or formal market for any of it. Interventions of all kinds are opportunistically negotiated, according to the client's knowledge, context, type and degree of suffering, illness or discomfort.

These practices, with their clienteles and practitioners, are not mere reflexes of history then. They are not simple reactions to 'neo-liberal' capitalism or conquest or colonialism. They are neither antique Africanisms, nor simply 'invented' for the dubious purposes of mass marketing or mass culture. The inchoate nature of much of what I call 'healing' and others call 'African tradition' or even 'African traditional religion' is one of the key challenges I have encountered in writing about healing – it is difficult to describe since it lacks a history, a community and even a 'culture', yet it certainly has a clientele and a diverse membership. For these reasons, and despite the lack of formal, regulated practices of exchange, pricing, supply and demand, I use the concept of 'market' in its broadest sense to give coherence to this subject matter, in this particular place and time.

The social history of southern Africa in the twentieth century began with the destructive Anglo-Boer War, during which the life of virtually every community was disrupted. The rise of industrial large-scale mining and its demand for labour further disrupted families and settled communities, driving many to cyclical patterns of migration and a precarious existence. While some degree of stability was established between 1910 and 1940, the imposition of apartheid led to further dislocations resulting from the imposition of racially defined 'group areas', partly in pursuit of what was already a gradual process of urbanisation that still continues. Today uncontrolled migration from surrounding countries combines with the crippling legacy of apartheid to make stable settlement and family unity more or less impossible. The relative coherence of cultural traditions in much of the rest of Africa simply does not exist in South Africa.

Accordingly, I present healers *as if they operate in generalised market-like forums* of knowledge, therapy and healing.

Healers and their clients seem to balance scepticism and belief in their search for therapy and in their therapeutic experiences. While there is always a market for medicine and healing in any society, the institutional forms of 'the market', or even the notion of markets, is often challenging in the African context. This is especially true in southern Africa, including this ethnographic context, since – unlike in much of the rest of Africa – precolonial markets did not exist. Exchanges were personal, networked and usually embedded in kinship. More generally, Marcel Fafchamps (2004) points to the frequent lack of hierarchy, bureaucracy and enforceable contract in African markets. He notes that:

> We know little about how [African] markets operate in practice. Perhaps the best measure of this lack of knowledge is our propensity to call 'informal' everything that is not of Western inspiration. The truth is that market activity in Africa is *not without form*; it is only without economic formalization (Fafchamps 2004: 4; emphasis added).

The market for healing in South Africa is frequently informal, but 'not without form'; it is also more than what some have called a 'search' or 'quest' for therapy (Janzen and Feierman 1992; Janzen 1978: 70; Janzen 1987: 70; Nyamongo 2002; Turner 1968). Radical scepticism and a search for 'belief' exist in equal measure; they do not balance each other, but rather compete in what can be called a kind of 'market' for acceptance of one or other type of healing. In other words, the choice for any patient is whether and how to become a patient for some particular therapeutic intervention. There is no shared system of meaning and no shared assumptions about the causes of illness and misfortune, or the therapies that may be appropriate to the patient (Feierman 1981: 356).

Many people express considerable scepticism about tradition and especially about traditional healers and traditional authority. There is a great diversity of opinion, debate and contestation and, consequently, an historical process of change and adaptation. Indeed, one aspect of people's logic is to stay as far away as possible from the influence of cities and central government laws and legal frameworks. Recent legislation on traditional healing often has little real impact on the way healers operate. Indeed, in 2016 several small movements resistant to government attempts to regulate these practices have emerged. Sangomas, like other representatives of 'tradition' such as 'traditional leaders', called chiefs and kings, respond far more strongly and creatively to local contingencies and politics than they do to national policy.

The appropriate social metaphor is the network rather than the 'structure' or institutional form. The beliefs and practices of healers and their patients are communicated today through networks of social media – Facebook, WhatsApp, WeChat and many others. Every sangoma has at least one cellphone. Cellphones have even been incorporated into the regalia of the dance – *ngoma* – suspended on beaded lanyards and bandoliers that also contain *muti*, the protective 'medicine' that no sangoma can be without.

Medical parallelism

The personal agency that is expressed in this market-like social network has its own 'small-town' dynamic. I show that traditional healing is neither 'traditional' in the orthodox sense, nor strictly 'healing'. It is, rather, a deeply contested and emerging element of a complex *medical parallelism* which accepts the paradoxes that arise from competing and contradictory notions of healing, health and the nature of the individual, and exists primarily in South African small towns. Karen Flint, for instance, in her historical study of the role of 'African medicine' in South Africa from 1820 to 1948, notes that 'the region's medical "traditions" and cultures often have been treated as their own "systems", bounded and separate from each other, [but] this was not the case' (Flint 2008: 7). By contrast, the more stable traditions of Tanzania (Langwick 2011), for instance, and of Central and West Africa, show far more cohesion as systems of thought and practice.

The concept of medical *pluralism* is, however, deeply embedded in medical anthropology discourse (e.g., Cant and Sharma 1999; Crandon 1987; Flint 2008: 18; Janzen 1978; Reis 2002; Sujatha and Abraham 2012; Thornton 2010). I use the term *parallelism* here rather than the much more common 'medical pluralism' for the reasons outlined above, but also because South African history and culture have been plagued by the idea of cultural or political *pluralism* in a region where – over several centuries – ethnic identities have emerged in relation to each other and in interaction with each other. Ethnic identities did not meet each other 'fully formed', as it were, and they interact with each other at their margins as already well-established identities. As Max Gluckman showed in his important study of political and cultural interactions in Zululand (the northern part of the current KwaZulu-Natal province), it was impossible to separate the political identities and processes of 'Zulu' and 'English', or of the government of the province of Natal in the Union of South Africa and the Zulu kingdom (Cocks 2001; Gluckman 1940, 1942). I, among many other South African anthropologists, have argued the case thoroughly too (Thornton 1987, 1994, 1995, 2000a, 2001, 2002). These observations also apply to *bungoma*, despite the fact that there is a deep continuity between today's practices and those of the previous thousand years or more.

The apartheid system was partly based on the notion that South African cultures were authentically separate and must develop apart from each other – hence *apart*-ness, the English meaning of the Afrikaans *apartheid*. In the small town context in which I worked I did not see a meaningful *cultural* distinction between the way people understood and used biomedicine and the other types of healing and therapies. Biomedicine is deeply established in South African minds and daily life. The same is true for *bungoma* and other healing and medical systems. In the context of their usage in a South African small town it makes little sense to call biomedicine 'Western', while designating *bungoma* as 'African', or other practices as Indian, and so on. Increasingly, non-black people either resort to *bungoma* in various ways or become sangomas themselves.

Thus, the concept of *pluralism* raises more problems than it solves. Therefore, I call the interaction of multiple medical systems 'medical *parallelism*' as opposed to the more usual 'medical pluralism'. Many therapeutic interventions are available, but all of them are subject to scepticism. Advertising pervades the airwaves in a town where no one is out of reach of television, radio and the Internet. More than 30% of the population of Umjindi has direct or significant, but somewhat limited, access to the Internet. The ANC and government advertise themselves constantly. And yet, almost nothing actually works 'as advertised'.' This is true of the cheap goods offered in the Chinese and Pakistani shops, but it is also true of government, the medical and educational institutions and much else. Doctors, healers, prophets, therapists of all kinds – even practitioners of biomedicine, the overstretched medical doctors on the margins of southern African society – operate within a market for healing. Since no therapies seem to be entirely effective, at least in the experience of the townspeople in the time span over which they judge efficacy, the elasticity of belief is tried every time: how far can the practitioner stretch the credulity of the patient, and how far can the patient trust the practitioner? This struggle over 'belief' often lies more at the core of medical plurality in Mpumalanga than the efficacy of any specific therapy. Credulity is stretched and sceptics warn but people still explore their options.

In order to practise as a 'traditional healer' or sangoma an individual must first undergo training and eventual graduation and initiation into the group of fellow students and teachers of *bungoma*. When students 'eat *intwaso*', they incorporate their own experience and knowledge of healing into their own body, and thereby bring it under their own control through 'eating'. In a step-by-step two-day process, they are initiated into the ways of *bungoma* as new healers.

Healers are not just chosen by ancestors, as is often stated both in academic texts and by the healers themselves (Hammond-Tooke 1989, 1994; Ngubane 1977, 1981). They are taught through an exhaustive and exhausting process. Knowledge is transmitted to the new healer through 'ritual' and also through straightforward teaching. The process of teaching and learning the traditions of healing will be explored, as will the methods sangomas use in learning how to innovate and build on tradition.

In the work of the healer there are four principles of South African political culture which, at the local level, govern social relations and help to determine the nature and form of conflict. These are ideas of 'respect', 'equality or 'equivalence' (especially of men of the same generation or age), jealousy and suffering. They play important roles in the calculus of evil and misfortune. The correct interpretation of these motives in others is one of the fundamental reasons that rites of divination – *kupengula* – exist. Again, these values can be theorised in the terms of generalised markets. In particular, the marginal utility of ritual and magical interventions – that is, their efficacy 'in the last instance' – is one of the chief reasons for their continued existence in the face of modernity. The 'hidden hand' of zombies – tangible persons whose autonomy has been taken from them – can act for or against 'business'.

In the context of 'medical' parallelism, multiple causal mechanisms, agents, influences or persons can affect the health of an economic actor and his or her economic enterprises. Human actions, especially economic actions involving money, are exposed to evil or misfortune as much as persons are. The action of a witch or other malevolent actor or agent affects the *actions* of persons as much as their physical being. (Once, for instance, when I accidentally slipped off the edge of a bad road and seemed headed for the ditch, my local travelling companion wondered aloud whether this fall was caused by witches.) What a person does, especially if this is seen to bring fortune, is understood as part of the person or, rather, as an augmentation of the person. The witch or malefactor may indeed be jealous of success and fortune, but it is not a jealousy of the person's possessions as much as a suspicion that, by acquiring wealth or good luck, a person's being is changed. The person with wealth *is* wealth (a state of being), not just wealthy (an adjectival modifier). Wealth and good fortune are the ontological status of the person so affected, just as poverty or ill fortune are. These are states of being which affect the being of the person. Accordingly, acts that change one's material wealth also change the nature of one's being in the world. This implicit understanding explains, for instance, why and how a zombie can act to augment a person's wealth (Chapter 6), or why divination can ascertain whether 'money' and wealth – *imali* – may 'come towards' you or materialise magically in your life (or even in your wallet). It helps us, too, to understand the nature of 'jealousy' in this cultural context (Chapters 2 and 5), and why it is useful to understand 'healing' in terms of a market for the exchange of values and personal actions.

Chapter 9 explores the role of material objects – plant, animal and mineral – in the magical process of *bungoma*. Magical weevils and amaryllis flowers (the *Brachycerus ornatus* beetle and the *Boophone disticha* plant)[1] provide instances of the magic inherent in southern African ritual landscapes. Healers' uses of plant, animal and mineral materials and objects demonstrate the important role of *material* cultures of healing. This *material logic* involves the person-like elements of the 'objects' in the landscape, which are brought into play through their use to harm, heal, protect and attack others. In this chapter it is shown that sangomas are modern hunters and gatherers. They utilise the material of the 'bush' as *material*, that is, as stuff that can be used to heal lives, protect people and cleanse evil from the body. What is hunted, mostly by others, or that reaches them by any means become materials out of which

---

1   Accepted name; www.catalogueoflife.org/annual-checklist/2012/details/ species/id/9765593 accessed 25 Jan 2013. The taxonym is credited to 'L. f.' (Linnaeus fils, Carl von Linne's son).

powerful objects are made. Items such as python or lion fat, crocodile brains, animal skins, blood of goats and chickens, claws, beaks, feathers and shells become part of the practice, the magic, of healing. Similarly, *materia medica* of botanical origin is also collected in the bush. When sangomas go out to the bush to hunt and gather they say they are going to 'dig'. In fact, they may strip bark and collect leaves, seeds or pods in addition to digging. The significance of 'digging' is made clear by the fact that holes are not backfilled: the plant remains as if still rooted in the non-domestic, uninhabited space of the bush.

To have this magic, however, the material substances from which *muti* is made are conceived as if they are still connected to the 'bush'. The bush is not just a source of non-domestic animals and plants, it is the place of non-domesticity itself. This is its power. The 'bush' can be any area that is not inhabited; therefore, it is not full of the influence of other people and the intangible presences they create.

While sangomas are hunters and gatherers, they are also experimental scientists. The South African lawyer and anthropologist, JD 'Jack' Krige, noted especially that what was called 'Bantu magical mentality' involved an explicit empiricism and

> [l]ike the conceptual scheme gradually built up by physical inquiry in our natural science, the presupposition and logic of which determine observation, chains of reasoning and verification among us [educated, mainly white South Africans], this conceptual pattern or 'magical mentality' provides a framework of criteria, categories of thought and explanatory principles. The whole structure is considerably elaborated and often invoked in regard to health and disease ... an understanding of the pattern of the so-called 'magical mentality', its recognition of causality, its essential empiricism and its application, is very relevant to the effective execution of [South African] national health plans (Krige 1944: 1).

Jack Krige and his wife, Eileen Jensen Krige, based this assertion on their collection of more than 500 botanical specimens, of which 230 were part of the 'ordinary everyday medical pharmacopoeia, and 145 provided food eaten raw, cooked or in some other processed form'. They also documented the Lobedu 'magical mentality' in their book, *Realm of a Rain Queen* and in copious photographic documentation (Davison and Mahashe 2012; Krige and Krige 1943). Supporting the argument offered here, Krige (1944: 2) wrote that 'the 'magical' in all its forms, including the medical, is continuous with the empirical and discontinuous with the mystical'.

More specifically, I call this aspect of the sangoma's knowledge practices 'magical empiricism' because, while the logic is 'magical', the practice is empirical in the original and radical sense that the nineteenth-century physicist and philosopher of science, Ernst Mach, gave to the term. For Mach, knowledge came from sensory experience; what could not be seen or sensed (that is, measured) in some way was not part of the real world, and therefore no judgement of truth could be made of it. Mach was deeply influential in the development of anthropology through the work of Bronislaw Malinowski, who moulded Mach's empiricism into the deep and comprehensive ethnographic method for which he is known. Malinowski, however, neither mentioned this influence nor the influence of Friedrich Nietzsche in his published English-language work, although it is explicit in his early work in Polish, the language of his birth and education (Banks 2014; Thornton 1996a; Thornton and Skalník 2006). In as much as sangomas are a kind of anthropologist of the local, they adhere, in effect, to the empirical method. But there is a twist, as is shown in Chapter 10. For, while neither Mach nor contemporary scientific empiricists would consider dreams and knowledge acquired during trance as empirical knowledge, sangomas say that this experience is real, that it is empirical and that the knowledge it reveals is also real. Their sensory experience of a patient's illness, or of hidden objects, or of the power of a plant to heal is, for them, an *experiment*.

Chapter 10 explores the paradoxical relationship between the 'magical empiricism' of the healer and the empiricism of the biomedical practitioner, while Chapter 8 argues that the core of this practice is not therapeutic interventions but, rather, apotropaic magic. Apotropaic magic includes all magical gestures, amulets, substances and rites that are designed to protect rather than to cure. It is prophylactic rather than therapeutic. This move shifts the focus away from the sangoma towards the patient. Instead of seeing the healer as the central actor, the patient is revealed as an 'exposed being', a person who is vulnerable and whose 'natural' health will prevail only he or she can be protected. Above all, the patient must be protected from evil, 'badness' and misfortune of any kind. The material logic of evil leads the patient to seek 'healing' not as a cure but as a form of prevention through effective protection. The underlying philosophy is exposed as a distinctive regional cultural ontology and a theodicy (theory of evil) that offers 'healing' by 'augmenting' the self through ritual and other practices.

Chapter 2 proposes that instead of thinking of witchcraft and other types of malign influence as coming from sources outside of the self they should rather be considered as a distinctly *material* – or ontological – logic of evil. The response to this, for both patient and sangoma, is to augment or strengthen the person through apotropaic magic. Reflecting the information campaigns that have been conducted in an attempt to reduce HIV transmission, this protection or apotropaic magic is often talked about in terms of 'strengthening the immune system', a term derived partly from HIV/AIDS education programmes and partly from television advertisements for vitamins.

The patient becomes an *augmented* self through 'strengthening' and 'protection'.

The material logic of evil proposes radically different answers to the question of where evil and sickness come from. The historical arrival of Christianity led missionaries to search for what they believed should be universal 'religion'. But they did not find it in pre-colonial southern African cultural systems. Instead, as mentioned above, southern African cultures had developed a theory of healing as primarily a cultural ontology and a theodicy that offers 'healing' by 'augmenting' the self through ritual and other practices. This theory still underlies the southern African healing practice. It is a theory of the person rather than of society. It operates with the implicit images of the person as an exposed being and augmented self and builds upon a radically *material* logic of evil.

Language

Healers in the Umjindi district of Mpumalanga, as in surrounding regions, use a combination of languages and dialects. Swazi (siSwati) and Zulu (isiZulu) are both official languages, but in other contexts might better be described as significantly different dialects of the same language. While most of the healers identified themselves as Swazi (*mSwati*), they moved between Zulu and Swazi forms of language with ease. Many could also switch to Afrikaans, English or Sepedi (North Sotho) and could communicate effectively in several or all of these languages. Sepedi is a language of the southern African Bantu family of languages, but its phonology, lexicon and grammar are very different from siSwati and isiZulu. The latter are classified together with isiXhosa as 'Nguni'. English and Afrikaans are also mutually unintelligible, but share a common history and origin in north-western Europe.

I use the siSwati grammatical forms for the principal words here, that is, the words that are the focus or subject matter of this discussion. Thus, *lithwasana* (singular) and *emathwasana* (plural) are used instead of the anglicised versions *thwasa* (singular) or *thwasas* (plural). However, words of non-English origin that are commonly used in South African English, such as sangoma (traditional healer), veld (Afrikaans: 'the bush', or open grassland and bush) and sjambok (Afrikaans: long, stiff whip), are not italicised or treated as non-English words. This varies with context, however, depending on whether I am simply using the word as a label within the book, or whether the word itself is the subject of analysis.

'Sangoma' is derived from the Zulu, *isangoma*, and is used in popular speech, the press and other media to designate a 'traditional healer'. The Swazi form is *tangoma*. Occasionally *inyanga* or *nyanga* (common form) is also used in English and other South African languages such as isiZulu and Afrikaans, although more generally this means any kind of doctor or qualified healer.

Key terms often have different forms. Speakers of both languages/dialects make automatic perceptual adjustments to accommodate the different phonologies, thus these words tend to 'sound the same' to many speakers and vary with the context of speech. For instance, *emadloti* (ancestors, or spirits of the ancestors) is the siSwati form of the word more widely known in isiZulu as *amadlozi*. The dialects are mutually intelligible as long as account is taken of certain substitutions, for example /t/ is used in siSwati for /z/ in isiZulu. There are also differences in pronunciation, for instance the /d/ sound in isiZulu is pronounced with a slight /z/ sound on release of the consonantal stop in siSwati. *Mpande* in isiZulu becomes *mpandze* in siSwati, for example. The isiZulu /t/ is pronounced with a light /tz/ sound in siSwati, so *muti* in isiZulu becomes *mutzi* in siSwati. The

Zulu *abantu* (people), becomes *bantfu* with a more implosive or emphatic /b/ sound in siSwati.

It is difficult to achieve consistency because the forms used depend on who is being quoted, the situation being described, or if the word is being used as a label or descriptor. Generally I use the term that is more familiar to southern Africans, for instance *muti* instead of *mutzi*, and Bantu instead of *Bantfu*.

In general and anthropological literature the sangoma is often called a traditional healer, but this is misleading. The sangoma does many things. While healing is certainly part of the sangoma's activities, supporting other healers through drumming, dancing, knowledge exchange and travel often consumes more time than the actual healing of patients.

The sangomas of southern Africa, almost all of whom speak a Bantu language or especially a Nguni language (isiXhosa, isiZulu, siSwati, xiTsonga/Shangaan), also share much with the broadly disseminated *ngoma* cults throughout the large portion of sub-Saharan Africa in which Bantu languages are spoken. They are not associated with a particular ethnicity or language group, but constitute a regional guild of practitioners with secret knowledge. They control 'ancestors' (*emadloti*) who have originally come to them in dreams with specific demands and who usually 'require' them to become healers or *isangoma*. By becoming an initiated sangoma the uninitiated apprentice learns to control the *emadloti* that possess him or her. The process of learning to master these forces ultimately makes the apprentice, *mthwasana*, able to heal by controlling others forces of a similar kind.

In this discussion, I use siSwati versions of words that are similar throughout the Nguni language family (isiZulu, isiXhosa, siSwati). Equivalent words exist in xiTsonga, tshiVenda and the Sotho-Tswana languages (or dialects). English and Afrikaans healers and the lay public usually use the Nguni words when speaking about these matters. All southern African languages may be in play at any time within any gathering.

CHAPTER 2

The material logic of evil and the augmented self

> [W]hen one sees the people giving up their whole minds to it, sub-
> mitting without resistance to the circumcision and putting up with
> extreme hardships in the way of cold and disease in the lodges, and
> the entire suspension of their ordinary duties, it makes it difficult to
> dispel the idea that it is *their form of religion* or perhaps some cher-
> ished national custom handed down to them.
>
> *Olden Times in Zululand*, Bryant 1929

If *bungoma* is not a deficient or 'traditional' medicine, and not a science, is
it not then a form of religion? If traditional healing is not fully traditional,
can it be reduced to a single task that we call 'healing'? Does its use of
ritual, formulaic language, music, song and intangible person-like agents
make it a kind of African traditional religion? Some scholars have argued
that it is indeed a form of traditional religion (Chidester 1996; Chidester
et al. 1997; Dovey and Mjingwana 1985; Kruger 1995; Mbiti 1975, 1990;
Setiloane 1973, 1976, 1986; Smith 1929) and that it must be respected
as such. But the argument that traditional healing is a limited, early, or
'traditional' form of religion – or, in the words of the missionary Edwin
Smith (1929), a 'twilight religion' – has the same drawback as representing it as a simpler and alternative medicine. Both positions rest on the
assumption that *bungoma* is a deficient form of something else, either a

not-quite religion, or a 'barefoot' medical practice rooted in superstition and misunderstanding.

By presenting the philosophy of traditional medicine in its own terms we can ask in what sense it might also be a form of medicine or a form of religion. I would claim that *bungoma* is certainly a form of medical *practice*, even though it is *not only* a medical practice. It is not, however a form of religion, that is, it is not a *deficient* theology. Surprisingly, the earliest Christian missionaries agreed that it was not religion.

In order to understand how and in what ways southern Africans got along perfectly well without 'religion' we can explore why early Christian missionaries agreed that there was no religion in southern Africa. This had important implications for their own ambitious programme of proselytisation of its people.

'Their form of religion'?

Olfert Dapper begins his description of the Cape of Good Hope, published in 1668, with a declaration that the people of the region have no religion:

> The country or land of Kaffraria or, according to Marmol, Quefrerie is so named after the Kafirs, its native inhabitants. They are commonly known to our countrymen as Hottentoos or Hottentots, because their language is so clumsy and difficult; and they live without any laws of religion (Dapper, Ten Rhyne and De Grevenbroek 1933 [1688]).

This view did not originate with Dapper since he never visited Africa, and probably never left Amsterdam. But he draws on very reliable sources in the Cape that not only knew the 'Hottentots' well but were also integral members of Cape society. By the middle of the seventeenth century residents of the Cape seem to have agreed that the 'Kaffirs' or 'Hottentots' – Dapper and his sources did not make a distinction between them – 'lived without any laws of religion'.

When missionaries first began to flood into southern Africa in the early nineteenth century one of the primary questions they asked was: 'where is the religion?' This has remained a perennial question. 'As everyone knows,' David Chidester (1996: xv) writes, 'European observers entered southern Africa and declared that the indigenous people had no religion.' Since the sixteenth century Christian observers have said that religion, as they understand it, did not exist among southern African peoples. Instead, they reported that Hottentots 'worshipped' the mantis insect, or the moon, and that Bantu-speaking peoples worshipped their ancestors, or nothing at all. Christian missionaries believed, accordingly, that all they had to do was to bring 'enlightenment' to southern Africa with the Christian message.

Robert Moffat, father-in-law of David Livingstone and one of the first missionaries among the Tswana of Kuruman (Comaroff 1985; Comaroff and Comaroff 1991; Moffat 1846), was a case in point. In the dedication of his book *Missionary Labours and Scenes in Southern Africa* to His Royal Highness, Prince Albert, he wrote:

> Your Royal Highness is well aware that all methods of effecting the civilization of Africa, apart from the Gospel of Christ, have hitherto proved abortive; but...in every instance where the Gospel has been introduced, it has effected a complete revolution in the character and habits of its people. Philosophy must eventually confess her impotence; the pride of Science be humbled; and the fact be universally acknowledged, that the Gospel of Christ is the only instrument which can civilize and save all kindreds and nations on earth. This has been verified by the labours of Missionaries in South Africa...Nothing remains but to apply the means already at our disposal. In this high enterprise of religion and humanity, all may share (Moffat 1846: i).

Originally published in 1842, drawing on Moffat's southern African work over 'twenty-three years as an agent of the London Missionary Society in that continent' (Moffat 1846: title page) Moffat speaks of the 'revolution' and 'revelation' that Jean Comaroff wrote about 150 years later (Comaroff 1985; Comaroff and Comaroff 1991). The Comaroff texts, like Moffat's, treat Tswana knowledge as deficient and both purport to show that while Africans could resist its influence, ultimately the power of Christianity and capitalism would overwhelm them. While some anthropologists and historians have moved considerably beyond this formulation today (for instance, Landau 2010), the notion that southern African thought was simply deficient in 'religion' has remained a dominant motif.

In southern Africa, unlike in other parts of the world, missionaries did not have to struggle against an earlier, or other, religion such as Islam, or Hinduism, nor bring backsliders and apostates back to 'their proper faith', as in Britain or Europe. Instead, as people like Moffat and the other missionaries saw it, they simply had to bring religion *as such*. Ever since, anthropologists, theologians, missionaries and others, have worked with a 'deficit model' of southern African pre-colonial culture. Southern African concepts of causation, creation, life and being simply lacked a 'true' concept of God, time and creation. Referring to an episode that took place in 1815 Moffat wrote:

> I cannot do better that repeat the substance of a conversation between our missionary, Mr. Schmelen, and a native, on this subject. Mr Schmelen had at that time better opportunities than any other man of becoming acquainted with the views of the Namaquas in their native state. In his journal of the 23d May, 1815...Mr S[chmelen] writes thus: – 'Addressing a Namaqua, I asked, did you ever hear of a God' 'Yes, we have heard that there is a God, but we do not know...we heard it from other people'...'Who made the heavens?' 'We do not know what man made them.' 'Who made the sun?' 'We always heard that those people at the sea made it; when she goes down, they cut her in pieces, and fry her in a pot, and then put her together again, and bring her out the other side...They said the moon had told to mankind that we must die, and not become alive again; this is the reason that when the moon is dark we sometimes become ill.'...'Do you know you have a soul?' 'I do not know it' 'How shall it be with us after death?' 'When we are dead, we are dead ...'
>
> [Later in the journal entry, dated July, Moffat quotes Schmelen:] 'After service I spent some time conversing with some of the aged, but found them extremely ignorant; some [of] them could not conceive of a being higher than man, and had not the least idea of immortality of the soul' (Moffat 1846: 33).

Reading this out of the context of missionary rhetoric of a deficient religion – that is, in purely humanist terms – it would appear that the Namaqua had independently invented an anthropocentric or humanist worldview. But, throughout the rest of the nineteenth and twentieth centuries missionaries repeated much the same sort of conversations with southern African people in what Moffat and Schmelen called their 'native state'.

Taking words from southern African languages and redefining them in the process of translating biblical and religious texts remedied this deficit rather simply. *Utixo*, a Khoe word, was used to translate 'god' in isiXhosa, while the root words 'big' (*-khulu-*) and 'chief' (*-kosi*) were roped in to do the work in isiZulu. And so on. Moffat eventually used the word *molimo/modimo/morimo* as the word for God in his translations of biblical and church materials, even though he noted early on that:

> From the frequent conversations I had with him [Moselekatse, also Mzilikazi of the 'Matebele', or Ndebele, now in Zimbabwe] and his people on the subject of religion, and some of the strange ceremonies I witnessed, it was evident that though they were entirely ignorant of the origin of all things, and of a Creator and Governor, they used the name Morimo* – or Molimo according to their pronunciation – which they applied not to a being or power, but to the state of the dead, or influence of the *manes* [Latin term, usually translated as the 'venerated ancestors'] of the dead. (The asterisk points to the note: 'This being the Sechuana [Setswana] word, as I never could discover that the Zoolus [Zulu] had even the name in their language') (Moffat 1846: 152).

Of course, the 'Zoolus', like other people speaking Bantu languages in southern Africa, did have a name for what Moffat had thought of as the Latin '*manes*'. These were the *amathongo* or *amadlozi* (isiZulu and isiXhosa; *emadloti* in siSwati) in the Nguni languages, or *seriti* and/or *moyo* in Sotho-Tswana languages (for instance Mönnig 1967: 54ff; Schapera 1957), subsequently translated as 'soul' or as 'ancestor' (Hunter 1936: 231–235, 536–541; Krige 1950: 284; Krige 1944; Kuper 1947; but cf. Landau 2010: 17, 75ff concerning mistranslation and pervasive confusion among these terms). For the missionaries of the nineteenth century, however, none of these terms quite translated their own concepts of god-as-spirit, although they sometimes believed that they might constitute inklings of true religion.

The deficit model was also applied to the members of schools or guilds of magicians and ritual specialists, variously called 'rainmakers', 'witchdoctors', 'traditional healers', 'shamans' and 'African' or 'traditional doctors'. Moffat quotes the French missionary, Casalis, who was working with the 'Basutos' of Moshoeshoe in what is now Lesotho and the Free State province of South Africa:

> [T]he Basutos speak of Morimo, consult their rain-makers and their amulets, slaughter their victims, without appearing to attach the least religious idea to these actions. 'We have learned this from our fathers, but we do not know the reason of it.' This is the answer they make to the questions which are put to them on these subjects [of religion]. Perhaps it would facilitate our labours if they had some notion of this kind (Moffat 1846: 152).

But they did not. They were experts of a different kind, not priests.

According to the Christian missionaries, then, while the southern African peoples had no 'religion' they had plenty of magic and were 'heavily oppressed' by witches and witchcraft. As southern African people were only able to resort to magicians, charlatans and magic, their lack of religion literally condemned them to 'darkness'.

The 'rainmakers' were treated as doctors who lacked efficacy, that is, as 'charlatans' with pretensions to medical knowledge but without true medicine, much as they lacked true religion. They could only offer 'amulets'. Other ritual actions, or 'strange ceremonies', in Moffat's terms, such as circumcisions, were also treated as deficient forms of religious ritual (see epigraph from Bryant's *Olden Times in Zululand*). Again, this deficit model is still almost universally applied to southern African pre-colonial conceptual, healing, ritual and technical systems, as it is to contemporary 'traditional healing'.

Monica Hunter (Wilson), for instance, notes that 'there is no proof that the Pondo, before contact with Europeans, believed in the existence of any Supreme Being, or beings' (Hunter 1961: 269), while Hermann Mönnig (1967: 43) was able to remark, similarly, that 'Pedi ideas on religion are extremely vague'. Mönnig lamented that the 'labours of the missionaries have not…borne the fruits one would expect'. (Even the historical label 'pre-colonial' implies that, by being 'pre-', southern African cultures lacked the 'colonial', and, like religion, were simply waiting for it to happen.)

By the middle of the twentieth century, however, anthropologists and religious studies scholars attempted to resolve the problem by asserting that what had been called 'magic' and witchcraft, and beliefs concerning 'the ancestors', were just another form of religion. They were, in fact, 'African religion' or 'African traditional religion'. The identification of African ritual systems with 'religion' was strongly influenced by Victor Turner's work on the Ndembu of Zambia and by Mircea Eliade's universalist theories of religion (Eliade 1961, 1963; Turner 1969).

In order to 'dispel any lingering traces of a Frazerian hangover' Stanley Tambiah (1968: 176), for instance, argued that the 'magical power of words' was essentially the same in 'religion' and 'magic', and that the distinction – for instance, between 'prayer' and 'spell' – was therefore entirely artificial. 'Prayer' involved a communication with the divine, while 'spells' were 'mechanical' magic. Anthropologists, he claimed:

> Operated with the concept of 'magic' as something different from 'religion'…Frazer carried this thinking to an extreme by asserting that magic was thoroughly opposed to religion and in the interest of preserving this distinction dismissed half the globe as victims of the 'confusion of magic with religion'.

All these approaches imply that 'traditional' attempts to comprehend and manipulate material reality are, in fact, deficient. Rather than continuing to explore southern African cultural systems as deficient 'religion', as deficient 'medicine', or even as a defective indigenous science, it is better to explore them in their own terms.

As I understand these terms, it is a material logic that operates with and in terms of objects and persons. Some objects have person-like qualities, while some persons are like objects. Some persons and objects are tangible and some are intangible, but nothing is regarded as fully external to the material world in which we live. This might be called a 'this-worldly' orientation, or animism, but it is more accurate to call it simply 'material' orientation to life as such. There is no transcendent or metaphysical parallel or 'other' reality. This is one of the most significant features that distinguishes this African set of knowledge practices from the category 'religion'.

In order to avoid engaging other polemics directly I do not call this 'materialist', in part because there is no opposing immaterialist, transcendental, or metaphysical philosophical perspective with which the southern African material logic habitually engages. I also do not wish to call it a 'science of the concrete' since it does not fully conform to the structural characteristics that Claude Lévi-Strauss defined for the 'science [or logic] of the concrete' (Lévi-Strauss 1978: 10). For my discussion of *bungoma*, and to distinguish its logical form from both religion and the sort of myth and well-structured systems that Lévi-Strauss analysed, I use the term *material logic*. But, as Lévi-Strauss (1966: 12) wrote:

> The real question is not whether the touch of a woodpecker's beak does in fact cure toothache. It is rather whether there is a point of view from which a woodpecker's beak and a man's tooth can be seen as 'going together' (the use of this congruity for therapeutic purposes being only one of its possible uses), and whether some initial order can be introduced into the universe by means of these groupings.

Magic, then, is a logic of the material, or a material logic, but not necessarily a deficient science or a deficient religion. It is a magic because it achieves its results through juxtapositions and manipulations of tangible objects such as animal parts, plant and organic substances, mineral earths and objects made of metals and glass. It is a logic because it has formal properties of thought: a logic that links these things together in causal frameworks. Above all, a material logic of this sort makes sense. It makes sense in two ways: first, it is easy to *see the sense* in its juxtapositions, metaphors and metonymies, especially for someone who is fully at home in the universe of the specific things it comprises. Second, it *makes sense* by creating meaningful sentence-like structures of real objects. These composite objects – so called fetishes, medicine bundles, totems, *muti* – are 'sentences' of this type, not simply tokens (single marks, items or symbols) of complex meanings. In other words, magic makes meanings. It aims to achieve health, life, and the well-being of human bodies as embodied persons by making *statements* through reasoned combinations of objects that are themselves linked to other objects and to persons.

In the southern African context, however, not all persons have bodies, and not all bodies are 'persons'. For instance, 'ancestors' (*emadloti/amadlozi*) and even the 'shadow' of a person (*isithunzi*) lacks a body, but nevertheless has the characteristics of a person. Zombies, on the other hand, are bodies that lack autonomous 'person' qualities since their active intentional selves have been stolen in order to be controlled by other personal agents. This magic does not necessarily cure or even seek to generate diagnostic knowledge or therapeutic interventions.

In *A fundamental question of religious sociology* Bronislaw Malinowski (1993: 243) asked:

> Is there a sharp and deep cleavage between *religious* and *profane* matters among primitive peoples? Or, in other words: Is there pronounced dualism in the social and mental life of the savage, or, on the contrary, do the religious and non-religious ideas and activities pass and shade into each other in a continuous manner?
>
> This question is of utmost importance for the general theory of religion. Professor Durkheim postulates the existence of a perfectly sharp and deep cleavage between the two domains of the *sacré* and *profane*, and his entire theoretical construction stands and falls with this assumption (Thornton and Skalník 1993: 243).

Malinowski generally concurs with Émile Durkheim's sociology, but rejects his distinction between the sacred and the profane in favour of a broader cultural domain that does not necessarily include 'religion' as a fundamental and necessary domain of culture. His exploration of the Trobriand Islanders' magical logic of concrete things set anthropology on its current course. Malinowski, however, treated Trobriand magic as a linguistic problem involving the efficacy of spoken 'spells'. Here, I wish to distinguish the 'magic' of southern Africa from the linguistic approach of Malinowski, the 'sociological' binarism of Durkheim, and the Structuralism of Lévi-Strauss. Specifically, I want to make clear that this is not a 'materialism' in the sense that Marx and Marxists use this term because the southern African philosophical system does not pose the possibility that an *im*-material, transcendent or metaphysical reality stands in opposition to Marxian material*ism*. Thus, *muti* and associated material culture cannot be meaningfully described as 'fetish' because there is no dichotomy between man and nature, mind and body.

The material logic of southern African practitioners, it seems to me, is a logic that deals primarily with persons and person-like agents in relation to each other, rather than abstract cosmologies and transcendental causal hierarchies. Persons may be embodied, and therefore tangibly real, but also disembodied, and therefore intangible. The logic does not easily dissolve into binary 'structures' but is, instead, conceived as networks of multiply linked agents that include persons but also comprise certain elements of 'nature' called '*muti*'. This is integrated into an ontology of flows and mutual forces that include powerful agents that might otherwise be conceived as 'natural', 'cultural', 'personal', 'animal'/'animistic', 'social' or even imaginary.

What I call the material logic of the southern African ritual and healing specialist, then, does not imagine a purely transcendent immaterial world of spirit and then ascribe to it moral value as 'spirit' operating within a soteriological discourse. The southern African ideas comprised radically material logics and practices that focused instead on augmenting and thereby protecting the person in a complex network of materially constituted but nevertheless intentional agents. The logic of causality relied on the image of mutually causal 'persons' – some tangible, some intangible – as well as agents with plant, animal and mineral form. Thus, all objective, living persons were understood as possessing 'power' constituted by their physical, material presence but also by their intentions, 'blood', 'name' and other qualities that made up their 'shadow' (*seriti, isithunzi*). The more powerful living persons became influential 'ancestors' or intangible persons who lacked only a physical form but who retained their person-hood, or personality. There were also other types of 'partial-persons', such as witches, witch familiars, zombies and magical animals (*tokoloshes*, rain-animals), among others. Similarly, mineral substances like ochre, iron, gold and glass, animal substances such a python fat or hyena hair, as well as vegetable matter (*muti* or herbs), possessed causal powers. Together, these persons and 'things' constituted a complex network of causal agents. It was deficient primarily in that it lacked the

Aristotelian causal hierarchy of final, proximate, and efficient causation that is fundamental to Christian thought as it was developed from earlier philosophies of antiquity.

Moffat, like other evangelical Christians of his age, was keenly aware that the ancient philosophers thought in terms of a materialistic philosophy:

> Many heathen [here meaning ancient pre-Christian] philosophers who possessed advantages vastly superior to any of Africa's sons, instead of inferring from works of creation the existence of a Supreme Being, generally maintained that the *matter*, and even that the *form* of the world itself was eternal, and other again substituted part of the visible universe for God himself...It appears evident, then, from what has been written that all the relics of theology to be found in heathen lands are only the remaining fragments which have been handed down by a vitiated and defective tradition. But more than this, we find people not only in Africa...from whose intellectual horizon the last rays of tradition have fled, – proving what the Scriptures affirm, that man's depraved nature is such, as to choose darkness rather than light...(Moffat 1846: 72).

The logical structure of southern African conceptual systems, like those of antiquity, could not be mistaken, therefore, for 'religion'. 'Their systems are *radically defective* [emphasis in original]', Moffat insisted. Instead of positing a causal hierarchy with a 'god' at the top to act as both 'final cause', and 'creator' – the latter being simply a 'prior' cause, and therefore logically symmetrical to the Aristotelian 'final' cause – southern African cultural systems understood causation as radically mutual, diffused and 'flat', that is, non-hierarchical. Human beings, as well as a range of intangible 'persons', possessed power (*emandla*) over all others, including themselves. The network of causal agents also included plants, herbs, animals and animal products, as well as geological and material-cultural objects such as beads, cloth, coins, shells and metal objects.

All had, or could have, if manipulated correctly, power over other elements in the causal network, including humans. Thus it was possible to misunderstand this as a kind of deficient 'medicine'. The specialised technologies of magic also included actual fabrication of material-cultural objects such as beads, beaded objects, metals and other 'powerful' objects of fur and fibre, glass, wood, stone, bone, gum, ivory and many other materials. These technologies were all devoted to 'strengthening' people by protecting them from the complex causal network that surrounded them and in which they were embedded as similarly causal agents.

The 'augmented person'

Given the forces arrayed against any single person, the principal aim of these technologies, then, was *to augment the person* in a way that would enable him/her to withstand the influence of the many forces around that person. This involves a literal augmentation of the person with 'charms' and 'amulets', but also a 'cleansing' of the person through vomiting, enemas and blood-letting to clear out other, dangerous, causal agents that had come to reside inside the body. This is a technology aimed at creating persons. (The need for a first, or primary creation, or origin myth, is thus practically obviated.) As causal agents were not hierarchically – top to bottom – arranged, but rather laterally, from all sides, it appeared that 'natives' were afraid of everything and were 'bound in darkness', as the missionaries said, by superstition and fear of witches. This was true to a degree, but failed, as it still fails, to capture the fundamental and radically material logic of southern African conceptual systems relating to life and health, *imphilo*.

Southern African cultural systems, then, were not simply deficient religions, or deficient medicinal systems. What have been deficient are the broadly Mediterranean-Christian social philosophies that have been brought to bear in the effort to understand the cultural systems, which are a radically alternative philosophy of time, space and causation that has little in common with the 'Western' philosophical and religious conceptual apparatus. This distinctive ontology supposes a universe of material objects, including persons, that has mutual causal force, intentionality and integral continuity over time and space. Each person is such a network and is exposed to the power (*emandla*), the presence (*isithunzi*) and life (*imphilo*) of all other persons.

This resembles E B Tylor's concept of animism as 'pre-religion', except that it does not posit ontological being to an *animus* (Latin, 'soul') in non-human objects as his theory of animism does. Tylor's concept was developed primarily in relation to South American native concepts of a 'life force' or 'soul' that spanned human and animal beings. It has elements of James Frazer's 'contagious magic', in that objects are held to maintain their connection to place and the animal, plant or earth from which they originally came. But the southern African system is not entirely accounted for by either a Tylorian animism or a Frazerian magic

Animism and magic both posit a complex ontology of mutually causal material beings that maintained links across time and space. For instance, one's 'ancestor' maintained the link with a previously existing person, communicated across time with the living and was of the same substance as future generations that took the ancestor's names. Ancestors were simultaneously future children and the living persons of any current moment. Through blood and semen as shared substances, the living communicated directly with the children of future generations. These 'intangible persons', the dead and the yet-unborn, had discoverable intentions, needs and powers, and through the shared substance of 'blood', had direct influence over tangible, living persons. Like other social persons, intangible persons possess intentionality, identity and agency and their effect on the living demonstrates, in terms of these assumptions, causal efficacy.

Material derived from 'the bush' and used in the home or homestead similarly transcended place or space, but less in the European philosophical sense of 'transcendence' and more as consubstantial being. *Muti*, as mineral, plant and animal substances, connected the power of the wild with the space and needs of the domestic environment and served as a medium, or tool, to manipulate other persons, but also had its own character, intentions, and efficacy. All such objects, for instance, possessed gender and social roles (as enemy, friend, father, child ...) and had their own spatial orientation (front/head, back/top, feet/bottom, lateral direction) and even a 'mouth' by which they could be 'felt', smelt or heard.

The southern African approaches to the person and healing constitute a distinctly different ontology. Bruno Latour's ideas about different ontologies are useful here since the 'exposed being', the augmented person and the role of *muti* constitute what he calls 'artificially produced objective fact' (Latour 2014: 2). In the context of Latour's laboratory science, facts are 'artificially produced' by the entire scientific enterprise. In the context of *bungoma* we would call them 'cultural facts', but their objectivity is of the same nature since they are 'produced' and made 'objective' by the healing enterprise itself, the practice of its 'science'.

Latour (2014: 2) explains that

> [e]ven though 'ontology' has been defined as the science of 'Being as Being,' I take it as a relational and highly practical term. Ontology is what you engage whenever you wish not to shock those you are encountering by granting the wrong type of reality to the agencies that keep them moving.... [W]e practice ontology...when we realize that we had entered an interaction with too limited a set of templates to account for the realities mentioned by our informants.... So, ontology emerges over the course of encounters where the inquirer feels him or herself corseted by too narrow a set of legitimate agencies.

The 'Western', largely Christian ontology with which writers (including African writers) have sought to understand *bungoma* simply does not have the intellectual 'templates' to comprehend this form of African healing. An alternative ontology is required.

This radically material logic of southern African 'healing' effectively defeated the European logics of transcendent cause or 'spirit', causal hierarchy and categorical logics of space and time. The material logics of southern African cultures were not 'religions'. This is not to say that they were 'deficient' in 'religious knowledge', as the missionaries said, and as many observers, including social scientists and historians, have believed. It is simply that this cultural system or philosophy was sufficiently different from what Europeans, as inheritors of the great traditions of the Neolithic Middle East, had come to normalise and naturalise as the very essence of culture itself. The Anglican theologian and academic Matthew Arnold equated religion with culture. The more religion a culture had, in his view, the closer it came to 'civilisation'.

Congregations and sacred spaces

There are other reasons why the early Christian missionaries were unable to find 'religion' in southern Africa. The religious congregation is clearly a fundamental element of the Abrahamic and other Mediterranean religions of antiquity and achieved its fullest development in post-exilic Judaism and Hellenic temple worship (Robertson-Smith 1927 [1894]; Weber 1952 [1917–1919]: 156–165, 298–299, 379). During the late Neolithic period in the Levant those who attended sacrifices around an altar began to define what Durkheim later called 'the church' (1995 [1912]: 38–44). Similar altar structures, defined sacred spaces of temples, and communal sacrifices before a congregation are also present in the ancient Asian and Indian cultures Buddhism and Hinduism. The formation of a *congregation* at a sacrificial ritual before or on an altar is visible in the temple architecture of European and Mediterranean antiquity. This also defines the 'sacred space' that Durkheim thought was one of the key elements of 'religion' *per se*. Durkheim's definition is still the theoretical bedrock of academic understanding of religion. It is worth repeating here since it also helps us to understand why southern African *bungoma* and other ritual practices and systems of belief did not constitute *religion* in these terms:

> We arrive thus at the following definition [of religion]: A religion is a unified system of beliefs and practices relative to sacred things, that is to say, things set apart and forbidden – beliefs and practices which unite into one single moral community called a Church, all those who adhere to them. The second element thus holds a place in my definition that is no less essential than the first: In showing that the idea of religion is inseparable from the idea of a Church, it conveys the notion that religion must be an eminently collective thing (Durkheim 1995 [1912]: 44).

The ritual congregation, as the 'eminently collective thing', became the model for subsequent social identities such as the 'People of Israel' or the beneficiaries of Christ's sacrifice or those who submitted to the will of Allah as revealed by Mohammed. The importance of the congregation can scarcely be overstated, especially as evidenced by the demarcation of the sacred space of a central temple at the pinnacle or centre of a hierarchy of sacred spaces and sacred architecture as 'sacred things' that were 'set apart'. This architecture of space is central to the layout of cities even today.

Indeed, the word 'hierarchy', meaning priestly or holy (*hiero-*) precedence (*-archy*), points precisely to this system of hierarchical religious orders that define a hierarchical order of sacred sites, temples and holy places.

Southern African ritual systems were not organised in this way. Specifically, they lack a congregation as a 'moral community', even though there is a common set of beliefs and practices. They are not organised hierarchically in a pyramid of priestly precedence with a high priest at the top. There is no final authority defining belief (*doxa*) or ritual performance (*praxis*). And finally, there is no altar of the sort described in biblical and other ancient texts and as seen in the archaeology of the ancient Mediterranean and Middle Eastern cultures. Their focus was on the person as intentional agent linked through mutual influence to many other intentional agents, some of them also persons.

While social gatherings that focused on ritual performance might be called a 'congregation' in the southern African context, the very notion of a set of people all of whom are beneficiaries of a magical, ritual or sacred intervention of any kind is simply unthinkable. All such gatherings focus entirely on 'healing' or benefaction of only one person at a time. In trance dances and healing ceremonies involving dance and drumming – that is, the essence and central meaning of '*ngoma*' – it is the supplicant, the sufferer, the patient or client that receives the power (*emandla*) of the ceremony (or 'work', *sebento*). The 'congregation' consists only of interested observers and is in no way considered to be a sacred community of worshippers with a common transcendental focus or sacred object. The audience is just an audience and its members do not see themselves as recipients of blessings deriving from their joint participation in a religious act. They are nevertheless involved in the performance and can be addressed by the sangoma and the spirits at any time.

Above all, sangomas are not priests as they do not lead a congregation. They provide individuated services to clients, drawing on a broadly construed cultural tradition. They are experts who possess expertise not conduits of sacred knowledge or shepherds of flocks. It is above all their *personal expertise* that makes them who they are and allows them to do what they do, not sacred orders or hierarchical office-bearing.

The lack of a congregation, as such, and the role of the personal expertise of the sangoma also point to fundamental differences in the organisation of sacred spaces and to the relationship between sacred specialists, or 'healers', and 'society'. People who have been called healers, rainmakers, herbalists, witchdoctors and so on, were all members of what amount to secret guilds of ritual specialists and practitioners possessing proprietary knowledge about herbs, pyrotechnologies, beads, metals, earths, animals and animal substances. Typically held to be dangerous and powerful, but also useful, these possessors of specialised knowledge and practices served many different needs in the southern African social order and were bound together by their shared knowledge, which is owned only by the expert. Because they were feared, the very possession of such knowledge separated them from those who did not possess it. They were feared because they had extraordinary influence, or power, over the sources of evil and misfortune.

From the point of view of the client, that is ordinary persons who lacked specialist knowledge – expertise – or access to it, members of these 'guilds' provided two things: First, they were able to narrate a coherent account of the nature and sources of evil and misfortune. Second, they were able to provide protection against it. Protection came in the form of ritual interventions, often mediated by trance, or in the concrete form of 'amulets' made of metals, glass beads, and many other powerful substances. The technology to create these was also controlled by the specialists.

Unlike the hierarchies of priests in control of congregations and presiding over a hierarchy of sacred sites and holy places, before the advent of Christianity the early southern African social landscape consisted primarily of small groups of people – hunters, herders, planters, gatherers, chiefs and warriors – who moved relatively rapidly across the land and who gathered or divided as circumstances required. These groups were probably served by guilds of specialists who provided both the rationale and the means for 'protecting' against the evils and misfortunes that life brought their way.

'Witchcraft' or theodicy? An ontological theory of evil

Though not sharing much with the Mediterranean peoples, southern Africans still had to deal with the nature of evil and its sources in the world. This was done by means of the distinctive southern African material logics of regarding the nature of evil and misfortune.

While sociological theories about the nature of causation of evil and misfortune may have merit in the context of medieval Europe, or early colonial North America, they are not particularly relevant to southern Africa. As I understand it, the concept of witches, understood in its context, is itself an African theory of the nature of social evil. Thus, witchcraft, witches and sorcery do not need to be explained by means of a theory of social stress, historical, or structural violence, but already constitute a social theory of relations between persons.

Specifically, southern African 'healing' systems constitute complex theories of the ontology of evil, by which I mean a theory of the physical nature of evil, misfortune and bad luck, or the absence of goodness, or simply the inevitable personal and corporeal exposure to evil that afflicts everyone. I use the etymological sense of theory as 'seeing' (> Gk, *theorein*, to look at, to see), in the sense that theory allows one to see the world in a specific way. By 'theory' in this context I mean a specific way of 'seeing' evils and illness as embodied in patients, but also as existing in myriad physical substances and in either physical, tangible persons or intangible ones (*baloyi, batsakatsi, emadloti, inzunzu, ndzau* and others).

By 'ontology' I mean the sense of what is real and what is empirically knowable or given to the technologies of healing, including trance, dreams, divination, intuition, smell, 'feeling' and direct empirical experience, for instance, of textures, colours, 'heats', 'coldness' and other properties of physical substances. In Western ontology trance, dreams and intuition would not be classified together with smell and other 'physical' sensations. The knowledge of the senses, of course, was the guarantee of 'reality' for philosophers from Aristotle's realism through René Descartes's rationalism and Ernst Mach's empiricism, and such sensory knowledge, however much extended by microscopes, cyclotrons, or photography, is still the basis for empirical knowledge. For sangomas, however, what is smelt, or dreamed, or encountered in trance is also real, and therefore empirically knowable. In this sense, they possess a different ontology on which a different empiricism is based.

In trance the healer enacts an ecstasy that mimics a sexual ecstasy that would be called – if seen independently of its meaning and context – an 'orgasmic' event. It is a solitary orgiastic mania that serves as a sign that the spirits have come. The mouth foams, the body runs with sweat, the voice changes to deep groans of ecstatic character and high-pitched shouts rhythmically repeated. The body is possessed in a ritually induced mania that mimics a sexual arousal, plateau phase and culmination in orgasmic release. As in sexual ecstasy, the consciousness is altered but does not cease to be conscious of its surroundings. It is, specifically, wild.

The contrast between civil social behaviour and the wild ecstatic behaviour of the healer is like the contrast in the African imagination of the landscape between the settled civil area of habitation and the wild open area of the surrounding landscape. Just as the healing power of the environment comes from the bush, the healing power of the ecstatic possession comes from the wildness of that possession. It brings this power into the heart of ordinariness of everyday pain and suffering, just as the *nyanga*, or herbalist, brings the wildness of the herb into the daily life of the patient. The 'wildness' of both bush and ecstatic possession are powerful and closely aligned in the healing process. In order to function both require a distinction between 'bush' and 'town' and between the 'ordinary' and the 'ecstatic'. These contrasts must be present and available to everyone. The sangoma's trance, then, is not a form of unconsciousness, or loss of mind, but an alternative mode of processing information, especially social information that is usually unspoken, 'secret' and hidden. The trance, human relations, evil, pain and intuition become objects of thought, albeit of a kind that cannot be called 'rational'.

As Lévi-Strauss (1962: 3) remarked in *Savage Mind*: 'the universe is an object of thought at least as much as it is a means of satisfying needs'. Every civilisation tends to overestimate the objective orientation of its thought and this tendency is never absent.

If southern African societies had no 'religion' in the sense of the Abrahamic religions derived from the Mediterranean Neolithic, they also had no concept of 'spirit' as fully non-material 'substance' without place or time. In the Christian concept of spirit, the only property of this 'substance' is causation since, as immaterial 'thing', it cannot also have spatial or temporal coordinates. Saint Augustine, the Bishop of Hippo, insisted on this as he struggled to come to terms with Christianity without leaning towards Manichaeism or Gnosticism, which, given the ferocity of his argument against them, he seemed to have naturally preferred.

This is not to say that the Mediterranean religions did not also possess a material logic. They certainly did, but this theme ran a continuous counterpoint to the non-material essentialist notion of spirit and god. This is the reason why Judaism, Christianity and Islam all forbid what they called idols. In the ancient Mediterranean world philosophical combat took place between the Abrahamic concepts of immaterial transcendent essence and the physicalism – or 'materialism' – of the 'also ran' religions that did not make it into the modern age. Among these are Manichaeism, Mithraism, Zoroastrianism, the religions of Egypt, the Hittites, Canaan, Babylon and Minoa, the religion of the Pharaoh Akhenaten, among many other smaller cults and religion-like philosophies and practices that were eventually supplanted by the Abrahamic religions 'of the Book', including Judaism, Christianity, and Islam.

For the monotheistic religions of immaterial essence the 'idols' of other religions represented gods that could not, or should not, be worshipped, venerated or empowered in any way. For the people of the other religious traditions, however, the idols, statues, paintings and other forms of the god were not representations or symbols, they *were* the god. The god was the *thing*, and vice versa. From the earliest evidence of Neolithic ritual sites at Göbekli Tepe, with its 20 000kg monolithic stones arranged in circles or 'rooms', dating from the tenth millennium BCE, it appears that people put a great deal of effort into these images and places. Even earlier, the delicate sculpturing of the 'Lion Man' from the Stadel Cave in the Hohenstein of Lone Valley in south-west Germany is one of the earliest examples of anthropomorphic art. This ivory figure is now dated by carbon-14 methods to around 40 000 BCE. It is clear from the vast archaeological evidence and the history and texts of ancient religions that the sculpted or painted image of a 'god' or venerated being of some sort was central to the earliest religious forms in the Mediterranean and Eur-Asian region.

The difference between a material god and an immaterial or transcendent god was one of the chief problems that kept Augustine awake at night as he wrote *The City of God*, which helped to define the social architecture of the Roman Catholic Church just as the Roman Empire itself fell to the barbarians. Early in *The Confessions* Augustine (1961 [ca. 398 CE]: 62) tells us about his struggles with 'the flesh' and sexuality, and 'the outer world that lay before my eyes':

> There is another reality besides this [the 'outerworld', 'the flesh']
> though I knew nothing of it. My own specious reasoning induced me

to give in to the sly argument of fools [the Manichaean philosophers] who asked me what was the origin of evil, whether God was confined to the limits of a bodily shape, whether he had hair and nails, and whether men could be called just if they had more than one wife at the same time, or killed other men, or sacrificed animals.

Augustine confesses his fruitless search through the Manichaean, Aristotelian and Platonist philosophers for the solution to what was essentially a Manichaean problem: was evil a material substance or being, opposed to good in a cosmic struggle between darkness and lightness, Good and Evil? 'I was trying to find the origin of evil,' Augustine tells us. Before his full conversion to Christianity, he

pictured the whole of creation, both the things which are visible to us, such as the earth and sea, the air and the stars...and everything spiritual – for I thought of spiritual things too as material bodies, each in its allotted place. I imagined the whole world of your creation as a vast mass made up of different kinds of bodies, some of them real, some of them only the bodies which in my images took the place of spirits (Augustine 1961 [ca. 398 CE]: 62; Book III, 7).

Augustine believes that God is infinite and good and 'utterly and entirely better than the things which he has made' and is forced to ask, 'Where then is evil?'

In short, Augustine comes to the conclusion that the true nature of spirit is formless, timeless and without place or spatial reference. It can only be 'known', in a sense, through faith, and evil has no real – that is formal, material – existence, apart from the evil that men do and think. 'Either there is evil and we fear it, or the fear itself is evil.' This is the nature of sin and the source of evil in an otherwise perfect creation of a perfect creator. Augustine appears never to accept this conclusion fully, however, and touches repeatedly on the problem of evil and his troubling conviction that there is some other reality besides the one we know though 'the flesh' and see in the 'outer world'.

This continued to be the central problem of Christianity that the missionaries brought to Africa. The problem is still, naturally, one of the central differences between the Christian religious philosophies in Africa and the African traditional systems of thought, often called 'African traditional religions'. Christians, especially African Christians, insist that the mere practice of an African traditional ritual is in itself evil. The missionaries taught that what the African feared most – the witch, and 'superstition' – did not exist and, like Augustine, concluded that what Africans feared was the fear itself.

Here I have posed the Christian system of thought against the southern African traditional one as though there were a simple opposition, calling one 'Christian' and the other 'African' as shorthand. I take the Augustinian Christianity as a sort of 'basic' Christianity, since Augustine's works, especially *The City of God* (Augustine 1890 (ca. 410 CE)), have defined Catholic thought since the beginning of the fourth century. Moreover, Augustine's views are worked out precisely in the context of strong opposition from deeply materialist philosophies that did not posit a domain of pure immateriality called 'spirit'. Since these were also the questions that motivated the missionaries who brought Christianity to Africa, and as they have daily relevance to most Africans practising some form of religion, the juxtaposition makes good sense.

Let us take as given that all humans 'see' some other reality behind, or other than, the visible one. This seems a feasible premise since all anatomically modern humans, beginning with the first burials involving ochre, art, sculpture and sacred architecture, seem to be premised on the concept of some other reality, no less real for its otherness. Let us assume further that all human beings have a basic and universal *a priori* concept of space, time and causation.

Given these assumptions we can conclude that Africans in southern Africa had no religion at all, as most missionaries and Christian observers wrote from earliest European contact. This does not imply in any way a moral deficit but rather a different philosophical orientation to human life. Yet, if there were no God and no concept of sin what would constitute a comparable cultural framework in the southern African context?

It seems to me that the answer lies in Augustine's troubling question, which he never answered to his own satisfaction: 'What then is evil?' This is the problem that Gottfried Leibniz called 'theodicy'. Leibniz was concerned by the question of why evil exists in a world made by God, who is perfect and omnipotent. But the problem of theodicy itself dissolves entirely if no 'god' is posited, that is, no ultimate force or power, since evil is simply present and natural. The problem of *what evil is* does not dissolve so easily, however.

What has come to be called 'witchcraft' answers the question of why evil exists, even – or especially – because it does not need to posit a good 'God' who nevertheless permits evil to exist. It is an effective theodicy, but one without reference to a 'god' or even to another unseen or immaterial world. It is a radically material, this-worldly account of the nature of evil. Evil, in this view, is the consequence of a world in which all beings are directly exposed to one another in a vast web of mutualities.

This includes human persons, but also intangible human persons as ancestors and the yet-unborn, beings still prefigured, however, in the blood and semen of the current generation. It also includes plants, animals and minerals, especially those that have some perceptible, metaphoric or syntactic ('contagious') connection with human persons. Witches are not alone in this worldview.

Anthropologists and historians, together with missionaries, the Christian public, and southern African popular culture have isolated 'witchcraft' as a uniquely African affliction. This appears particularly problematic because the notion is isolated from the cultural context in which it makes sense. 'Witchcraft' in the African context is also explicitly compared with the phenomenon in European and early Euro-American contexts, even though it has little in common with them. But 'witches' are not alone in the *bungoma* philosophy and do not act alone. They are part of a complex system of causation involving earth (metals, ochre), water (rain and 'rainmakers', streams, foam, water 'spirits' or *inzunzu*, 'rain animals', among others), fire (pyrotechnologies including metal smelting and smithing, glass and ceramics), and air (*moya*, breath). This also includes plants (*muti*), animals and animal parts (*nyama* 'flesh', *mafuta* 'fat'), and materials from the earth such as ochre, specularite, clay and other earths and ores.

This solves the problem of evil, since evil simply circulates in a closed system of causes that have some good and some bad consequences. The southern African solution to the problem of evil is to see it as an eternal regress in an undirected, non-hierarchical and dense network of causation and intentional actors. Without having to resort to a hierarchy of causation with 'God' at the top, this flat logic of the materiality of evil in a densely interconnected system of causal relations seems complete. It does not need, and therefore does not 'lack', religion.

Witches are persons, according to *bungoma*. They can either be present or not present and more or less conscious, possessing intent, or fully unconscious, lacking intent but possessing efficacy. The witch is simply one of many sources of evil in the system and, as such, does not 'deserve' special attention. Together with that of many other entities, the notion of the witch provides an explanation of evil and, at the same time, a defence against evil. The witch's 'magic' can be turned against it, reflected, like a physical force. Only those who are inadequately protected, or caught unawares, are fully vulnerable to the witch. But this is true of any other form of danger, including that of the ancestors.

It is wrong, therefore, to isolate 'witchcraft' as a specific form or consequence of 'social stress'. This is also why so-called 'witchcraft' has been more or less immune to the Christian denunciation of it and to government attempts to eradicate it. It seems also to be immune to the ostensible 'knowledge' that it does *not* exist.

The exposed being

In this cultural framework the person is an *exposed being* that can either be augmented and protected or diminished and therefore made more vulnerable. Each actor in this system, including non-humans and intangible persons – such as witches – is similarly vulnerable or protected. The dynamic of any human practitioner, or any sufferer, is whether and to what extent protection can be afforded in particular circumstances. Divination, and other modes of knowledge, expose the context of other causal agents, while material objects of the sort that are often called 'charms', 'talismans' or 'amulets' are made to protect the person. Those with protection are therefore augmented, or 'greater' than others to whom they still remain vulnerable, and the others to them.

This implies a hierarchy of protection or augmentation. Each person can be regarded as more or less protected against others, or vulnerable to them. This is the essence of so-called witchcraft. Importantly, the hierarchy or relative protection of one person against another does not have a necessary pinnacle. There is no ultimate cause and thus no need for a god, or gods, to account for the regress of causes. All causation is an endless regress into a network of witches, persons, amulets, animals and all other active substances and presences.

Power (*emandla*), here, is a personal attribute rather than a role or position in a social hierarchy of people who command or follow one another. The followers of a chief are not directly controlled by his command. Indeed, chiefs almost never give commands of the sort that Weber (1978: 33) made central to his definition of power. Rather, the person has power or not, and to varying degrees. This determines his or her share of evil, illness, and misfortune, but also his or her health, wealth and good luck.

Persons thus differ from one another by virtue of their greatness (*bukhulu*) and the degree to which they are protected from others. It is not only witches who can pose a threat, any other person can do so, despite the literature to the contrary. The greatest (*mkhulu*) is the chief (*inkosi*) or simply, 'Mr Big' (*umkhulu*). In the missionaries' efforts to harmonise – and colonise – the African understanding of the world with Christian concepts they adopted the neologism *unkhulunkhulu*, 'the big bigness', as the name for God. This is logically impossible, however, in a strict interpretation of the pre-colonial African logic since all 'greatness' is simply relative to the network in which all others are embedded.

This working misunderstanding continues to define the interaction between Christianity and African indigenous philosophies. On the other hand, the lack of fit between these two fundamentally different accounts of evil and suffering allows them – paradoxically – to co-exist. This was not the case, of course, for other Mediterranean religions, or those of pre-Christian Europe or the Americas. They came into direct conflict with the Christian theodicy and were either destroyed or forgotten. The success with which Christian theology and practices have been blended with the 'pagan' in southern Africa, as was the case in the Mediterranean world of antiquity, is due to the fact that they do not compete for the same ground.

Most accounts of this interaction, such as those offered by John and Jean Comaroff (for instance, Comaroff 1985; Comaroff and Comaroff 1991, 1992), see it simply as a modality of capitalism and colonialism. Christianity as a form of colonialism, or a tool of capital, has simply overpowered and defeated what they understand as 'African religion'. This, however, is clearly an inadequate explanation in the face of the growth and persistence of *bungoma*. In fact, nominally Christian, yet clearly indigenous ritual forms such as *bungoma* are pervasive in southern African today and are becoming stronger, with more numerous followings. At the same time, these indigenous, syncretic cults are more adamant in their identification with Christianity.

The indigenous African system works without the need for a god/God, since other persons, objects and substances do the philosophical work of the god figure. They provide an account of a non-local causation and an account of the 'origin' and the nature of evil in the unlimited regress in a network of persons as exposed beings.

Ancestors: 'spirit' or intangible persons?

The word 'ancestors' implies a genealogy and a social relation between persons, living and dead. Moffat radically confused the issue by assimilating the southern African ideas of the *emadloti* with the Roman notion of 'venerated ancestors', called *manes* in Latin. For these reasons, the southern African term '*emadloti*' [siSwati] *amadlozi* [isiZulu], or *molimo* [Sesotho, Setswana], usually translated as 'ancestor' in accordance with Moffat's usage – especially in his translation of religious texts such as the Bible – is a venerable mistranslation. In place of this, I suggest that it might better be understood as 'intangible' persons with social links to real persons and therefore with power over them. A genealogy implies a long-term temporal continuity with formal recognition of a kin group. A group implies an identity. While some might object that it is difficult to imagine an *intangible* person, it is no less difficult to imagine than a *completely non-material being* called 'spirit'. The phrase 'intangible person' at least captures the sense of how *emadloti* are conceptualised and how they are believed to act, according to southern African traditional beliefs.

In the southern African traditions the *emadloti* do not create 'identities'. The social name, the so-called praise name, *isibongo*, that is inherited or often adopted, provides an identity. This is often only loosely connected, if connected at all, to a proveable genealogy or heritage. The characters called *emadloti* are only a selection of all possible genealogical ancestor, and are often, in fact, names chosen in dreams to reflect a claim on imagined power (*emandla*). Very few people can recite anything like a genealogy. It is true that ethnologists of the Native Affairs Department in the middle of the twentieth century obsessed over genealogical records of people who they called 'chiefs', but genealogies seemed to exist mainly for chiefs, and these are, at best, always contested, never codified.

Few today accept these Native Affairs Department genealogies of people who were sometimes, but not always called chiefs (*inkosi*). These genealogies determine who has claim to what are considered fortunes in salaries for the chief and a retinue of retainers, but there is endless and constant debate in almost every locale where chiefs still 'rule', including in Unjindi and Barberton, about who is 'really' the chief. In other words, the genealogies have little legitimacy. They often also determine the disposition of large tracts of land under the 'land reform' policies of the ANC government. Since the legitimacy of these can rarely be 'proved' in a way that satisfies even a corrupt legal system, the land reform programme has ground to a near halt, especially in the rural areas.

In short, there is very little reason to assimilate the southern African term '*emadloti*' into the notion of the genealogical continuity and identity of formal groups, even though they clearly denote a genealogical connection across generations. What I wish to argue here, however, is that this is not so much hierarchical and temporal in the sense of European concepts of genealogy, but rather social and contemporary.

Beings that are universally called 'ancestors' in English exert influence over the living and are often held to determine the life course in fundamental ways. Ancestors 'speak', have needs that can be fulfilled, appear to people, direct divination processes and have strong, sometimes indomitable personalities. In other words, they seem to act in many respects like *persons*, not names or positions in a genealogy.

For this reason, I call the *emadloti*, simply, intangible persons. This formulation assimilates the *emadloti* into a material logic and allows an understanding of their 'magical' qualities.

Divination as a statement of ontology

Divination (*kupengula*) – throwing the bones (*emathambo, tinhlolo*) – is clearly a logic of material objects. It looks very much like a game of pieces and indeed, insofar as it entails a narrative, formal moves and tokens on a board or mat, it is a game. But it is a game of logic of a clearly material sort.

The practice of 'divination' in southern Africa has largely been understood as if it were cognate with ritual or religious practices of the oracle in Mediterranean antiquity.

As I have come to understand the process of divination (*kupengula*) in southern African *bungoma* practice, however, it is largely concerned with two things: Identifying the context or environment of threats and evil for the client (and also for the healer) and identifying threats to relationships with others such as wives, husbands and lovers – especially in relationships involving sexual contact and desire, wealth (*imali*) and family or generational relations. The ultimate aim of divination, then, is to augment the person in a way that either protects against evil and misfortune or reflects evil back to its source. By reformulating the client's own narrative of being it augments the person directly, and therefore protects.

It is not generally diagnostic of any particular complaint, nor does it necessarily reveal any therapeutic approach, except in a general sense. A client usually emerges from a '*pengula*' session with some sense of a diagnosis and of a therapeutic process that must be followed, but these determinations are usually made before the actual divination begins, or after it is over. Before the session begins the sangoma has usually already intuited the location of illness and specific pains in the body. This is part of what a sangoma is expected to 'know' when the client approaches. It is often among the first words spoken to the client when the healer tells the client what is troubling him of her. This demonstrates the intuitive credentials of the diviner, who receives this knowledge directly through a direct, corporeal empathy with the suffering client. Clients believe that unless the healer is able to do this, any further consultations are probably worthless.

After the session the divination kit is cleared off the mat and put away in its container, thereby quieting or deactivating the 'bones'. The healer and the client then discuss the results. This may involve further specific identification of illness – that is, diagnosis – or it may involve giving a prescription for therapeutic interventions. Such interventions include cleansings, protection, ritual acts of acknowledging the *emadloti*, sacrifice(s) or ascetic practices such as abstention from specific foods or sex. Only rarely does it involve drinking a tea or a concoction of herbs designed to act in a physiologically therapeutic way. Divination, then, in the *bungoma* practice I encountered, is directly therapeutic rather than, or sometimes in addition to, being diagnostic.

Material logic and the augmented self

In contrast to the approaches that attempt to 'explain' witchcraft as an isolated anomaly and as a consequence of 'social stress' ranging from family conflict to the contradictions of capitalism, I argue that 'the witch' is only one element of a complex set of forces and sources of evil characteristic of the southern African regional culture. It plays a role in a larger discourse and it is not sufficient to explain the whole in terms of one integral element, the 'witch'.

But witchcraft has been explained as deficient religion, and as deficient science and the sociological perspective has taken it to be a reflex of 'social dynamics'. But this takes as given a particular vision of 'society'. As Marilyn Strathern (1988) has observed, we must not expect cultural others to solve the problems of 'society' for 'us', the 'Europeans'. In other words, in so far as 'society' is a concept central to Euro-American modernity it is not fruitful to try to solve the problems that arise from our use of this concept through the frameworks by which other people seek to understand themselves.

If the problem of 'witch' is to be explored adequately and explained with sociological rigour we must take the concept itself as true of some social reality and then seek to understand the nature of the reality in which the concept, and practice, of witchcraft makes sense.

The figure of the witch makes sense in the context of a network of independent social actors, or persons and para-persons, who directly influence each other through a causal network that includes other person-like entities that are not tangible or not (fully) human, together with apparently lifeless 'objects' that nevertheless have personal qualities such as spatial orientation and intention. In terms of such a vision of the social the witch plays a fundamentally important role in a philosophy dealing with the origin and work of evil in the world. But it is only one element of a much more complex material logic of evil and operates in a world characterised by a *flat*, rather than a *hierarchical*, order of causation.

This vision of the social is radically different from the 'modern' concept developed during the nineteenth century in European thought and in the philosophies and sociologies of Marx, Durkheim and Weber, among many others. It is, above all, a vision of the social that lacks a concept of institutions and political actors as mediators of social conflict and instead places its emphasis on *the exposed being of the person* in direct, unmediated social interaction with other persons and person-like beings.

The fundamental character of the southern African 'healing' – or 'religious' – culture is its commitment to the ontology of the 'person' engaged with and enmeshed in a web of other material beings that – though some are intangible – are directly opposed to each other. I distinguish this construction of social from the European notion of 'society', with its distinct, and distinctive, commitment to a separate 'religious' domain. In the southern African conception each person can only seek to protect himself or herself against the pervasive influence of others by growing, supplementing or augmenting his or her person. The interaction of *augmented*, and therefore *protected*, persons with diminished, and therefore vulnerable or *exposed*, persons is the essence of the southern African cultural system in which the figure of *both* the witch *and* the sangoma makes sense.

CHAPTER 3

'Cleaves Water', eats *intwaso*: Becoming a healer in the *bungoma* tradition

A person becomes a sangoma primarily through a sustained period of training, often triggered by a period of illness described as being under water, or in a river. Many sangomas insist that they truly experienced a long period 'under [or in] water', *eyamanzini*. They say they have met the snake that lives in the water. This figure of speech expresses the flow and transmission of knowledge that allows the novice to acquire control over those disembodied, intangible 'persons' we call 'spirits'.

For the sangomas of eastern Mpumalanga, knowledge (*lwati* [siSwati]; *ulwazi* [isiZulu]) is the ocean, *lwandle*. Water (*emanti; amanzi*) flows like blood and semen (*igazi*) across generations and flows like knowledge from teachers to students; the bodies it flows into and out of only contain it temporarily. The snake (*inyoka*) is sinuous, like water. The sangoma feels the pressure of the persons around him or her and is exposed to them as one is exposed to water. Some of this pressure comes from other people, but it also comes from spirits and ancestors and from medicine or *muti*, the magical substances that heal or protect. All these constitute forms of the person, have intentions and motives and can pressurise like deep water. The eyes are closed but the mind sees in this medium. To carry this burden is like being submerged, while to emerge means the burden can be carried successfully. The constant allusions to water, blood, foam, rain, rivers and the ocean are references to the master trope of water as flow and pressure and of becoming and being a healer.

One can never rely fully upon a supply of water. Like knowledge and rain it can come in torrents or not at all; it evaporates, it soaks in, or falls on, another place, another person. While Michel Foucault taught us to think of power as flowing like water in the channels that knowledge and 'discourse' provide (Dreyfus and Rabinow 1982: 184; Foucault 1972, 2008; Gordon 1980), for the healer knowledge is water and water is the medium

FIGURE 3.1: The healer is under flowing water, the basic metaphor of *bungoma* education.

through which power and knowledge move. That is why the healer experiences being 'under water' as knowledge. It is the central mystery of *bungoma*. Becoming a healer entails intense flows of blood and water. These are the power to heal.

Ultimately, the successful student healer proceeds to the status of sangoma, a 'traditional healer'. In the literature this is called 'initiation' in the community of sangomas, 'graduation'. The ritual process described here is typical of the many ceremonies I have observed over five years in the Lowveld. This example is relatively elaborate and comprehensive, but most other ceremonies include some or all of its parts. The discussion deals with the first part of the procedure, which has to do with the *emadloti*, the 'Nguni' spirits, who are the immediate and local ancestors of the practitioners. The second part of the ritual introduces the *lindzawe* – the foreign spirits associated with water in rivers and streams, who offer special kinds of healing and power.

In the case I describe here, Magodweni, a highly respected sangoma and my teacher (*gobela*), oversees and directs the initiation of his student, or *lithwasana*, who has taken the 'healing name' of DabulaManzi ('Cleaves Water'). The name is a powerful one since it indexes water (*-manzi*) and because the most famous person of that name, Dabulamanzi kaMpande (1836–1885) was a son of the Zulu king Mpande kaSenzangakhona (1798–1872) and commander of the Zulu regiment at the famous battle of Rorkes Drift during the Anglo-Zulu War of 1879 in which the Zulu armies were victorious.

DabulaManzi's graduation event takes place over three days of intensive activity at Magodweni's modest homestead in Extension 11 in Barberton. During this time Magodweni is also training several other sangomas, coordinating a band of drummers and dancers, coping with a crowd of visitors, kin and neighbours and, through it all, engaging critically and creatively with his tradition of healing and interaction with the spirits. He works from principles rather than rules. He actively develops relationships with his clientele and colleagues and performs the key elements of his practice as the event unfolds.

But to call this event an 'initiation' of a 'student' into the arts of 'traditional healing' is also to misconstrue it. It is not so much an *initiation*, that is, a marking of a beginning or initial point of a new status, although it is this too, but rather a public aspect of a process of spiritual unfolding or 'upliftment' (the English word that Magodweni himself uses to describe it). DabulaManzi is not so much a *student* as a sufferer who is attempting to achieve mastery over his own internal spiritual world in order to achieve both health and status as one who can assist others on the same journey, as fellow sufferer and master.

He is called *lithwasana*, the personal nominative derived from the verb *ku-thwasa*, meaning, roughly, 'to develop or uplift one's spirit or soul so as to become fully aware of one's own spiritual power' but also meaning to emerge, as if from deep water. He does this according to Magodweni's instruction, and as the most junior member of Magodweni's household.

He begins by entering into an intense apprenticeship as Magodweni's servant and student. He wakes early (4am) to drum and dance. He washes and cleans for his master; he collects, dries and grinds herbs while learning about them; he maintains the ritual clothes, skins, drums and other implements; keeps the fire and, at all times, does whatever he is told by Magodweni. Eventually, he is ready to leave. At that time, and through the events described here, he becomes *mthwasa*, 'spiritually aware', and is ready to be declared a sangoma.

The graduation of a *lithwasana* is the highlight of the healing process. Through the ceremony the *lithwasana* achieves the respect of his peers and becomes a sangoma. This means that the initiate has acquired the knowledge to heal others through the effective control of his own ancestors, who become his spiritual aids rather than the pests they had been before.

Exposure to *emadloti* can manifest in many ways, and it is often not obvious. If parents, friends or siblings suspect that the *emadloti* might be involved they will have taken the sufferer to a sangoma, who may or may not diagnose *emadloti* and if he or she does, there is always a choice. Will the diagnosis be accepted? If so, corrective action may or may not be taken. In the end, those who ultimately seek to heal themselves by training to become a sangoma do so after serious ongoing attacks of 'illness'. The illness itself may take many forms: physical, emotional, social or cognitive. DabulaManzi had been diagnosed several years previously but had resisted. He could not concentrate at school, was depressed, and felt, he told me, that he was 'afraid of what might happen' either way: if he continued to resist or if he acceded to the calling.

Initiates show, through the public performance of tasks that have been set for them during the ceremony, that control has been asserted over their spiritual partners and that they are competent to join the ranks of others of this calling. They become members of their new *mpandze*, the group of *emathwasana* who have been trained earlier by the master, the *gobela*. While the training has been carried out under the private guidance of the *gobela*, with secrets of the healing process revealed slowly, this public performance demonstrates power and achievement.

An important aspect of the ritual is the deliberate exposure of 'secrets' or something that is hidden. This happens during the public part of graduation ceremonies since these events serve to heal ('to make to live', *kuphila*) but also to assemble the local healers in order to exchange medicines and stories, and to 'support' each other through dancing and drumming. The 'secret' or hidden thing (*timfihlo*, from *kufihla*, 'to hide') might be something like a coin or box of matches that is hidden in the homestead or on the person of someone in attendance. The new sangoma, in trance, seeks to find the object and bring it out, or expose it to the crowd. This is as much a display of skill as it is taken to be guided by 'ancestors' or other intangible persons in the gathering. The *timfihlo* or 'hidden thing' is also a part of the sangoma's regalia and consists of *muti* that is 'hidden' within a medicine bundle incorporated into the bandoliers, necklaces or armbands that are worn during dance. To find the hidden thing is a form of cleansing of secret evil and sin, but it is also potent protection against exposure in the form of hidden *muti* in the form of an amulet.

The practice of deliberate exposure of 'sin', 'witchcraft', or other unseen factors and influences draws in many of the onlookers. The audience that has gathered has arranged itself around the outside of a rough circle, with the drums placed along this margin. In the centre sangomas take turns to dance and to display trance-like states of dissociation.

They fall on their knees in front of members of the audience and, after introducing themselves through a recitation of the names of their ancestors – those possessed/possessing them – and the lineage of their teachers, *emagobela*, they begin to expose the 'secrets' of members of the audience in the surrounding circle. The selection of a 'target' often looks random, and it is sudden. Once the sangoma has knelt in front of the person and begun the recitation almost no one leaves, although some try to flee the circle if they think the sangoma will land in front of them. The recitation begins when the drums stop. It maintains the rhythms of the drums, however, in the cadence of the language, with the crowd adding the counterpoint phrases: *Siyavuma!* 'we agree!'; *Thokoza Gogo*, 'peace, grandparent'; *Yiza!*, 'listen!'.

The new sangoma will continue to express his or her submission to the authority of his or her *gobela*, but from the moment of graduation he or she may begin to acquire his or her own clientele of patients and may accept a *lithwasana* of his or her own for training. The *mpandze* will grow and, as the knowledge and competence of the new healer grows he or she has the opportunity to achieve higher status and respect from his or her peers.

First day

DabulaManzi's ceremony took place from 5 to 7 December 2003. DabulaManzi is the healing name, or spirit-name, of Penuel Tsabedze (name used with permission), a young man who arrived at Magodweni's house on 7 July 2003. He had failed his Matriculation (high school leaving examination) and was clearly intelligent and educated. He told me then that 'the ancestors first came when I was eight years old'. At that time his family had begged the ancestors to allow Penuel to complete his schooling. After completing high school he became very ill. He did not find employment and his family agreed that his difficulties were due to the ancestors, who still wanted him to become a sangoma.

He first went to train with a young Swazi woman whose healing name was Nomalanga and who had been trained by Magodweni. She felt that she could not handle the case and passed Penuel on to Magodweni to train. From July until December he stayed at Magodweni's house as a *lithwasana*.

From the moment he arrived at Magodweni's he began to grow his hair and to plait it into dreadlocks. It was rubbed with fat and haematite (black iron oxide) to make it shiny and black. He now wore it in the *siyendle* style of the sangoma. A small cowry shell (*litdvumane*) had been tied onto a lock of hair at the crown of his head. This was a symbol that he now belonged to the *emandzawe* (pl; sing. *lindzawu*, *lindzawe*) spirits as they belonged to him. The *Concise siSwati Dictionary* (Rycroft 1981) defines these as 'hostile evil spirits'. Magodweni said that they were 'foreigners who died in South Africa' and who had their own language. There is, it seems, little consensus, and categories appear to be a complex mix of traditions that have in common simply that they are not 'our ancestors', *emadloti*, that is, not Nguni. All agree that they are unpredictable and that only some healers can deal successfully with them. DabulaManzi's task was to learn to control their power as well as the power of his own ancestral spirits who had called him to become a sangoma.

DabulaManzi was now dressed in the red, white and black cloths of the Nguni spirits. He had acquired the habits of humility, sitting always on the ground, never on a chair, and always greeting guests and clients who came to the house with head bowed. '*Thokoza*' (peace), he said, while clapping his cupped hands together in the respectful greeting given by the healers to each other and to guests and clients. He was now called DabulaManzi, his 'healing name', and was no longer Penuel Tsabedze for the duration of the ceremony. Later he would decide how he wished to be known – by his healing name alone, as Penuel, or by both depending on context. Magodweni always used his healing name and corrected those who called him by his given name, Fani Nkosi. The new healing name, DabulaManzi, implies a change of identity in other ways. His surname, Tsabedze, is tshiVenda and he was originally from the tshiVenda-speaking area of Limpopo province, but he no longer had relatives there. His primary language was English, but spoke isiZulu/siSwati fluently. By taking a strong Zulu name he aligned himself strongly with the 'Nguni' ethnicity that includes Xhosa, Zulu and Swazi peoples and languages.

He looked young and frightened when we first encountered him at Magodweni's five months previously but through his period of training he had grown in stature and confidence. By December he had learned much of what Magodweni could teach him about herbal healing and control of the ancestors. He had learned divination by throwing 'the bones' (*tinhlolo*) and had learnt to smell out witchcraft substances from the body of a client (*kufemba*), the ritual required for greeting and talking within the spiritual domains of ancestors and *Ndzawu* spirits, and other knowledge of the *bungoma*, the special knowledge of the healer. He was ready to be initiated.

He had come to Magodweni's household to take advantage of Magodweni's renowned skills. Magodweni is at once gentle and demanding. He respects his *emathwasana* and never abuses them as some other *gobelas* are often alleged to do. His following of former *emathwasana* is large and strong and they clearly adore him. The *mpandze* of Magodweni had gathered from surrounding settlements and towns – some had travelled 150km or more to be there. Magodweni had called them all to participate in the initiation of the new member of the *mpandze*.

Late on 5 December the first day's activities commenced. Normally, activities would begin in the early morning, at about 6am but DabulaManzi's uncle, his father's younger brother, had passed away the previous morning and the funeral was scheduled for the following morning. The late start on the Friday allowed his relatives time to take care of arrangements for the funeral. The members of the *mpandze* had been arriving all day and were now almost at full strength.

Magodweni set up a small shrine (*ligandzelo*) in the yard. A forked branch of the *umsinsi* tree (*Erythrina caffra* L., or lucky bean tree, *kaffirboom* in Afrikaans) had been dug into the ground. The *umsinsi* tree is a 'spirit tree' that is always home to African spirits. It 'calls' the spirits wherever it grows and, at the start of the ceremony, the spirits must be called to sit in the *umsinsi* branch of the *ligandzelo*. The *umsinsi* is never cut in the veld. A live *umsinsi* tree grows in Magodweni's yard. Around the branch the earth is dug in a circle approximately 1.5m in diameter. Several new healing herbs, including the *Boophone disticha* plant (*incoto* or *incwadi*, see Chapter 9), and the reed, *umhlanga*, have already been planted here. The lees of home-brewed sorghum beer have been poured out on the ground for the spirit and a small plastic canister of snuff has been placed beside the branch in the middle of the garden. A white cloth is draped over the branch. The white cloth, says Magodweni, is to call the *emadloti* for help, although ordinarily it signifies the *ndzawu* spirits. In this case it seems to call the Nguni spirits, DabulaManzi's new Nguni ancestors (as a consequence of his new name) and the *ndzawu* spirits. 'It is white because the person for whom he is performing the ritual is not his real child,' Magodweni explains. If it had been his 'real child' the cloth would have been the brown and white pattern that is especially reserved for the *emandzawe* spirits. In practice, however, it is very rare for sangomas to train or initiate their own children.

In this case, the colour points to the fact that Penuel Tsabedze, newly named DabulaManzi, is not Swazi, but Venda. The ndzawu spirits are said to be from the north and Vendas live to the north of Mpumalanga province. Venda history also links them to the Shona people of northern Zimbabwe. The white colour signifies here a 'foreign' spirit. DabulaManzi will later again wear the red, white and black clothes of the Swazi sangoma, the colours in which he trained.

As the ceremony begins the members of Magodweni's *mpandze* and other *emathwasana* (trainees) come out of the house to the shrine. They

FIGURE 3.2: Magodweni prepares the goat for slaughter beside the garden with new herbs and the lees of beer spilled for the ancestors under a white cloth on the *umsinsi* tree branch.

are all wearing at least one African cloth in the colours of the healer, red, black and white, with a picture of a lion, leopard or other symbol of power (such as King Mswati's picture) on it. Magodweni and his common-law wife, Mahlasela, together with DabulaManzi's first *gobela*, Nomalanga, sit by the tree and *pahla*, to call the spirits. They do this by clapping their hollowed hands to make a resonant sound and call the spirits by name to join the gathering. The other participants bow their heads and join in the rhythmic clapping between calls to the spirits. Each participant announces his or her own spiritual lineage, that is, the line of spirit ancestors that are known to him or her. Each announces his or her own name, too. Finally, they formally greet Magodweni.

Magodweni, meanwhile, has taken a seat on a carved stool. He is dressed in his full regalia, including a red robe with his name, 'Magodweni Dlamini', stitched in white letters on the back. The robe is very much in the style of African Christian robes worn by some worshippers during services. In fact, Magodweni was consecrated as a priest of the Antioch Church of Zion in 1994, but is no longer active in this church. He now devotes his time entirely to African traditional healing. He is wearing his red, white and black beads and has a spotted cat-skin fur hat on his head with red and white beaded pins on it. Seated on his stool he looks regal. He thanks the ancestors and the audience for their participation.

A line of drums has been set up beside the yard where the ceremony is taking place and drummers file into place to begin the drumming. As the *pahla* at the shrine ends, the first beating of the drums begins and several of Magodweni's recently 'graduated' students begin to dance. At first Nomalanga and Magodweni's 'senior girlfriend' dance together, then others join. This first dance is low key and restrained. While the dancing goes on a young, white, male goat is led to the place where Magodweni is sitting. The cord around its neck that has been used to lead it is cut and several helpers restrain the goat.

Magodweni speaks to the gathering, saying: 'We only slaughter one goat. We will all eat from one dish. Let those of you (*emadloti*) who want more go elsewhere! I do not slaughter for nothing! I am only slaughtering this goat for you.' He thanks [*siyabonga*] the *emathwasana*, the members of the *mpandze* and other participants and claps his hands to welcome the spirits. 'We are doing this thing in the afternoon,' he tells the spirits,

FIGURE 3.3: Magodweni sits on his stool, looking regal.

'because there has been illness and death in his family. Even the father is not well. The mother and father are here.'

The ritual is solemn, serious, and practical. Its aim is to achieve the correct process, rather than coherence or continuity of the event *as event*. Indeed, throughout the ceremony – as with all ceremonies I have witnessed in Barberton – there is always some disruption. In fact, the ritual was halted for a time while I went to fetch a number of students who had accompanied me. In general, drunks almost always make a scene, someone can be relied upon to play the fool, crucial participants arrive late, family quarrels intrude, someone feels that they have not been adequately acknowledged or there has been a lack of respect – all these incidents can and do interrupt the ceremony. People endeavour to 'look through' the disruption, to ignore it as if it is not happening, or, if that is impossible, to move the offending person to the side as quietly as possible. As long as the process unfolds appropriately and fully, and according to expectations, the actual pace is of little consequence.

Mahhashe, another male sangoma, helps Magodweni to feed the goat with some *muti*. One holds the goat's chest and head up while the other administers the herbs – by stuffing the powdered plant material down the goat's throat. As the goat is prepared for sacrifice DabulaManzi kneels in front of the shrine. Magodweni speaks to the two people before him as well as to the crowd of onlookers, telling them 'the ritual ('work', *sebenti*) is starting now' instructing that their minds and spirits must all be here, focused and alert. The drums reach a sustained crescendo.

Four or five substances from large trees found in the bush have been mixed together, including powdered material from the *sigugu*, *msenge*, *kampeni*, *sivangatane* trees. All are used also in trials before a person can become a *lithwasana*. In particular, a *lithwasana* is not supposed to have sex before he/she enters training and these substances 'test' whether a person has had sex. If the person has had sex immediately prior to taking the herbs it is believed they will make him or her ill. If not, 'it can also protect you'.

According to Magodweni:

> In fact, it protects you from the medicine that you are going to eat because you are still going to eat strong *muti* and it [these medicines] can protect you. During the ritual process the ritual can kill you without this protection. The medicine is put in the goat and the *lithwasana* eats the same medicine.

In this way, the goat and the *lithwasana* are paired. This exemplifies the exposed nature of the person undergoing the procedure, but here the exposure is to 'medicine' itself. When the goat is killed the *lithwasana* might also die, but as the goat bleeds the *lithwasana* will suck the life force out of the goat by drinking its blood. This, too, can kill. The herbs are given both to test the purity of the *lithwasana* and to 'protect' both goat and human from external influence. 'Giving it to the goat protects in a lot of ways,'

Magodweni elaborated later. 'Even where we buy the goat...we don't know what has been done to the goat; people might have done other things to the goat. It protects the goat and purifies it for the ceremony.'

Among the 'other things' that people might have done to the goat is the possibility that someone has had sex with it and polluted it, or that someone has deliberately treated it with other herbs that may make the ceremony fail or that may kill the *lithwasana*. In this time of AIDS there has been increasing panic throughout the Lowveld about who (or what) to have sex with. Some have resorted to animals. The goat might also be a conduit for witchcraft.

All of this must be protected against since this is a moment of utmost ritual risk for the *lithwasana*, and a time at which his or her resolve and clarity of purpose – as well as his or her (and the goat's!) abstinence from sex – will be tested. DabulaManzi is not expected to undertake this alone. He is joined by another sangoma, Mpande, a woman who has already gone through the ritual successfully but who has not yet had a *lithwasana* of her own. She will act out the same ritual events in parallel with DabulaManzi to support him by being united with him. She will also be learning to become a *gobela* so that she can train her own *lithwasana*. As the goat dies she will shadow DabulaManzi's actions and thus strengthen him and protect him. 'When you are about to eat the *intwaso*,' Magodweni told me, 'there must be someone there to back you up.'

DabulaManzi now appears to have drifted into trance. The drums are beating as Magodweni invokes both his ancestors and those of DabulaManzi to witness the event of his 'dying' as a *lithwasana* and as an ordinary person and, as the goat dies, becoming an *inyanga*, healer and the possessor and actuator of special knowledge. Ndaye, another member of Magodweni's *mpandze*, hoists the goat above DabulaManzi's head as DabulaManzi kneels quaking on the ground. A knife appears in Magodweni's hand and then at the throat of the silent goat. It spasms as its carotid artery and jugular veins are cut. Blood both spurts and runs onto DabulaManzi's upturned face. He embraces the goat and stuffs his face into its neck, mouth open, sucking its blood, bathing in the flow. The blood runs down his back in rivulets, jets over his chest. In drops and streams the life of the goat runs into DabulaManzi's mouth and over his body. Blood spurts towards the crowd that has now pressed in close to witness – and to *feel* – this act of death.

They are dying, the goat and DabulaManzi, but DabulaManzi will live if he has performed his rituals correctly and if he is able to purge himself of the blood he has consumed. He is delirious. He does not know where he is. The goat, now drained and dead, is taken to the back of the yard where it is laid out on a tin sheet to be cut up.

There is more blood to be shed. A white hen is brought and its neck is cut over the earth in the shrine. The blood is caught in a small white enamel basin and the twitching body of the chicken is thrown to one side.

After the ceremony Magodweni explained:

> For a male *lithwasana* a female goat is used; for female a male goat is used. But they were only able to get a male goat for DabulaManzi. Fortunately, they were also able to get a hen for him. When he is initiated they must not say that he has not been initiated properly. That is what the chicken is for.

He elaborated:

> I gave DabulaManzi blood to drink. The goat's blood has been drunk and then he has to drink the chicken blood so that when he has the goat blood there will be female blood in his body. It doesn't matter if it is chicken or goat blood, it is all the same. What is important is the sex of the blood, not the animal. The female blood mixes with the goat blood. The animal is important but, because they could not find the female goat, the chicken was used.

Again, the practical rather than the formal is emphasised. Magodweni's stature as a master healer and as a *gobela* comes from his ability to make these choices well, at the moment they are required, so that no one can say afterwards that the ritual was not performed properly. In many cases, especially among young and inexperienced *emagobela*, inappropriate choices or substitutions mean that the ritual has failed and must be done again. This does not happen to Magodweni, although he has re-initiated many other aspirant healers where rituals have indeed failed. Thus, although not all rituals can be performed precisely according to 'tradition', there is usually a way around the problem and Magodweni finds this through a practical logic rather than a formal adherence to rules. The goal is to achieve the proper blend of female and male substance through the medium of blood (*ingati*). The way of the sangoma blends male and female virtues. The men wear skirts (as do the women), and the women dance with spears and sjamboks (like the men). All wear the same beads and ritual regalia.

DabulaManzi's first *gobela*, Nomalanga, and his mother begin to cry hysterically. They retire to a room in the house, lie face down on the floor and continue crying. The reason for the tears, it emerged, was that 'DabulaManzi was between life and death'. 'If he does not vomit the blood it will kill him. Humans do not drink the blood of animals and it must be brought up successfully.' This is his next test. His mother wails in a closed room. She cannot bear to watch.

Magodweni confirmed the explanation:

> She thought that DabulaManzi might die. If DabulaManzi *wecile*, that is, 'skipped over' or missed something, or did something wrong – for example if he was having sex with someone, then the blood could kill him. On the morning that you are drinking the *intwaso* you have to admit your sins, almost as if you were going to communion; if you stole something or committed a sin, if you skip over this process then the *intwaso* will kill you. It's the *intwaso* [that does this, not the blood] because it hardens the blood and it can't come out and it closes your breath. Even if it does come out, it will get stuck in the throat and choke the person.

DabulaManzi is helped to stand and taken over to a trench that has been dug on the margins of the yard. Mpande goes with him. Although she has not drunk the blood she will carry out the same procedures to support him. A large 50 litre galvanised washing basin has been filled with warm water and powdered herbs from the veld. This is the *intwaso*, a special liquid that will both test and heal him. It will make him strong if he is virtuous and the ancestors truly intend him to heal others or kill him if they do not. The vat is stirred. A two-litre plastic tub is used to scoop up water for Dabula and Mpande to drink and they begin to vomit by pushing their fingers down their throats. Soon the water is jetting out of their mouths. Everyone watches from close by. They are fed more and more water from the tub and keep vomiting. They become soaked with the water in the tub. At first the liquid is clear or yellow, then the blood comes up from DabulaManzi's stomach into the trench. His companion has not drunk the blood, but she keeps vomiting as well. It is now night and candles are brought to light the proceedings. If DabulaManzi does not bring up all the blood, and consume, with Mpande, all the water, they will die. They vomit for their lives.

DabulaManzi and Mpande continue to vomit for half an hour. Their helpers rub their bellies and splash the *intwaso* water over their heads and backs with a whisk (*lishoba*). Finally, the *intwaso* water is gone, and the vomit is clear. He has brought up all the blood and will live. When he finishes he is led back to the house to recover in the *indumba* (the 'surgery', or healing house, where all healing implements are kept). He lies on the floor panting and exhausted, but recovers quickly. Half an hour later he is fully recovered and chatting with Mpande. Both are pleased to have accomplished their trial.

Meanwhile, the goat is laid on a corrugated metal sheet and cut up. The skin is removed for use as the sangoma's jacket (*ijazi langoma*) to be worn the following day. The jacket will be prepared from strips cut from the raw hide and will be worn untanned and raw as it dries out on the body of the new sangoma. The meat just under the skin over the shoulder – the meat that 'quivers' – the subcutaneous muscles that shake the skin to ward off flies in life, the 'meat that is the softest' – is carefully cut off and laid to one side. According to Magodweni, 'The pieces are taken from the *imphungane* ('fly') the meat that shakes the skin; where the meat is wobbly. Don't know why. I found it like this.' This is the *luhlelo*.

The entrails are removed and put into a basin. The stomach contents, *umswane* or chyme, are removed and put onto a flat basket where they are smeared over the bottom and outside, *lihlelo*, because this 'keeps the soup from going through the basket' and 'when he eats the pieces of meat, it protects the meat'. The small pieces of subdermal muscle are cut into nine pieces, cooked briefly in boiling water and placed in the basket. The hooves are severed and the knucklebones are cut out, with the gall-bladder, and placed in a separate basin. The knucklebones will serve as part of the kit, *tinhlolo*, that will be used by DabulaManzi when he begins to *kupengula* 'throw the bones' for divination. They will be the basis of his first set of 'bones'.

FIGURE 3.4: The gall-bladder and the knucklebone (astragalus) from the goat.

Other pieces will be added later to make up a full set. One of the knucklebones will be put on his wrist in a bracelet and one is put between the horns of the goat, which will be removed and put with the *tinhlolo*, the divining bones. *Muti*, protective herbs, are put in the horns of the goat in order to protect the *emadloti*. The horns are tied, decorated and incorporated into the bandolier that will be put around DabulaManzi's shoulders on the following day.

The gall-bladder, *inyongo*, which has been cut out and laid with the other ritually significant pieces of the goat, will serve an important purpose later the next day. The *inyongo* is handled carefully so that it will still contain the bile. The two men who have taken charge of the cutting, take out the liver and carefully excise the gall-bladder. When DabulaManzi is ready for the next step on the following day – finding the gall-bladder that has been hidden by someone the initiate does not know – the gall (also called *inyongo*) is poured up his nose and he must drink a bit of it. 'It is done so that it can trace the *inyongo* [to] where it has been hidden. Like the dogs once they smell someone, they can find that person.' The spirit world of the ancestors is also an inversion of the normal world in some ways.

Accordingly, what is bitter in this world is sweet in the other world, and vice versa. Thus, the intensely bitter gall is sweet to the ancestors and, upon tasting it they will be willing to help with the task of finding the hidden *inyongo*. Without this, the ritual fails.

Next, the *lihlelo* in the flat basket is pulled across the ground towards the vomiting trench. As it moves, DabulaManzi follows on his knees, straining to keep up with the basket as it is pulled before him, always just out of his reach. He may not use his hands. He strives as hard as he can to keep up with the moving basket; the meat must be taken up with his mouth only and swallowed whole. 'It is a law, it is the ritual,' Magodweni says. 'This is a sign that the *emadloti* are meeting you. You are recognised by the *emadloti*. They are leading you.'

Mpande, DabulaManzi's companion through all of this, joins him on her knees. She follows him as he reaches for the nine pieces of meat in the basket, but does not eat. DabulaManzi eats all the meat and, when they reach the trench, they begin to vomit again in the same way as before. It is dark and a candle is lit to see if the meat is coming out in the vomitus – eight of the nine pieces must be seen as they come out of his stomach or he is judged to have failed. The audience, including children, all stand very close, close enough to be splashed by the water from the tub and by the vomit, and watch. DabulaManzi's first *gobela*, Nomalanga, helps him by holding him and using a cow-tail whisk, *lishoba*, to bathe him with water from the tub, over his back and chest. She kneads his stomach while he is vomiting to help him eject the pieces of meat. Nomalanga holds the *intwaso* for him to drink. Magodweni says, 'She is being taught practically. She is experiencing the way to perform the ritual.' Magodweni is always teaching, assisting, appraising the quality of the performance, and giving himself wholly to the practice of healing. He is greatly admired by his colleagues.

The *intwaso* mixture this time contains the same mixed *muti* as before but with other things added. Herbs called *liphambo*, *mhlaru*, and powdered *umsinsi* (the same tree that grows in Magodweni's garden and is used for the *emadloti* shrine) have also been added. *Mhlaru*, in particular, makes him vomit uncontrollably. Everyone presses close to see if the eight pieces of meat appear in the trench.

It is now very dark; there is no moon. Candles have been lit and wide leaves of a grass have been placed in the bottom of the trench to help the observers see the meat as it is brought up. The pieces are counted: one, two, three, four…He must vomit all but one.

There is some uncertainty about whether he has vomited them, but eventually Magodweni calls an end to this part of the ceremony. He tells us it is 'just the ritual', part of the trial to see if DabulaManzi is worthy and pure:

> There must be one that remains in him of the pieces of meat that are fed to him; he vomits eight and one stays inside. The *emadloti* hold it back so that they can also feast on it. The ones that come out show that he is following the ritual that he needs to go through. If he has been bad they do not come out. If they don't come out he must pay a fine and he will be given *muti* that will bring them out.

For tonight, though, he is satisfied that the ritual has been performed successfully.

DabulaManzi and Mpande are helped back to the *indumba*, both exhausted by this final ordeal. They will do nothing more this evening but rest. Tomorrow the ceremony will begin again at first light.

The dancing of the sangomas who have observed and supported the event begins. The drums start, beaten by a troop of young girls. Dancers, dancing for their own spirits, and guided by them, take it in turns to dance. After each dance the dancers kneel before Magodweni or another member of the congregation who is significant to them (another member of their *mpandze*, a relative, or a guest) and recite, in cadenced verses, the greetings from the ancestors who possess them. They declare their names and the names of their spirits and thank the hearer for listening.

As the dancing continues dancers are applauded on their performances, or criticised. One man comes from 'down over there'; he is apparently not well known, or is despised. His performance is ignored. He does not find anyone to listen to his recitation of the spirits and his greeting. He is from a different *mpandze*, perhaps trying to win favour. No one professes to know what he is about or why he is there. Eventually he just talks into the corner of the yard, out into the darkness, shouting his recitations from and to the spirits into thin air. The drums falter; the drummers lose their enthusiasm. The stranger persists and eventually goes into his dance again.

He finally begins to attract enough attention to keep the drums going and to attract a small audience. But he dances for too long. People say he is boring, that he does not know when to stop. Meanwhile, another dancer begins to dress and starts to roar in the *indumba* as the spirits possess him. He comes out dancing, but in slow motion.

People expect another boring dancer. As he comes out into the arena of the yard the first 'boring' dancer is encouraged to leave. He eventually goes into the house to change out of his dancing gear and leaves the field to the other. The other man also dances for far too long. Although he dances well and the audience participates, they insult him gently, and encourage him to finish. At the same time several women have clustered around him to support him. Members of the audience have to be told to leave the arena 'to give him room to dance'. But he does not seem to be a real sangoma. He does not restrict himself to the usual sangoma style, but incorporates the popular 'Zulu warrior' style into his dancing, kicking his leg up and bringing his foot down hard on the packed ground. This is enjoyed, but some people comment that it is not appropriate. He dances for a long time, and eventually retires. Even Magodweni criticises the length of time he has danced.

'This man can dance for an hour!' says one member of the audience.

'An hour! More like two,' says Magodweni. 'He has only just begun. He doesn't stop!'

Second day

The continuation of the ritual gets off to a slow start the next day. It is after 10am before everyone is ready to proceed, and the sun is already hot. This is the day that DabulaManzi will search for the *inyongo*, the goat's gall-bladder, which has been hidden somewhere in the bush while he was sleeping. He must find it through his own intuition, unaided except for help from his spirits. If he does this, he graduates and becomes an *inyanga*. The *inyongo* will be inflated and tied into the hair at the back of his head as a sign of his new status. It will stay there until it dries and eventually falls out some months later.

DabulaManzi kneels on the ground in front of his *gobela*. With the *lishoba* (whisk) now in his hand, he assumes the qualities of trance, his voice changes to the deep hoarse voice of the spirit-possessed and he recites the names of the spirits. He is quizzed by Magodweni about what he is looking for and where he will find it.

> DabulaManzi [chanting]: *Yeva! Yeva! Yeva!* [It hears/hear me, hear!]
> Magodweni: It is your thing. I give you it.
> DM: It is by the tree. I'm an orphan. You have given it to me. I haven't given birth yet.
> M: No.
> DM: There is a tree. From somewhere...Mpumalanga! [the name of the province].
> M [testing him]: Where? This is not Mpumalanga. What you say is wrong.
> DM: *Yeva! Yeva! Yeva!* I see a road.
> M: Where is it from? Where is it going?
> DM: Mpumalanga [towards Nelspruit, the capital of the province].
> M: You are running away from the secret. You stay there.
> DM: It's called dunusa [?].
> M: No.
> DM: I am walking by a road...Running away from the secret.
> M: Where?
> DM: By the big road [the highway to Nelspruit].
> M: What is next to the tree?
> DM: I'm running away from the secret. *Yeva! Yeva!* [Listen! Listen!] I'm running away from the secret. There is farming next to the tree!

The interview concludes and Magodweni sends DabulaManzi off into the bush to find the *inyongo*, issuing a mild threat: 'If you don't find it, I will kick your ass!'.

DabulaManzi rushes out of the yard, down the track towards the bush that separates the township section (Extension 11) from the main road out of town. Mpande and Nomalanga accompany him. They are gone for about 30 minutes. They return with large group of children and others running with them. They are singing and ululating. The *inyongo* has been found. The drums start as they approach the stand.

DabulaManzi and the two *tinyanga* who went with him kneel before Magodweni and thank him. Magodweni replies:

> M: I thank you! I praise you! You have learned from me. You may speak badly of me later, but remember that I am the one who taught you.
>
> DM and others: Thank you, thank you! [*Siyabonga, Siyabonga!*].
>
> M: I want you to keep your healing alive. I have suffered for you. You are thanking me for taking you out of your home, for making you work hard for nothing. I have made you suffer. I thank you for showing passion and a need to learn.

After the *inyongo* has been found other things are hidden for DabulaManzi and the two *tinyanga* who have accompanied him to find. Several coins are placed somewhere among the bodies of audience. They find the items easily.

Magodweni's sister, who has been hovering around the margins since the beginning with a chip on her shoulder, is now very drunk. She had been given the task of hiding one of the important beaded necklaces. The *tinyanga* fail at first to find it. She is too drunk to remember now where she hid it, and she cannot interact appropriately with the sangoma who asks/ tells her where it is. This is done through a period of rapid questions and answers in a ritual manner in which the sangoma kneels at the feet of the one who has hidden the item and makes statements about where he or she feels the item is. The respondent must disagree (*Xa!*) or agree (*Siyavuma!*). Musa, another sangoma attending, makes an announcement. He tells the people that if they want to hide something for the sangoma to find they must not be drunk when they do it.

I had been asked to hide some money and had put R20 in my shoe. DabulaManzi addresses me, eyes closed, sweating from exertion, switching the *lishoba* up and down, breathing heavily: entranced, enchanted.

> DM: It is outside.
> Me: No.
> DM: It is on the body.
> Me: Yes, that's right! [*Yebo. ngiyavuma!*]

M [prompting, teaching]: Where on the body?
DM: On the body. [I look blank]. Down! It is down.
M: Where?
DM: On the foot.
M: Which foot?
DM: On the right foot. Under the right foot.

This is correct and I give him the R20. He does not take it with his hands. The money is too 'hot' for him to handle. I put it on the ground. Someone else picks it up and puts it into a cup with some ashes in it. This is to cool the money so it can be touched by the sangoma.

They dance. DabulaManzi is now no longer a *lithwasana*. He is a full member of the *mpandze*. The drums are being beaten by a posse of girls and one or two older *tinyanga*. As one tires of beating the drums – it is hard work – another moves in to take his or her place. The drumming and dancing will now continue for the rest of the day as various members of the company take turns to dance. Each one dances to exhaustion and to the point of trance, then exits. The next emerges from a side room where he or she has gone to dress in a dancing outfit. Males and females dress almost alike, but each is different, reflecting their own collections and careers. Each carries a dancing stick, or a wooden representation of an axe, knife or spear. These items were once made of both metal and wood, but there are no iron smelters or blacksmiths today. Each begins to dance as the previous dancer fades back into the changing room.

One woman wants to consult (*kuphengula*) with DabulaManzi. She puts down R50 on a mat. It is covered with ash to cool it before it is taken.

Then the company of healers, Magodweni's *mpandze*, and all the other sangomas who have come from far to be present, kneel in front of the shrine and invoke the ancestors' names. Kneeling in front of Magodweni, Mpande gives him one of the parcels that has been found. It contains strings of beads and bracelets, a ring, and a fresh goatskin 'jacket' cut in crossing bandolier fashion. The time has come for DabulaManzi to don the clothing and the beads of the professional healer.

Mahlasela, Magodweni's wife, and Makadingane, Mahhashe's wife assist in the dressing. First, strings of red, black and white beads are placed around his neck. Then the beaded spherical parcels of protective herbs

FIGURE 3.5: A ring is tied to DabulaManzi's forelock.

and medicines are brought out and also placed around his neck. The gall-bladder (*inyongo*) that has been taken from the sacrificial goat and that he has found again in the bush is tied to the back of his hair. Large bands of red and white beads (*umgaco timfiso*) are placed in crossed bandolier fashion around his neck. A brass bracelet is put on his wrist as are beaded wristlets (*tigcizo*). Mahhashe puts a brass ring on his finger (right hand, third finger) then takes it off and ties it onto the front of his hair above his forehead. Magodweni is seated on his stool, in his full regalia, watching. Magodweni instructs him:

> Mahhashe is putting on the ring to show that you have married your ancestors. This is tied onto the front of your hair. It shows that you have agreed for the ancestors, and that you have agreed to everything that they are going to bring and that they want from you. This is a commitment or promise. Once you take it off your hair, you put it on your ring finger.

When all the beads have been put on Magodweni stops the dressers and tells them that they have done it all wrong. Everything must be taken off and done again. They divest DabulaManzi of the beads and start again. First, the bandoliers must be placed on his body (not the necklaces around his neck). The bandoliers must be placed first on the right shoulder, then on the left. They do it correctly this time. The strips of raw goatskin (*lijazi*, 'coat'), still wet and fleshy, are pulled over his head and arranged around his body like a jacket. In the next few days they will dry (and stink) on his body. Then the necklaces are put around his neck. Finally, the new red, black and white cloths of the sangoma are draped around his shoulders and waist. He is fully dressed as an *inyanga* now, and declared 'graduated' to become a fully qualified *inyanga*, 'doctor', in the *bungoma* tradition, that is, a sangoma.

Makadingane, Mahhashe's wife, will now join him as his companion for the rest of the ceremony. Her training and graduation had not gone well. There had been errors that needed to be corrected. She was also there to learn how to initiate a new sangoma, to be taught by Magodweni, so that she might take a *lithwasana* of her own. In particular, she had not been initiated into the ways of the Ndzawe spirits. Her re-initiation in the Ndzawe part of the spirit realm will make her a member of Magodweni's *mpandze*.

At this point DabulaManzi has completed his training under the tutelage of the ancestral Nguni spirits of his own line. He, too, has yet to be initiated into the ways of the Ndzawe. This could only be done at the river the next day, early in the morning. But for now, he was finished.

Two other *tinyanga* also receive new beads after DabulaManzi has been dressed. We are told that they are being graduated to a 'higher stage' that will allow them to begin to take *emathwasana* of their own. We break for a lunch of chicken and *mieliepap* (white maize meal porridge). Dancing continues for the rest of the day.

DabulaManzi's demeanour immediately changes. He is no longer ducking and subservient. He sits up straight on a mat by himself. He begins to tell the drummers what to drum by singing snatches of songs that have been taught to him during his period of training, and the drummers seek to take up the correct beat. Magodweni takes one of the drum sticks and corrects the drummers. They get the new beat and sustain it. For most of the rest of the day DabulaManzi sits by himself on the mat in his new, clean clothes and beads, no longer the object of attention but now an honoured, respected (*hlonipa*) member of the party. (Later I accidentally spilled beer on his shoulder cloth. Without a word, he gets up to change it for a clean dry one. He is proud and aloof.)

The party is relaxed now. There is an uninterrupted sequence of dancers. After sitting for a while, DabulaManzi gets up to change into his dancing uniform. He ties strings of rattles on his feet and takes up a carved wooden spear and a *knobkerrie* (fighting stick). He emerges from the *indumba* in a state of high energy, entranced, enchanted again. At the end of each dance each sangoma kneels before a member of the audience and tells him or her what the spirits have revealed. The person addressed enters into dialogue with the spirit through the medium of the sangoma. This is public, and often embarrassing, or worse. There is no shelter from the spirits' knowledge and no control over when they choose to reveal it. DabulaManzi dances and then kneels before Magodweni's wife, Mahlasela. He begins his chant, thanking the people for being there, revealing the names of his ancestors, and repeating what the spirits have revealed to him in the dance. He speaks in the voice of the spirit.

> DM: Why are you married [to Magodweni]?
>
> Mahlasela: Why do you ask me that?
>
> DM: It is because I am wondering why people are bad-mouthing you.
>
> Mahlasela: Why, is it because I live in my house comfortably? I am telling you that this man is mine.
>
> DM: I am saying this: that this man is ours; he also belongs to me.
>
> Mahlasela: So what? He loves me.
>
> DM: He also loves us all.
>
> Mahlasela: Are we fighting for [over] this man?
>
> DM: What I would tell you is that he is ours, not yours alone.
>
> Mahlasela: He is going to use you as he is using you now, but he loves me.
>
> DM: Why are you staying with him, because he is busy with us outside. Do you think he loves you? No way! I feel pity for you as you are really suffering.
>
> Mahlasela: As we are sharing this man, are you bothered that he lives with me, not you?

> DM: But he spends time with us [his *emathwasana*]. You have to wash and cook for him, so he comes to me very clean. You do the dirty job.
>
> Mahlasela: You spend money to be with him [through paying for training]. You are the buying type.

The 'exposure' is both a confession and an apparently involuntary exposure of secrets. Once a person's 'secrets' are revealed in this way he or she is expected to accept the exposure as a form of cleansing by way of confession.

In fact, Magodweni and Mahlasela have been estranged for some time. It is well known that Magodweni has another girlfriend, and that Mahlasela is unhappy about this, but tries to accept it. She moved out of his house some time ago, but still acts around him as if she were his wife. Magodweni, for his part, also continues to act towards her as if she were his wife. DabulaManzi has formed a very close attachment to Magodweni, and through the guise of spirit-revealed knowledge expresses this. When in possession of his spirit, DabulaManzi is female and feminine. He has been having sex with Magodweni and confesses to it here. Since his spirits cause him to be female, this not surprising or wrong in this context. The drums begin to play again and DabulaManzi dances again, but returns to Mahlasela who has remained seated close to Magodweni, and apparently unmoved by what has been 'revealed'.

> DM: Why are you so sure of yourself, is it because of this person [Magodweni]?
>
> Mahlasela: I have to be sure of myself; he is important to me.
>
> DM: I am telling you it is not that we are against you. It is your attitude.
>
> Mahlasela: What attitude?
>
> DM: This Magodweni is our child, that is, a person we care for; you must know that.
>
> Mahlasela: But I have a child with him, why are you involving yourself in our affair?
>
> DM: There is a man that you are seeing besides our child.

Mahlasela: You are always saying a lot of things all the time that are not true!

DM: That is the problem we have with you, you are cheating.

Mahlasela: You may think what you think; the problem is that you want our child's money.

DM: Why is it that when we suggest that you all come and live with us you refuse? What is it that you know that we do not know?

Mahlasela: It is always a problem; there are always misunderstandings.

DM: That is why you say we want your husband's money. You know the truth.

Mahlasela: But it is true you are always asking from him, so you want to control everything, including me. That's why you claim that I am seeing another man, as you want our child to leave me and stay with you to do everything for the whole family.

Magodweni remains aloof from this dialogue. Although public and heard by everyone nearby it is also a 'private' consultation between the person addressed and the spirit. Everyone seems to conspire to pretend that this is not happening in front of them.

Dancers break periodically from their dancing to go to a member of the audience to tell them something the *emadloti* have communicated during the dance. These messages are invariably delivered deliriously and with passion and great energy. The sangoma kneels at the feet of the respondent, panting and heaving, sweating profusely from the exertion of the dance. No eye contact is made, for the eyes are unfocused and wild. The sangoma's body quivers, rocks rhythmically; the voice is strange – hoarse and deep, or high and shrill. The interaction is rapid and responsive, with the sangoma speaking in short phrases, punctuated by the respondent's reply: '*Siyavuma*! [We agree]', or '*Thokoza*! [Peace]'.

It is as though the sangoma does not know who he or she is addressing and indeed, afterwards, when they have returned to their ordinary clothes and normal demeanours, the sangomas deny all knowledge or consciousness of what has gone on. Though the manner of delivery is the same for each sangoma, the message is different. Each consultation begins with a greeting to the ancestors ('*Thokoza!*') from the recipient of the message and ends with thanks (*Siyabonga! Siyabonga kakhulu!*). The spirits have chosen the particular recipient of the message and they must be thanked, even if the message itself is painful. Both the spirit and the sangoma are addressed as' '*Gogo* [Grandmother]'. One dancer, a male, interacts with a woman in the following way:

> Respondent: *Thokoza mkhulu, thokoza gogo* [Peace great one, peace grandparent].
>
> Male sangoma: You sometimes get headaches, and your waist can be very painful.
>
> Respondent: *Siyavuma* [We agree]!
>
> Male sangoma: As you walk around your legs ache a lot and they get cold and stiff sometimes.
>
> Respondent: *Siyavuma, thokoza gogo, kunjalo mkhulu* [We agree, peace grandmother, enjoy elder one].
>
> Male sangoma: It is something they put for you, that you jumped over without knowing that you are being bewitched.
>
> Respondent: *Thokoza gogo.* [It is true]. *Siyavuma.*
>
> Male sangoma: You will have to get medication that you must drink, as this will destroy you, you will drink *imbiza* [herbal medicine or muti].
>
> Respondent: *Thokoza gogo thokoza mkhulu.*
>
> Male sangoma: Some people want to walk over you; they want you underground. They want to see you dead.
>
> Respondent: *Thokoza gogo.*
>
> Male sangoma: You may ask what you need to know.
>
> Respondent: I have heard you clearly! *Thokoza.*

Here the respondent has heard well but has also heard enough or more than she wanted to hear. It is not possible to disagree under these circumstances. Whether or not she had pains, or felt threatened by someone trying to bewitch her, she assents to the sangoma's message. In fact, almost everyone has pains of this kind at some time, and almost everyone can feel paranoid or spooked by potential enemies, so the message usually rings true to some degree. In some respects, these interactions amount either to a sales pitch for *imbiza* (herbal medicine prepared by *tinyanga*) and other services, or sound like proselytising for the cause. Most *tinyanga* urge their respondents – many of whom are neighbours and curious onlookers who have been attracted by the party atmosphere and the drumming and dancing – to take the *emadloti* seriously. Ultimately, this can lead to becoming a *lithwasana* and paying the fees for graduation. The following interaction shows this clearly:

> Male sangoma: Why is it that you do not praise [*pahla*] your ancestors? Why do you not slaughter an animal for them, as your ancestors are angry that you do not do anything for them? They are very angry with the whole family.
>
> Female respondent: *Thokoza Gogo.* I do not know much about *emadloti* as I am not exposed to them at home.
>
> Male sangoma: But you must tell your family what I am telling you! This is a serious issue! Go home and tell them so.
>
> Female respondent: *Thokoza Gogo! Siyavuma.*
>
> Male sangoma: For you to be here, the *emadloti* brought you here! Hear their cry. You must tell them at home that you all need to praise the ancestors.
>
> Female respondent: *Thokoza Gogo*, I shall do so.
>
> Male sangoma: That is why there are a lot of mishaps in the family. There is no happiness in your family. You are not united, and the ancestors do not want that. Your grandmothers and fathers acknowledged the presence of the ancestors, but you do not. If you can do as the ancestors are saying you will see the change in your family.
>
> Female respondent: *Thokoza Gogo*; *kunjalo Gogo*, it is so.

The interactions between the *tinyanga* and the audience continue for hours. Most of the dances are formulaic and apparently routine. People comment on the passion and energy of each dance, and on the dancers' skill. Although the ceremony is held in one yard or stand, Magodweni's, the stands are small and there is little to separate the yard from the road or from neighbours. Some neighbours attempt to ignore the high energy drumming and go about their business. Others join the audience, whose membership changes as passers-by join the observers and people come and go.

A few dancers stand out from the others. Skwayela, a female sangoma from Emjindini, dances with a sjambok [a stiff whip traditionally made of hippopotamus hide, but today usually made of plastic] that she holds between her legs like an erect penis. She thrusts her hips and dances in a sexually suggestive way. She is very aggressive and people run from her when she swings the sjambok. Later, when she has finished and has changed her clothes, I sit and play with her baby and talk to her. She is sweetness itself; calm and reserved, as I had known her before. She tells me that when I visited her last in Emjindini, and gave her R100 for throwing the bones for me, she bought bread and a canister set for tea and coffee to remember me by. Majuba ['Doves'], a small woman with a square jaw and sharp features, dances with a masculine frenzy but also with feminine grace. She dances several times, sometimes with other female *tinyanga*, echoing the others' moves in a high-energy *pas de deux*. Her stamina is remarkable, and she takes turns to beat the drums between her dances.

Nhlahlo, from Shakastad, a town 50km away, has come because he wants to be part of Magodweni's *mpandze*. His *gobela*, Mahhoyana, has apparently not been able to teach him the secrets of the *Ndzawe* and has not performed some of the rituals correctly. Magodweni must redo part of his initiation and take him back to the river to introduce him to the *Ndzawe* in order to make him part of his *mpandze* and to teach him the secrets. He dances with aplomb and gravitas, masculine authority, almost frightening in its force. Bhoko, from Middleburg, similarly exudes a purely masculine power, his muscles etched beneath his dark skin.

The dancers express an unambiguously gendered persona in their dance, but this is independent of their sex, depending instead on the gender of the primary spirit that they possess (and that possesses them). Skwayela, though feminine in ordinary life, expresses masculine aggression in her dance. DabulaManzi is feminine in both dance and daily life. Bhoko is all male in dance and ordinary demeanour. One cannot doubt Majuba's femininity in her quick and flighty style. Indeed, if this were a dance floor in New York or London, one might say each was very 'camp': gender is acted out – performed – in a hyper-real way that is both sincerely felt and mocking of gendered styles. All dancers wear the light cotton printed fabrics around their waists as a skirt, the beads and rattles, and most display the long, plaited or dreadlock hairstyles. Each, too, carries a small carved wooden assegai (short stabbing spear) and fighting stick or sjambok. In other words, the costume mixes characteristics of both genders as they are imagined to have been 'traditionally'.

As each sangoma ends his or her dance and the drums stop, a new one emerges from the *indumba* to begin his or her own dance. They fall on their knees several times during their performance to bring a message from the ancestors, the *emadloti*, to someone. Most of the cadres of *tinyanga* in attendance have been initiated by Magodweni. Many, but not all, bring a message to Magodweni, greeting him with great respect as they do so. Magodweni, in turn, addresses the spirit/sangoma with his own message. Always, he endeavours to teach.

> Male sangoma: I am greeting you, father.
> Magodweni: *Thokoza mkhulu* [Peace, Elder, literally 'great one'].
> MS: *Thokoza mkhulu.*
> Magodweni: Others have gone this way and that way, but you said you are staying, this has been a journey for you.
> MS: *Thokoza mkhulu.*
> Magodweni: I am asking you to hold on tight to this *bungoma*, heal people as you got initiated [*udle ntwaso*] – once only. I want to tell you to hold on to healing, as you have to be serious in this. You have taken this kingdom. There is no better kingdom than this. I am going to tell you what I want: go and heal people. I do not have *inhlanga* [a pattern of evil, madness]. I do not teach people to bewitch. I give healing only; people should heal by your powers. *Thokoza. Ngiyabonga* [I thank you] *mkhulu.*
> MS: I thank you father for telling me this message and all the advice you have given me. I thank you father, as you have cleared the way for me. I am asking for respect as I respect people, too, as you have taught me.

Magodweni himself does not dance until after 5pm. He attends to various matters around the house and yard and makes sure everyone is comfortable and enjoying themselves. He sits with small groups of people and talks with them. Late in the day he sits with us and I ask him, impertinently, if he is going to dance too. Shortly afterwards he suddenly begins to 'roar' (making the sound of the beginning of spirits coming) as he becomes possessed by his spirits. He goes to prepare to dance in the *indumba*. He must dress in his dancing gear first and reach the correct state of mind. Most of the other *tinyanga* attending have already completed their dances. Magodweni then dances. He has huge presence and style. He is known for his excellence in dance – everyone who has seen him says they are astonished by his skill and finesse – but today he does not dance with the flair for which he is noted. Instead, he draws in all of his *mpandze* and all of the *tinyanga* who are still there that late in the day, to dance with him. He is fussed over by the female *tinyanga*, who praise him for his short bursts of accomplished but apparently uninspired dancing. It is, perhaps, the best dancing of the afternoon, but lacks some passion, it seems. They wipe him with cloths when he sweats and attend to him. He leads several dances with one or two or four *tinyanga*, all of whom are his *emathwasana* or his 'grand-*emathwasana*' or 'grandchildren' (people who have trained with his previous *emathwasana* who have now become *gobelas*).

A group of young girls has come with one of the other *tinyanga*. The girls stand on the margins of the dancing area in a group under the *umsinsi* tree. They criticise and heckle Magodweni constantly from the sidelines.

> 'Yeah, yeah, we've heard enough!'
> 'What nonsense!'
> 'You are talking rubbish!'
> 'Well, are you going to dance or not?'

Magodweni mostly ignores them, but it is harsh and surprising since they are sitting under his tree on his stand. He is patient. He talks with them briefly. They do not shut up.

Magodweni's sister has also caused a disturbance because she is drunk again. He quietly leads her out of his yard into the sandy dirt road in front of the house. She stands outside and shouts at him, before coming back in and making a nuisance of herself. She is aggressive with other *tinyanga*, who look through her and try to ignore her. Another woman attempts to lead her away. She comes back and someone tries to block her way inconspicuously. She seems too drunk to notice, but continues to try to wriggle her way into the centre of the ceremonies. She feels that Magodweni, her brother, has neglected her. She stands by the door to the *indumba* sobbing loudly and conspicuously for a while. Everyone, including her brother, ignores her pointedly. Finally, she wanders out of the compound, still sobbing, and is gone.

Eventually, all the participating *tinyanga* have danced and addressed one or several members of the audience. The second day winds down slowly. Some pack their bags to leave early the next morning if they have come from out of town. Others will stay to go to the river the next morning for the final stages.

The education of a sangoma

Magodweni conducted the entire ceremony as a sort of educational exercise, presenting it as a 'text-book' example to the other *tinyanga* who gathered to help him celebrate the graduation of one of his own, and to learn from his knowledge and critical acumen. Although he is aware of his role as a performer, he carries it out more like a chemist than a priest. He does not present these rituals and procedures with any sense of irony or metaphor, or even as symbolic of some other reality – as, for instance, a contemporary Anglican priest in Johannesburg might do – but rather as a practitioner of a certain and material art that has determinable, though perhaps intangible, outcomes. He is no Socrates, therefore; there are no abstract entities that are ultimate or more real than the physical reality we see. Although the spirits are not seen, they are 'real' in determining life and behaviour. The *emadloti* are like the unseen DNA that a modern popular culture, drawing on science and its special imagination, understands as controlling the person. The reality of the ancestors, the *emadloti*, is simultaneously genetic and immanent. It is in the blood that flows from the physical ancestors' bodies into the bodies of the living, their descendants, and is as real. The *emadloti* are both 'blood' (as bodily forbearers) and 'spirit'; that is, intangible powers that come from bodily forbearers but which are no longer embodied themselves, achieving embodiment in the person of the *inyanga*. The bodily-ness and spirit-ness of the *emadloti* cannot be separated. Through the sacrifice of the goat, the body *and* spirit of the *mthwasa* are elevated and awakened (*kuthwasa*) and the healer-to-be is healed (*kwelapha*) and given life (*imphilo*), which is also health.

But, like Socrates, Magodweni convenes and acts as master of a school like the Ancient Philosopher's Academy, or Aristotle's Lycaeum. I, the anthropologist, interpret as a thoughtful scribe. Magodweni is not the priest of a cult or a master magician: he does no magic and does not claim to do any. He sees himself as an educator of youth and he sees the knowledge he conveys as critical of the established institutions of state and religion that he sees around him. Building on tradition, he interprets it and teaches it to the new generation. And, like Socrates in ancient times, he is mocked and abused by some. Christians often fear the very notion of traditional knowledge that lies at the core of the *inyanga*'s practice and belief. The young girls mocking him from within the boundaries of his own yard express this. There are many sceptics in the crowd, some of whom openly mock the proceedings. As one woman confided: 'I do not know much about *emadloti* as I am not exposed to them [at home]'. For many in contemporary South Africa, this practice is anything but 'traditional', it is a challenge to their own sense of order and reason. While they might recognise it as coming from an African tradition to which they feel they also belong, it is not their own way. Thus, as Magodweni insists, it must be taught and explained.

The sceptics and abusers, however, seem to strengthen Magodweni's power in the way that the ritual abuse of the Swazi king in the *incwala* 'first fruits' ceremony ultimately strengthens him. It makes real the adverse opinions against which these healers know they are struggling. They suffer the abuse gladly, drawing, too, on Christian images of persecution. Although alarming to me at first, it now seems an essential part of the context in which suffering is portrayed, tamed and domesticated through the ritual practice of healers. (See Chapter 5.)

To 'eat' *intwaso* (*kudla ntwaso*) is to inherit the tradition (also expressed by the verb 'to eat'), to carry it on by embodying it. Eating is a metaphor of acquisition in general, especially acquisition as a right due to position, suffering, or chance, crime or graft. In South African English, one 'eats' ill-gotten gains, or the benefits of chicanery, deceit and fraud; one also 'eats' one's inheritance, or one's salary (especially when no discernible work is done to get the salary, for instance, from a sinecure post in government). Thus, to 'eat' the *intwaso*, is to acquire the knowledge of the *bungoma* by right of status. One must reach the status of *thwasa*, being 'lifted up', or of 'heightened awareness' of the spirit in order to achieve this status, but to 'eat' the *intwaso* is to absorb fully, through the cross-flow of *intwaso* into the body, and blood and vomit out of the body, the quantum of spirit-being that is the virtue of the sangoma. This imbues the sangoma with the qualities of insight and the mastery of healing techniques that *intwaso* both enables and licenses. The *intwaso* is eaten, but causes suffering again. DabulaManzi vomits for half an hour, gagging and choking as the blood that has flowed into him flows out again. Through the flows of water, blood, and vomit comes a flow of knowledge as suffering.

With the *intwaso* comes an awareness of doubleness; of being both controlled by a spirit and under control of the self. Although many who have written about the *inyanga* describe the state of transcendent consciousness that is reached as a 'trance', it is neither an 'out of body' experience nor a loss of consciousness. As the term *kuthwasa* makes clear, it is a state in which the spirit of the ancestors is aroused and raised from within. It is not possession by an external spirit. The spirit of the ancestors is already possessed by the *lithwasana* who seeks control over it. By means of this control, the 'spirit' is now conceived as knowledge (*ulwazi*) and consciousness (*liphaphama*), which enables 'dreams' (*liphupho*).

It is not trance into which the *lithwasana* rises, but rather *enchantment* in a double sense: the etymological and the popular. This state of mind is created by dance and singing (enchantment, from *en-* + *chant*, 'song', 'to sing'), by the drums, as *ngoma* ('deep knowledge'). It is not an 'out of mind' experience or loss of consciousness to the control of some other consciousness, or other 'spirit'. It is, rather, the creation of a system of control through music and dance to entrain the spirit. It is a rhythmical entrainment of the mind to serve a mystical purpose, rather than a loss of mind caused by mystical forces. It is a heightened sense of 'enchantment' and of consciousness. *ukuthwasa* means to 'lift up' or 'heighten', not to subject or to control. Despite the *lithwasana*'s submission to rules and instruction during his/her training, the process aims at the upliftment of spirit in the body of the person, not the access to disembodied spirits beyond the realm of direct experience. The rite of 'eating *intwaso*' combines many different aspects of a complex of healing arts and systems of bodily, political and mental control.

The power of herbs and the power of spirit are different. The power of herbs comes from the landscape and from the bush, while the power of spirit comes from the person. Through eating *intwaso*, the power of the bush is consumed by the body that already contains the spirit. The combination of male and female blood, the combination of different 'streams of blood' from different ancestors, and the combination of powerful herbs are fused and located in the body of the *inyanga*. This imposes a duty of control on the *inyanga*, for he must control both the power of the herbs and the power of the spirit.

In the end, DabulaManzi's incorporation into the *mpandze* was incomplete. Several months after this ceremony was performed he had still not paid his fee to Magodweni for 'eating *intwaso*'. He was still Magodweni's *lithwasana*. Although he had completed all the steps, without payment – payment to the *emadloti*, the ancestors, as Magodweni says – he cannot

FIGURE 3.6: Magodweni and DabulaManzi.

practice as an *inyanga* or claim the full status. Formally, he remains a member of Magodweni's household, although he returned to his own home about a month later. He had achieved his upliftment (-*thwasa*), but not his *setifikat* ('certificate').

A year or so after his ceremony DabulaManzi applied for nursing college but failed to get in. He took a job selling fabric at Sheet Street, a low-end chain of shops that sells bedroom linens and other domestic goods. He ceased practising as a sangoma and reverted to his given name, Penuel.

And, a year later, Magodweni went into a stand of dense bush near his house and hanged himself. When he was found, months later, his body was dried and black like a smoked fish, with a puddle of detritus on the ground beneath it. All his remains were collected, including the dark material in the soil under the body. We buried him with his beads in his red cloak and impala skin hat. He was a master, but never fully mastered his own demons.

CHAPTER 4

The transmission of knowledge in *bungoma*

Much of the work of the healer actually has to do with teaching and learning. Many sangomas do not practise 'healing' at all, but rather specialise as teachers, or as herbalists. For them, the knowledge of *bungoma* is an end in itself. Learning *bungoma* eventually leads to initiation into a 'school' of sangomas under a teacher.

The knowledge sangomas acquire, however, is diverse and depends critically on the *gobela* (teacher). As in any educational system, not all teachers are competent. In many cases, the *lithwasana* changes teachers or even returns for further education under a new *gobela* once graduated and inducted into the *mpandze* 'alumni' group.

But whatever the quality of education, the fact that knowledge has been imparted and received confers *expertise* on the aspiring sangoma, who becomes, though education and practice, a technical expert. It is precisely the expertise of the sangoma that confers legitimate authority or capacity (*emandla*) and gives the sangoma a special presence (*isithunzi*). The expertise in the person of a specialist is one of the most important criteria for a healer to be taken seriously. It is also one of the primary characteristics of any practice of magic, especially in the context of craft and healing, as many have remarked (Childe 1949; Malinowski 1935; Rowlands and Warnier 1993; Schwemmer 2011; Tambiah 1968).

Sangomas are initiated only after experiencing a process of *ukuthwasa*, 'enlightenment', or 'lightening' that is described as being 'under water'.

They say that is 'not *like* being under water, but *being* under water' (Chapter 3). The process through which a student learns to be a sangoma, that is to acquire expertise of *bungoma*, is a hard one, but so is the role of the *gobela*. The student will have to learn to dance in the prescribed way to the rhythms of the *ngoma*, to enter trance and to learn from dreams. The student will also acquire a basic botanical knowledge of herbs and trees and of the animal products and minerals that go into healing potions. The process of teaching and learning is also never complete since the senior teacher can never transmit all that he or she knows. The initiated student will continue to learn over the duration of his or her career. Sangomas share knowledge constantly and support each other in the process of acquiring knowledge as much as in teaching it to others. The intensity of belonging to such a school is constantly manifest in their lives.

Sangomas in Mpumalanga province are organised into schools around a senior teacher and becoming a sangoma is understood to be a profession, not a religion or even a spiritual exercise. Healers actively assess the effectiveness of their healing methods, transmit their knowledge to each other, and evaluate each other's performances in ways that stray far from the mere transmission of 'tradition'. Clients are likely to pay as much for their services as they would medical doctors and the services are not limited to the medical. Their practices can be divided into roughly six 'disciplines': divination, herbs, control of ancestral spirits, the cult of foreign *Ndzawe* spirits, drumming and dancing, and training new sangomas. The status of sangoma is achieved through an arduous process of teaching and learning through which the student or initiate is simultaneously 'healed' and educated to become a member of the profession that coheres around these knowledge practices.

Bungoma and the public

Since the promulgation of the new South African Constitution in 1994 by the ANC government traditional healing has become prominent in public discourse. Increasing numbers of people today become sangomas. Both clientele and practitioners come from all 'races', including South Africans of European ancestry. For many, sangomas appear to preserve a sense of a distinctive 'African' identity in an increasingly globalised and 'Westernised' country. Conservative African Christians, on the other hand, revile them as 'primitive', dirty, and spiritually dangerous. They remain outside the experience of many South Africans but are fully part of South African life and consciousness. The beliefs and practices of traditional healers have been well described over the years (Cumes 2004; Du Toit 1980; Hammond-Tooke 1975, 1978, 1985, 1989; Junod 1912; Sundkler 1948: 220–237) but these practices continue to change and show great regional variation.

The sangoma tradition has multiple roots that extend across time, cultures and languages and it derives partly from pre-colonial African systems of belief. While its appeal is broadening, it is also changing, as sangomas are exposed to a wide range of other healing traditions and religious views. Today (2017) many of their practices scarcely resemble the older traditions reported in the early ethnographic monographs, although some, such as divination, remain. Sangomas consider themselves to be members of a profession with a distinct intellectual tradition; one that undergoes critique, modification, and change in the light of experience and myriad influences.

Sangomas offer a wide range of counselling, divination/diagnostic, medical and other services. The sangoma's art is rarely directed simply at organic causes of physical disease of the body. They prepare *muti* to protect clients from motor accidents, theft, witchcraft, infection, unemployment, and loss of love, or to attract and retain lovers or spouses. They relieve anxiety and depression, assist clients to make decisions and help to find lost or stolen objects. The governments of South Africa, Zimbabwe and Mozambique have attempted to formalise them into a national health-care system (Last and Chavanduka 1986; Cocks and Dold 2000; Green, Zokwe and Dupree 2000; Last 1986; Maclean 1982; Pool 1994; Yoder 1982), including recent legislation in South Africa. Indeed, many sangomas compare themselves with other medical professionals and believe that they should be treated in the same way and accorded similar respect, with appropriate remuneration. Despite this, sangomas and medical practitioners remain in separate spheres (Wreford 2005). Sangomas also remain ambivalent about government attempts to regulate them. A limited formal protest against more forceful attempts to implement legislation requiring registration began in late 2015 (Moatshe 2015; Mthethwa 2015) under the banner 'Vuka Mngoma' [Wake up traditional healer]. The protest was organised through a Facebook closed group called VukaMngoma. Other sangomas resist state efforts to regulate them by simply ignoring the regulations. Since there is no enforcement of the regulations, or any mechanism to do so, a large majority of sangomas simply remain outside of the state registration system.

The core of the profession is the school, called the *mpandze*, meaning 'root' or 'branch.' Wim van Binsbergen (1991) calls them 'lodges' in the context of Botswana. These are not 'churches' in the Durkheimian sense, but rather 'secret societies', or guilds of specialists that provide a sense of professional identity based on specialised expertise and knowledge. This is transmitted through a formal system of education involving teachers (*emagobela*) and students (*bathwasana*), who enter into formalised relationships.

Traditional healers are often called upon to 'cleanse' the nation of the damage from its apartheid past and to open government functions. Since the ANC government attributes virtually every political difficulty to the period of apartheid, South Africans seek political healing in many ways. The public hearings of the Truth and Reconciliation Commission, for instance, attempted to distinguish between 'political' and 'criminal' forms of violence in the past, and explicitly offered healing within a broadly religious framework (Tutu 1999).

This discourse of 'healing the nation' attributes political and social problems of today to the political 'ancestors' of the current 'dispensation'. In this respect it shares some characteristics with other forms of healing in South Africa, from the occult and 'traditional' to the 'New Age' and Pentecostal faith healers. On the other hand, the past is also held to be the source of true healing and health. According to the philosophy of African ubuntu and, indeed, of many sangomas, the past is also the purified and romanticised pre-Christian Africa of kingdoms and warriors, usually imagined in mainly Christian terms.

For instance, Manto Tshabalala-Msimang, the Minister of Health in the 1990s, insisted that a diet of beetroot, lemons and olive oil will cure AIDS. She did this in contravention of section 49 of the Traditional Health Practitioners Act No. 35 of 2004, which specifically stipulates that it is an offence for anyone who is *not* a traditional healer to treat or otherwise suggest that they can treat HIV or AIDS, among other 'prescribed terminal diseases'. The Act does allow, however, for traditional healers to treat HIV and AIDS if they wish and feel they are capable of doing so. Even in this competitive environment it is popularly claimed that 70–80% of all South Africans make use of the services of traditional healers. A questionnaire that I administered to 75 people in Umjindi district suggests that around 80% of residents of the Emjindini Trust, the communal tenure area of the municipality under the nominal authority of Chief Kenneth Dlamini, use traditional medicine (unpublished questionnaire results 2004). This is fully consistent with the often quoted, but unsubstantiated, number of 'up to 80%' of Africans use 'traditional medicine' (Green 1999: 10; Richter 2003; World Health Organization 2002).

The disciplines of African healing

South African law treats traditional healing as a single practice, but *bungoma* healing is conducted through several separate disciplines, each with its own history and teaching styles. Rituals and activities appropriate to each are performed and employed in distinct environments or contexts, with different aims and functions. All can be practised separately although in most cases it is the integration of these that constitutes the full practice of traditional healing in the region. Not all healers command the same degree of knowledge of each of these separate institutions.

I distinguish six such disciplines or divisions of traditional healing:

1. **divination** (*ukupengula*) using the 'bones' (*tinhlolo*) a collection of natural objects that are thrown onto a mat and jointly 'read' by the healer and the client (Hammond-Tooke 1989; Cumes 2004);
2. knowledge of **medicinal herbs** and animal products together with an environmental ideology of the source of their power (Hirst 1997);
3. knowledge of '*Nguni*' **ancestors** (*emadloti*) and the methods used to communicate with them *(kupahla)*;
4. knowledge of *Ndzawe* spirits and *inzunzu*, the **'foreign' and water spirits**, together with the ritual used to heal through their agency (*kufemba*);
5. experience and **knowledge of *ngoma*** ('deep' embodied knowledge), expressed through singing, dancing, drumming and the

'trance' or 'enchantment' of the dancers (Janzen 1992: 1; Ngubane
1981);

6. the **teaching relationship** between *gobela – lithwasana* and the
   school (*mpandze*), together with systems of knowledge transfer and
   criticism (Van Binsbergen 1991).

Each of these areas requires specific knowledge and individuals are more
or less expert in one or several of them, and each discipline must be taught
and learned separately during a period of apprenticeship. It is rare for one
person to be an expert in all these disciplines.

Magodweni, my teacher, who became a healer at the age of eight,
commanded knowledge of all these areas. One day, just before he was to
begin a talk to my class at university, he told me that if the spirits had not
called him he would have been a professor like me. Instead, he became a
healer, and because of his broad knowledge and expertise he specialised in
training other healers. Some healers who have already graduated came to
Magodweni for re-training because their earlier training had been faulty,
partial or incomplete, or because they wanted to learn another discipline.
The rarity of such breadth of knowledge highlights the complexity and
internal completeness of each of the separate disciplines.

The system of divination

The system of divination (*kupengula*) is the most widely known of the practices of southern African traditional healers. It has a wide regional distribution in southern Africa, with regional variants, and all sangomas learn to
do it. Stable central features include the spatial arrangement of diviner and
client at opposite sides of a restricted ritual space, symbolised by a grass
mat, and the use of a set of objects whose juxtaposition signifies events,
persons and relationships. Most clients expect to receive advice, a diagnosis
or herbal remedies. The actual divination involves the release of a set of
objects ('bones', *emathambo*, or *tinhlolo*) from the sangoma's cupped hands
onto the grass mat between the diviner and the client. This set of objects
consists of twenty to forty small pieces of bone, shells, ceramic fragments,
dice and dominoes, among other things, each signifying a range of meanings. Each set of *tinhlolo* is different, although there is a group of core

objects that signify social categories or types of people (children, adults, widows, the diviner) or relationships, actions, and emotions (jealousy, love, violence). When the *tinhlolo* objects are thrown onto the mat they land in a configuration that is 'read' through a rhythmic verbal interaction between client and healer concerning the meanings of each object, especially as it lies in relation to the others. A diagnosis or possible solution to the problem that is being addressed gradually emerges through the interaction between the client, the healer and the pattern of the objects.

A sangoma learns how to divine through observation and practice. A novice may practise with several clients and outcomes will be ratified or criticised by the teacher. In some cases, the client may decide the student's session was not up to scratch, and the senior healer will take over. Through this process of learning, techniques are discussed, critiqued and evaluated.

Joel Mnisi, a colleague of Magodweni's with whom I often discussed my interest in *bungoma*, explains the process. I quote Mnisi's lively teaching in full, since it shows the significance of failed teaching and the flexibility of the *bungoma* system:

> When they teach the throwing of bones, they give herbs that help them to remember, not to forget.
>
> When they teach the *thwasa*, they go to the forest or bush and tell them what to collect. When they first come to the *gobela*, the *thwasas* say 'So many herbs! Do you know what they all are?' The *gobela* tells them 'Of course I do!'
>
> The *thwasa* is taught by throwing the bones with a client and by discussion of the results afterwards. Sometimes the *thwasa* throws the bones for the *gobela*, or for himself, or for a client. Each item in the set is also taught and explained to the *thwasa*. All in all, the backbone of the teaching is the herbs that they eat while they are learning. Herbs help them to learn.
>
> First, they are given herbs to make them vomit. To purify their bodies and minds. Then they are steamed with herbs. The *gobela* makes cuts in the skin and rubs herbs into the body through the incisions. Finally, there is the *libudlo* (foam from a mixture of saponaceous herbs). When they eat the foam it lifts their spirit. Just as the foam is light and lifts from the water the spirit of the *thwasa* is

lifted and made light by the foam. *Lipakhamisa emadloti*, 'what lifts the ancestors' [to consciousness].

Foam in a container is put on the head of the *thwasa*, and it is foamed up by the *gobela*. The foam overflows the container and runs onto the head of the *thwasa*. After this the *thwasa* learns to beat up the foam, and eats it.

The teacher will also show how to teach other *thwasas*. The *thwasa* is not just learning what the *gobela* knows, but is also learning to teach other *thwasas*.

Libudlo is a combination of herbs. You must look at the spiritual side of the person and formulate the *libudlo* carefully. It is not the same for everyone. The foam must be formulated differently for the *Ndzawe* and for the Nguni spirits. Stronger herbs must be used to the *Ndzawe*. Sometime you will have to plead with the spirit to allow certain herbs to be used on whomever is being taught. The spirit might refuse some herbs and accept others.

Sometimes the spirit can refuse. You will know if the right herbs have been used if the *thwasa* is 'lifted up', 'awakened'. Sometimes the *thwasa* just does not awake.

If it fails it could be the fault of the *gobela*. The *thwasa* must then go to another *gobela*. The *gobela* is not doing his duty well. The *tinhlolo* show what kind of technique you must use (as a *gobela*), but the *gobela* might get this wrong. Other gobelas can be jealous. They feel that the *thwasa* is overpowering them. Then it doesn't work.

With me [Joel Mnisi], my first *gobela* was overpowered by my spirits. It did not work.

When he went to be initiated with this *gobela*, a man [Magodweni], he was still young. He threw the bones. He had a problem immediately. He could see my power. I threw the bones and started to divine. The *gobela* started swearing at me and abusing me. He was jealous. He said that I was making myself a *gobela* when I was merely a *thwasa*. I could divine better than the *gobela*. People [clients] wanted me to divine for them. The *gobela* was jealous of my power.

I stayed there until I got initiated. The *gobela* took me home, and I started to heal. I healed for a month or so then everything came to an end. I could not heal. The spirits refused. Nothing was working.

I had to go to another *gobela*. The second *gobela* started opening up the *tinhlolo* for me [teaching him more aspects of the *tinhlolo* divination]. The second one was stronger. She was not jealous. This was an old woman. She wasn't jealous of my power but taught me well. After that everything went well. I had to eat *intwaso* again and everything again. I learned more for the second one. I now belong to her *mpandze*. This was for the *Ndzawe*. The first one was for both *baNguni* and for *emandzawe*. Second one was just for the *emaNdzawe*. I had already done the *baNguni* initiation and it was OK.

If I can't heal a patient, I consult with another healer who tells me what to do and what to mix. Then I go back to the patient and try again with the new procedures and herbs. I constantly discuss with others because no one can know everything. I can discuss things with any healer. I don't just discuss with my own *mpandze*.

Sometimes, for some things, I can only discuss with my own *mpandze*. There are some things that are confidential to the *mpandze*. For instance, when going to initiate someone with *emaNdzawe*, we don't call the others. We do this with our own *mpandze*, people who know the *emandzawe*. BaNguni is open to all healers. They all come when we do the initiation for the *baNguni*.

Joel Mnisi shows us here that each process of teaching is individualised and formulated for each student. Teaching different subject matter also requires different methods. Mnisi's discourse also explodes the notion that *bungoma* is about a fixed tradition, passed on unchanged, and undermines any hope that it can or should be routinised as Public Health bureaucrats imagine it should (or could) be.

Medicinal herbs

As Mnisi explains, the system of medicinal herb use is often practised, taught and learned in conjunction with divination, for instance, when a healer divines a particular cause of a problem or a diagnosis of a disease. He may then prescribe a mixture of herbs (leaves, bark, seeds, roots, bracts, corms, and so on) or a mixture of herbs and/or animal products (bone, teeth, fats, burnt skin, and so on). Different *muti* can be prepared from the same plant harvested in different situations (at night or during the day, from wet areas or dry, from hillsides or valleys, and so on) or when it is in different stages of growth. The location of the herb on a hillside, for instance, may be as important as its species in deciding how it might be used. Often dreams tell the healer which herbs to use.

A single term for the whole range of any plant or animal agent, however, disguises a highly complex set of classificatory, evaluative and empirical judgements that are made with respect to the *muti* and its uses. Most sangomas – but not all – maintain a large collection of such substances. These are usually kept in unlabelled glass bottles and jars, the contents of which the healer must remember. The discipline of memory in this case is critical, and valued, although sangomas have also told me that the herbs themselves 'speak' to the true healer so that labels are unnecessary.

Most herbs are not used as pharmacological agents, but rather as part of a ritual, or for steam or smoke baths or inhalations, or as rubs, or for amulets. Herbs may be ingested orally, vaginally, anally via enemas, or through small cuts in the skin, but any chemically measurable pharmacological action the herb might have is often not part of the rationale for the treatment. Since there is no standard procedure for collecting, drying, storing or other treatment of herbs or other 'medicinal' products, much of the pharmacological potency may be lost, modified, or otherwise transformed. But their pharmacological attributes are rarely the point. Instead, herbs are classified by their colour, gender, age at the time of harvesting and the time and circumstances of collection, among other criteria. Botanical classification is not necessarily of foremost importance. This is partly because herbs are not used singly, but as mixtures, since balance (of gender, colour, heat, and so on) is the therapeutic objective. The goal of treatment is to cleanse and restore wholeness as a way to protect the 'exposed being'. It is the person who is treated, not specific organ systems according to a theory of physiology. Teaching, therefore, involves more than assigning specific herbs to specific illnesses. Environmental knowledge and a complex multilayered system of classification and balance is also essential.

The herbal system, then, constitutes a field of knowledge and expertise that is distinct from the rest of the healing practices, but is also distinct from Western scientific/botanical knowledge. This is learned by the sangoma as part of the process of becoming a healer, but most graduate well before they have acquired even a fragment of the knowledge of a master practitioner. Many teachers charge a separate fee for teaching the formulation of herbal remedies, field identification, preservation and preparation methods and ways to mix and prescribe them. It therefore constitutes a separate knowledge system that draws on earlier San (Bushman), Khoe, and European herbal practices, combining these with new knowledge and herbs 'discovered' in dreams (Hirst 1997).

The 'Nguni' spirits and 'ancestors'

Two sets of 'ancestors' are central to the healer's practice. The first is their own ancestors, called the *Nguni*. '*Nguni*' is a collective ethnic name that includes the Xhosa, the Zulu, and the Swazi, but excludes the Sotho and the Tswana of the Highveld, and the Venda and Shangaan (Tsonga) of the Lowveld. Most of the healers in Umjindi were Swazi, and thus classified (by themselves) as 'Nguni', but not all. DabulaManzi, for instance, was Venda. Those who are not 'Nguni', however, use this term to designate 'own' ancestors.

The ancestors are complemented by, but also contrasted with, the *Ndzawe* spirits, which are foreign. Healers are not possessed by spirits, but rather claim to 'possess ancestors' or to *have* ancestors. This is not simply a claim to special spiritual access, it is also a claim to an identity and a specific cultural and intellectual heritage. Learning to heal involves not only having ancestors but learning to use and to control their power. Learning to control them involves a transfer of knowledge and also the recuperation or creation of an identity.

Healing, then, is often primarily about establishing an ancestry or re-establishing a relationship with a living person and with the ancestors (*emadloti*) through the transfer of the *ngoma* knowledge practices. By being initiated into the family of the *mpandze*, 'having ancestors' is validated as a personal heritage. The lineage of the *mpandze* is the lineage of the *Nguni* spirits that they 'have', or that they 'possess' as empowering agents, and their members address each other as 'grandparent' (*gogo*). As the *lithwasana* (student) grows in skill and knowledge, he or she also becomes part of a family of healers. In this way the process of learning is also a process of acquiring knowledge of a new family.

In my conversations with several sangomas the notion of ancestors was sometimes compared with that of Christian saints since they were able to intervene in practical ways. No one compared ancestors with the Christian Pentecostal concepts of spirit or the divine 'gifts' of the Pentecost, emphasising instead the ancestors' humanness and their role in practical intervention. Magodweni once explained to me that while the 'holy spirit' of the Pentecostals often made them speak in strange languages (speaking in tongues) the ancestors spoke in their own language and the Ndzawe spoke in theirs (siNdzau). The extent of ancestors' power, however, is the extent to which they are known and can be named. The kinship that sangomas acquire through their association with other sangomas is paramount. When they recite their genealogies as healers, they recite the names of their 'grandparents', the *emagobela* that have trained them, and not that of their genetic or natural parentage.

The *emandzawe* spirits

Another set of practices that is specifically permitted or empowered by a set of non-material entities called *emandzawe* is distinct from practices associated with the 'own' Nguni ancestors.

The *emandzawe* are regarded as real albeit non-material presences. They are not 'spirits' in the Christian sense, nor are they the same as the *emadloti*, or 'ancestors'. They are specifically foreign. Magodweni describes the *emandzawe* in the following way:

> The origin of *emandzau* is from Maputo [Mozambique]. You will find that a Maputo man will come and settle in Swaziland [or South Africa]. Because of our Swazi tradition, a person is welcome. Maybe he eventually marries one of the daughters. Once they are integrated into the community, once he dies there, he is integrated into the community. Now the spirits of *mandzawe*, they connect to the spirit…to the family that he has been living with. This spirit is a go-between, as he is a spirit that has come to settle because he is not from this area; he comes from Maputo, and Beira [northern Mozambique].

While the *Ndzawe* are foreign spirits, they teach and enable a 'technology' of healing called *kufemba*, 'to smell out'. The *kufemba* is a dramatic technique for identifying 'foreign bodies' in the body of the client using a short 'whisk' made of hyena hair and a small beaded ring made of ritual substances wrapped in cloth. With this, the healer literally 'smells' all over the body of the client, and occasionally 'identifies' some active entity – sometimes human, sometimes animal, sometimes some other substance – in the body of the client. The healer then takes out this entity by allowing it to enter into his own body. When this happens, the healer takes on the character of the substance or entity that has been found in or 'smelled out' of the client's body. If the entity is human, the healer immediately takes on their personality and character. This enactment of its presence makes it 'visible'. The client and others who may be observing, then interrogate this 'person' to find out why it is dwelling in the client's body, and who, if anyone, has put it there.

This entity, now in the person of the healer who enacts it, may become violent and refuse to leave. If so, it is cajoled by others present at the healing session and persuaded with a gift to leave. The gift can be anything – a small coin, even a leaf or a twig – since the entity is not able to assess its value. If it is an animal, such as a dog or a pig, the healer will act the part of the animal. If it is a 'dead' substance, the healer will immediately fall down senseless on the mat and has to be restored to life by his helpers and others standing around. Accordingly, this method of healing is regarded as exceptionally powerful and dangerous. It is always performed with other healers in attendance who can assist in restoring the primary healer to his own senses at the end of the session. This method of healing is strictly the province of the *emandzawe* and cannot be practised by those who have not been specifically trained and initiated into its practice. Training in this technique is often not included in the ordinary training of a new sangoma. If it was not originally included a sangoma may go to a *gobela*/trainer who has specific skills in this area of knowledge and undergo a second period of training or *ukuthwasa* (apprenticeship).

Since this method involves the complex performance of different personas and is carried out in a group, it is dramatic in character and is always followed by critique and discussion.

The ngoma: Dance, singing, and performance

The dances of the sangoma, performed to intense singing and drumming (*ngoma*), are perhaps the best known of the sangoma's arts among the general public. Dances are public and have a degree of entertainment value for neighbours and observers, as well as for other traditional healers. This is also what South African practices of healing have in common with healing throughout the Bantu-speaking area of sub-Saharan Africa (Janzen 1992). It is perhaps the oldest historical substrate of the South African practices of traditional healing.

Dancing is taught by example and practice, but not all sangomas learn to dance properly. In an interview in 2004 Magodweni said to me: 'You teach them by actually doing it for the *thwasa* to see [show them] how it is done. Some never learn to dance properly.' I asked if that was a problem. 'The only problem with not dancing [properly],' he explained, 'is when you attend other rituals and cannot dance. It is not really important to dance. What is important is mixing the herbs, healing and divining. Even if the *thwasa* can't dance properly, they can still do other things.'

Dancing is said to 'wake up the spirit' or to 'lift up' the consciousness of the *thwasa*. When the *thwasa* first comes to the *gobela*, he or she is made to dance for long periods and learns the songs and drum beats that go with the dance. The *thwasa* is awakened in the middle of the night to dance. At other times, during the day, the ancestors are said to 'come out' and this requires more drumming and dance to quiet them. Like yoga, dancing is a form of intellectual or spiritual exercise that shapes and changes the mind, making it more receptive to the implicit or intuitive knowledge that the sangoma seeks and relies on. During special functions such as cleansing after death, or at the end of mourning, or for other reasons, large groups of sangomas come together and dance, one after the other, in night-long sessions over several days.

The dances are perhaps the primary expression of identity of the group, the *mpandze*, 'root' or 'family'. Each *mpandze*, in addition to the special knowledge that it commands, has its own dance steps, drum rhythms and songs that accompany the dancers. The dance is partly competitive, with different sangomas vying for a reputation as the best dancer. But even those who do not dance well are respected for their efforts.

The dance develops the consciousness of the student and gets the ancestors' attention. After brief (15 seconds to a minute) but intensely energetic bursts of dancing, the healer kneels at the feet of another person in attendance, and brings the greetings of the ancestors. This is the occasion on which the genealogy of the healer and his trainers (*emagobela*) is recited, and where the identity of the *mpandze* is declared to others in attendance.

The relationship between *gobela* and *lithwasana*

While the other five disciplines are essential to the practice of the sangoma, the teaching relationship confers an identity and membership in an *mpandze*. This evolves into a complex relationship between teacher and student, with personal, emotional, physical (and sometimes sexual) and economic dimensions, but it is always intensely intimate. Male or female *emagobela* teach students of either or both sexes, in groups or singly. The dress of men and women is essentially the same. The teacher-learner relationship is discussed, however, in a kinship idiom in which the teacher is addressed as *gogo* (grandparent) (never parent) to the student's 'grandchild' role until graduation. In Bantu languages there is no grammatical gender distinction between masculine and feminine so the 'grandparent' role of the *gobela* may be conferred on either sex.

Students usually arrive unexpectedly, afflicted by fits of mania or depression. Some say they have dreamed about the *gobela* and have come to fulfil this dream. Although these practices are often called 'cults of affliction' (Turner 1968), those who train to become sangomas must be reasonably healthy and well motivated, whatever else might afflict them. They have to be: the period of training is rigorous, exhausting and lasts for two months to a year. Those who are moderately or seriously ill or mentally incapacitated may not be able to endure the rigours of training. It is also expensive. I calculated the minimum cost of full training to the point of graduation, based on fees and the prices of the materials for making the ritual regalia in Barberton at the end of 2016, to be a minimum of R10 600, with the cost of other materials and rituals bringing this to approximately R19 000 in total. This represents six months' wages for a person employed as a casual labourer in 2017, or three months' wages for a receptionist in urban South Africa. Sangomas often go into debt to afford this, or borrow from family members. When the debt is not repaid it quickly generates more tensions between the sangoma and the family, or, commonly, results in further impoverishment when items like furniture are repossessed.

There is a hierarchy of knowledge that the *gobela* attempts to teach. First of all, the student learns to dance, to sing the songs of his school or group and to beat the drums. This is the first order of business in any new teaching relationship. As Magodweni explained:

> You need to teach a *thwasa* how to dance. Also, you must teach them how to integrate themselves with society and how to carry themselves in the society of sangomas. When you are a true sangoma, you have to drop everything and attend to people as soon as possible. Even if you are eating, the people might have come from far.

The disciplinary regimes of dance, singing and drumming lead to a sense of elation and intense involvement, or 'enchantment'. This state has often been called 'trance'.

The notion of 'trance', however, does not adequately describe what appears to be an extreme state of what could better be described as hyper-presence or hyper-consciousness, in which the healer becomes intensely involved with his or her own intellectual and emotional state. Trance, in this case, could be described as the intense mental effort involved in the critical integration of knowledge from intuition, from the senses and from the social environment. It is taught, learned and experienced as discipline, not as an other-worldly state. While the sangoma feels and experiences the world, especially the social world, more acutely, the dialogue the sangoma enters into with others in his or her immediate environment is often intense and personal. It is more of a release from other social conventions and a period of exceptional freedom for the mind to work on the 'dream stuff'. Healers in the *ngoma* dance are highly animated, sweating, working hard. They may be ecstatic, but they do not leave the 'world' behind or become unconscious. When the *gobela* attempts to 'lift up' the student it does not mean that the student is being trained for a spiritual exercise of disembodiment or transcendence, but rather for a method for making explicit the implicit understandings that emerge from dreams, the divination process or the interactions between the sangoma and the client.

The process of learning how to dance, drum and sing, then, is less a spiritual exercise leading to trance than it is an intellectual one leading to a specific method of evaluating knowledge and making it real and manifest. It is a somatic and cognitive technology that is taught and learned rather than 'naturally' acquired. It achieves its goals through specific drumming rhythms and intense physical activity combined with song, specific teaching and monitoring and correction of the student's efforts. Through this the student healer achieves insight and 'deep' knowledge (*ngoma*).

Learning as healing/healing the learner

The practices that fall under the label of 'traditional healing', then, are disciplines that are taught, shared, criticised and learned. Its practitioners consider themselves to have a profession comprising the six separate disciplines of knowledge described above. Each practice has its own set of expert practitioners and their clients. Each is taught and evaluated differently in different situations by healers and clients alike.

Despite the attempts by government (outlined in this chapter) to define and control these practices, they continue to operate outside bureaucratic and state-centred systems of control. This, perhaps more than anything else, is what gives it strength: it is explicitly *not* part of the bureaucratic South African order and is far from a simple, poor man's medicine.

The process of learning is also a process of healing, and vice versa. The teacher imparts specific and highly valued knowledge, but he also instils a discipline of mind and body that may effectively 'heal' the social chaos from which his patient/student often comes. The student/client learns to be healed, to be 'lifted up' and to acquire insight and, at least, an alternative account of his or her affliction. The teacher heals the learner and simultaneously transmits knowledge within the profession by teaching a new healer to heal and to teach. It is their shared knowledge, rather than any shared 'affliction' (Turner 1968) that creates a sense of family identity and which is expressed through a kinship idiom. In turn, the idiom of kinship between teachers and learners is what makes this African profession appear 'traditional'.

Sangomas share knowledge with each other through explicit teaching, apprenticeship, practice and example. They evaluate their therapies and results through discussion and observation. Their knowledge is not simply 'passed on' from the past; nor is it, as South African legislation states, obtained 'from the ancestors'. It is very much part of the present and part of a complex mix of therapeutic strategies that South Africans of all colours and classes might use. Sangomas see themselves as professionals and aspire to be accepted as equal players among the large diversity of medical and therapeutic practices in contemporary South Africa.

CHAPTER 5

Healing conflict: The politics of interpersonal distress

The politics of exposure

The arts of healing in the practice of *bungoma* are applied above all to relationships between persons, whether tangible flesh-and-blood or of other intangible kinds such as witches, *emadloti* (ancestors), zombies, *emandzawe*, or other 'forces' with apparent person-like agency, such as actual persons acting under the influence, or with the protection, of *muti*. Persons, in this sense, have intentionality and are believed to possess effective causal agency and, therefore, have 'power', *emandla* and presence, *isithunzi*.

If we may take a 'market approach' to healing, as I suggest in chapters 6 and 7, we may also take a 'political approach' to the influence of people in a social context that also includes other person-like agents. In this context people understand themselves to be exposed to other persons as active agents or as patients and victims. Since the patient is also a victim, and because the patient of the sangoma can also learn to be an active agent in control of others through the knowledge of *bungoma*, there is necessarily an implicit politics (in the broad anthropological sense) that underlies these roles and their relationships. By examining the problems that emerge from the micro-scale of social order we can, perhaps, create a picture of the environment in which the healer acts.

I have emphasised the importance of the 'small-town' environment in understanding how *bungoma* works in an otherwise 'modern' society such as South Africa. Here I explore the political culture of this small-town environment in order to provide the basis for understanding how persons interact in daily life and therefore to show how the ordinary politics of daily life sets up the categories of conflict in terms of which divination and healing therapies comprehend the kinds of conflicts and injuries that the 'exposed being' experiences.

Towards an analysis of local-level political culture

Anthropology and African Studies scholars (as well as political activists) have long resisted the idea that there may be different cultural bases to African political and social systems, preferring, instead, to rely on political concepts derived from European theory and experience. This chapter takes the risk of suggesting that there are indeed definable differences – specifically cultural differences – for political thought and action in local-level 'African' politics. They are different from those in the liberal bureaucratic democracies of the 'developed' world, or within the sphere of formal national and governmental politics of the state and of the formal parties and organisations that contest power within South Africa's constitutional structures. I am concerned here with the 'politics' of people in the small town/*edropini*, locations/*lokasi*, the township and the home/homestead/ *umuzi*. 'Local' politics in South Africa may be distinguished from the larger-scale politics of province and nation or even continent and world.

I evoke the 'political' in the context of healing because healing is about the power humans (and other agents) have over each other and is therefore 'political' in the broadly anthropological sense of the term rather than in the ways it is used in the discipline of political science, or in much of sociology and history. In these latter disciplines 'the political' includes the domain of institutional forms in which power is exercised and contested, that is, though the bureaucratic institutions of the state and by political parties, social movements and politicians.

Meyer Fortes and E E Evans-Pritchard introduced their anthropological notion of 'the political' in their edited volume entitled *African Political Systems* (Fortes and Evans-Pritchard 1940). They observed that 'the theories of [European] political philosophers' were of 'little scientific value' in the study of African political systems primarily because they were concerned with 'how men ought to live and what form of government they *ought* to have'. Instead, they believed they spoke 'for all social anthropologists when we say that a scientific study of political institutions must be inductive and comparative' and should seek to show the 'interdependencies [of politics] with other features of social organisation' (Fortes and Evans-Pritchard 1940: 5). That is what I intend here.

The bulk of a sangoma's discussions with patients concern the patient's relationships with other people, most of whom are considered to have power over the patient. Not all such persons are human, or even tangible: for instance, 'ancestors' are former or even virtual humans but are no longer tangible presences, while witches may be tangible or intangible persons (see Chapter 8) and zombies are not fully persons (see Chapter 6). All may be benevolent and healing, or malevolent, evil and destructive. In other words, the patient's problems involve a kind of politics of multiple agents that have power(s), but, by the same token, the patient, especially with the help of the healer, has the resources to resist, to react and to thwart untoward influences and to augment his or her own protective powers. This is a form of politics in which the 'political good' is health.

In divination (*ukupengula*), in 'smelling out' (*kufemba*), or even in simply addressing the realm of the intangible 'spirits' that surround everyone (*kupahla*) several features of these relations of power, health and illness emerge: the suffering (*buhlungu*) of the patient and of the healer, the jealousy of others (*umona, bukhwele*), the fundamental equivalence of all persons with respect to their own suffering and jealousies and, above all, the idea of respect (*inhlonipho*). These are the elements of dramas of power and resistance that, willy-nilly, embroil all persons. One can resist them by adequately protecting oneself using apotropaic magic, or one can react to threats by turning them back on the persons who have sent them. This could be called the 'social causation of illness' as it is in much of medical anthropology, but in reality it reads more like a complex political plot in which power is augmented, exchanged, transacted and directed by manipulating magic, jealousy, respect and the suffering of oneself and of others.

This is an interpersonal politics at the local level, but also a politics of persons in which health, well-being and even life itself is at stake. The sangoma also regulates the boundary between the 'normal' order of every-day life and the extraordinary disorder that is attributed to the 'bush'. Each person, each patient, is constantly concerned with cleansing him or herself of disorder, evil, bad luck and illness. This applies to the community of sufferers as well. Since all suffer, the entire community is at risk. By help-ing to determine who, or what, is to blame and by underwriting the belief in witches and witchcraft if not actually identifying such perpetrators by name, the sangoma performs a 'political' function of boundary creation and maintenance. The witch is exiled, and those who are no longer 'equal' to others are forced to exit. The dynamic of exile and exit is the communal equivalent of cleansing the individual person by smoke, vomiting, evacua-tion and water.

The processes of exile and exit link local politics to regional or national politics. Those who 'exit' usually do so in order to join or interact with higher levels of political integration, that is, provincial or national political groupings, or business activities that span at least regional econ-omies. In this way, joining a church may institute a sort of exit from local interpersonal conflict of the sort that sangomas typically deal with. Some 'exiles', such as suspected witches, may continue to live in local commu-nities but are ostracised and isolated, frequently living in marginal spaces between the formal towns (previously designated as white areas) and the townships or rural communal areas. Many migrate to the cities, where they participate in criminal gangs or activities such as begging, street trade or other activities in the 'grey' or 'black market' economy (the unregistered, untaxed and unregulated 'informal' trade).

The important point, however, is that this constitutes a one-way flow out of the local economy and polity into economic markets and forms of social organisation that return nothing to the local community. Unlike migrant labour, the other principal drain on the resources of the local com-munity, these processes of exit and exile do not return remittances or goods to the local community. This is a permanent loss that is the consequence of social forces originating at the local level rather than of the macro-politico-economic forces that drive labour migration. In this way, the beliefs that constitute the 'structure of feeling' (Williams 1977: Chapter 9) implicit in *bungoma* and mediated by the sangoma have much larger-scale political and economic consequences.

The sangoma's reach is sensitive to scale, however. It must operate at the local level. This is because it is, above all, about relations of persons, one to another, and this has scalar limits. Beyond the local level we can only see 'masses', populations, peoples and tribes, and these are entirely beyond the scope of traditional healing.

What is the 'local level'?

It is too often assumed that small-town South African life is explainable in terms of the fundamental concepts of Western philosophy and social science, that is, in terms of universal categories of understanding. These have been discussed since the times of Plato and Aristotle, with philosophers such as Adam Smith, Marx, Weber and Durkheim providing a basis for the social sciences today. Certainly, fundamental ideas about the 'market' and the notion of the 'maximising individual', of 'exploitation' and the nature of economic organisations, of the character and genesis of (mainly European) political economy, authority, power, the division of labour and the nature of social solidarity, 'community' and the primacy of the social remain as pivotal concepts in all the social sciences. These ideas have not, however, served African anthropology and African Studies particularly well.

Differences of scale are also important. Theories of power, polity and political economy that have been developed primarily in the West are concerned with large-scale polities, usually at least as large as a contemporary European state, and often at the scale of continents or the global. This 'political science' – liberal (such as J S Mill, de Tocqueville), Marxist (Marx, Engels, Lenin and so on), (free) market/neo-conservative (Adam Ferguson, Adam Smith, or Milton Friedman), state-bureaucratic (Max Weber), colonial (Henry Sumner Maine, Frederick Denison Lugard) and so on – has not been concerned, for the most part, with the small scale and where it has, it has been interested in aspects of the European-type bureaucratic state such as voting patterns, bureaucratic process and procedural matters. Even where political culture has been examined the focus has largely been on the larger scale. The small scale has been left to anthropology, but anthropology has not always fulfilled its mandate well with respect to local-level politics. While there have been excellent studies of political action along the way, such as Max Gluckman's analysis of the 'social situation' in rural Zululand in the 1940s or Philip Mayer's discussion of 'townsmen and tribesmen' in the Eastern Cape, what has emerged for the wider public and for the political imaginary has been an emphasis on so-called cultural difference associated with the African/European divide.

There are several primary organisational features of the 'local level' that distinguish it from the national, regional or global. First, social relations are networked rather than institutionalised or corporate. This means that forms of association and alliance are personal, or person-to-person. They are multiplex, involving many types of personal relations and functions rather than simplex ('single-function') relationships. Relationships involve overlapping bonds and associations with kin, family, workplace, sexual and economic relationships. The complex net of overlapping and often conflicted relationships severely restricts the scope for personal and political action. This frequently has long-term personal (rather than abstract or organisational) consequences.

Actors in these situations have limited resources that are not wholly or in part derived from this tangle of relations, and even fewer derived primarily from *outside* of the local-level political arena that might allow them to act with more freedom. This severely limited capacity to make or to enforce contracts means that they are exposed to the vagaries of others' actions and have little power to effect their own life chances. These and other features distinguish the local level from what could be called higher levels that exhibit larger scales of interaction and integration. These higher levels – that is, more formal, institutional levels of organisation with some elements of negotiable but binding contract – have greater access to economic resources. They also have a higher degree of institutionalisation and, consequently, a greater ability to make and enforce contracts. Political relationships tend to represent corporations of one sort or another (that is, they are 'politically representative') and are simplex, single-function relationships rather than full or 'total' social relationships with multiple implications.

In practical, empirical terms, the local level corresponds to those areas that fall largely outside effective administration or policing by municipal or provincial government such as communal or 'tribal' areas, rural and peri-urban shack ('informal housing') settlements, villages or farms.

These polities are often considered 'marginal' to the national politics that occurs within the formal structures of party politics and government.

Theirs is the only politics that matters because it may determine their access to land, the water tap, pasture for goats, systems of local justice and personal dignity. In addition, it may also determine the risk of being accused of witchcraft. The resources of national government come to people in these polities as if from 'outside'. They include (in rough order of importance and availability) pensions and social grants, schools, clinics, roads, water and sanitation (if any), electricity (if any) and finally policing and formal systems of redress and justice.

Residents of this small-town environment rarely feel that they have any control over these resources and have little voice in where, when and how they are provided. For them, the state is marginal to their concerns even though they are aware that it is (potentially) a valuable but unpredictable source of wealth. When they do participate in national politics – such as by attending the rally of a political party, or joining one, or voting – many people do so mainly in order to achieve access to this wealth that is perceived as coming from elsewhere. In this sense, their politics is 'local'.

These processes and activities are not reported in the newspapers. They leave no archives. It is a politics conducted primarily through the oral medium of talk, conversation and occasionally oratory and formal speech. But it is not written. It is not part of formal politics and, as such, is not formalised. We do, however, read of the *consequences* of these political processes when we read about witch killings, 'factional' violence within or between villages, or the failure of yet another well-intentioned and well-funded development project.

The intervention of a sangoma is especially welcome, and possibly uniquely effective in the special circumstances of the local. This is because the complex interdependence of multiplex relationships is never articulated publicly. Only the sangoma's divination allows the subjects to assemble and articulate a personal narrative of how these powerful, inescapable social networks might affect them, for good or ill.

In this context there is a small set of fundamental political beliefs, ideas, and motives that structure political action. Most of these are implicit, although many of the terms – suffering, jealousy, respect, and equality – are used frequently in daily discourse. Other terms – freedom, autonomy, exile, exit, and equivalence – are not explicit terms of daily discourse but capture aspects of political thought that underpin the structures of the social (political) action proposed here. These concepts structure local-level political interactions, motivations and expectations.

Four principles of local-level political culture

By examining social interactions in municipalities, chiefships, groups of traditional healers and other community-based organisations I identify four interrelated 'principles' that emerge from the way people talk about each other, and especially from how people understand their exposure to the power of others. These amount to primary representations in local-level political culture. The principles are 'cultural' in that they consist of meanings and values that are shared and that serve to motivate action and are political in so far as they are concerned with power and the boundaries of the polity.

I use four terms to label the 'principles' that occur regularly and explicitly in conversations about personal relationships. They are: *equality/equivalence, jealousy, respect* and *suffering*. In addition, more abstract notions of 'freedom', 'autonomy' and 'oppression' are also important, but these require a different treatment, as they are more explicitly political. Similarly, gender and age constitute important organising principles but, again, they demand separate treatment within the context of dynamics of gender conflict and sexuality, as well as the dynamics of age and generation. This quartet of terms, however, constitutes the practical vocabulary that emerges from real discussions of what are ultimately the abstract (or Western sociological) categories of 'gender' and 'age' (see Thornton 2008: 195–219).

By calling these 'principles' rather than social structures I move away from the more conventional medical anthropological explanatory frameworks of class, wealth/poverty, access or 'therapeutic citizenship' (Nguyen 2010), or, more generally, the 'social causation' model. I do this, in part, because the social and cultural structures in which sangomas and their clients and patients actually live are relatively incoherent. They do not have a common ethnicity, 'class position', language, religion, or even historical experience. Instead, they share a generalised 'market' of ideas about healing, health and the body and about how each is exposed to other persons in their social environment. This does not amount to structure in the conventional sense but can be better understood as constituting a network of persons with multiplex relationships and overlapping identities.

These terms, and the feelings that attend them, have special and particular meanings by virtue of their implicit link to a generative system. This is, in Raymond William's phrase, a 'structure of feeling'. It is culturally generative as it creates the conditions for the emergence and justification of other concepts and has real social, cultural and bodily effects. It is socially generative because it creates a 'feeling' of affliction, a perception of ill luck, or even outright sickness. These are the states of health that sangomas deal with. As Williams remarks, our descriptions of culture and society are habitually expressed in the past tense, thereby converting even the present into 'formed wholes rather than forming and formative processes [in which the] living presence is always, by definition, receding' (Williams 1977: 128). *Bungoma* shows its immediacy in solving the problems of the present. The 'principles' of equality/equivalence, jealousy, respect and suffering generate the dis-ease that each patient presents to each sangoma in the *indumba* ('healing house'). It is, as Williams remarks, 'grasped and defined as personal: this, here, now, alive, active, subjective' (1977: 128).

The groundwork of interpersonal conflict

Equality/equivalence
Equality is a principal value in South African politics but it might better be called 'equivalence' in this local context since it represents the value that all members of the community are, in principle, *equivalent* as human beings and as brothers and sisters. This is, in effect, Alfred Radcliffe-Brown's and Meyer Fortes's principle of 'equivalence of siblings' in Talensi political order, but also the equivalence of individual members of the 'mass' in radical and leftist African political thought (Fortes and Evans-Pritchard 1940; Hamilton 1971; Knight 2008; Radcliffe-Brown 1952: 27). It is the equivalence of the subjects of the chiefship and clients of the sangoma. Although 'equality' is often used in ordinary discourse at the local level, I argue that what is meant in practice can be better understood as 'equivalence', since every person has implicit power over all others, and thus limits the range and type of expression each person can use.

This notion differs from the concept of equality in a liberal bureaucratic-democratic sense. Equality in that context generally means equality of access to the market, to rights, security and to justice. Equality of access in the bureaucratic-democratic state is a property of a constitutional political or social order rather than a quality of the person or interpersonal relations. In the local-level politics of South Africa, however, persons, especially men, are held to be equivalent. This is not a concept that relates to access to rights, but rather a concept of fundamental *equivalence*, or even interchangeability, among same-sex members of a community.

Jealousy is often predicated on – and justified in terms of – the idea that all people (but especially men) should be (morally and ontologically) equivalent. In this sense, jealousy becomes a moral principle that maintains the value of equivalence through gossip and fear of witchcraft that jealousy might engender. Jealousy is not merely a moral weakness, it is a social value. Sangomas frequently say, for instance, that they are jealous, meaning that they assert their equivalent value and autonomy with respect to other sangomas. Similarly, suffering is often understood as the moral consequence of equivalence, since the larger community should (morally) experience suffering when one member suffers just as the sangoma suffers the pains of the patient. Political slogans such as 'strike one, strike all' express this value. Respect is due to the 'man of the people' who carefully guards his apparent equivalence to the common man, while working selflessly to ensure the solidarity of the community.

Respect
Respect is an end in itself, the acknowledgement of status, personal charisma, spiritual power (control of 'holy spirit', *amadlozi* or *ndzau*, for instance), or what Niccolò Machiavelli called 'virtue' (*virtù*) (Machiavelli 1998 [1513]). Respect confers a focus of attention on the individual by members of the community but it is not necessarily a means to further wealth or power. It should not negate the principle of equivalence, as ultimately all deserve (equivalent) respect, while some are worthy of special respect as long as it does not transgress equivalence. 'Some are more equal than others,' as George Orwell cogently observed (Orwell 1945: online).

Generally, larger than normal wealth or power is a threat to respect since only by effectively dispersing jealousy back into the community through diffusion of power and wealth can respect be maintained. The process of counteracting jealousy with diffusion of wealth and power generally means that respect and power are mutually exclusive. In other words, those with most respect often have little real power (that is power to command action and expect obedience). Chiefs who are most respected are those who seek only to 'help' their communities without demanding compliance with laws or coercing services from their subjects. Respect may constitute a kind of cultural capital but if and when it is exchanged for actual power – for instance, when a locally respected priest joins the ANC or a respected healer becomes executive officer of a development project – any respect they had may be lost. Respect is not always accorded to those in power, nor is power accorded to those who are most respected.

This concept can be compared to the notion of 'distinction' in a liberal democratic state. 'Distinction' is a legitimate quality of earned differentials of wealth, prestige, position or taste and generally operates within a hierarchy of power that is characteristic of formal political organisations within the structure of such states (Bourdieu 1984). For the most part, in the local-level politics that I am concerned with here, formal organisations are weakly developed and hierarchical orders of (Weberian) power are almost non-existent. In the place of formal organisations (that is, firms, political parties, corporations, and so on) business and other activities are organised through personal networks in which the links and transactions are largely covert.

Suffering

Suffering is part of what makes us human and what makes us part of the community: We suffer together and are therefore equivalent within the spiritual realm of imagination and action. People are said to suffer for one another in a community. Ideally, the mother suffers for her children and the father suffers for his family, while the chief suffers for his people. Priests and pastors suffer in order to guide their flocks; teachers suffer the indignities of poorly equipped schools. The traditional healer similarly suffers for his patient. Magodweni once said that he begins to *suffer the same pains* and trials his patient suffers and thereby comes to understand them and thus know how to treat them through this intimate participation with and exposure to the patient. The many churches, self-help groups, special interest groups such as the land committees set up as a consequence of the land restitution legislation, assemblies of traditional healers and their clients, among others, see themselves as held together by their suffering. All are conscious of this and make it explicit in daily conversation.

Suffering is held to justify position, with its attendant differentials of income, power, sexual access and other privileges that would otherwise negate the claim to equivalence, that is, to being at one with the community. Suffering, then, is a legitimate and valued form of distinction, one that others can never be jealous of, but which confers honour and respect. Most importantly, it 'drains' distinction of its offending difference and makes the claim to equivalence with others plausible: they suffer together. The suffering of the priest, the healer, the chief and the teacher legitimates what little difference they maintain from the community as a whole.

The quality of suffering can be compared with the notion of achievement in liberal democratic politics. It elevates the sufferer to a status of respect in a community of suffering. Those who suffer most achieve respect, while those who manage to transcend their suffering are held to possess special virtue or power (*emandla*).

Jealousy

This is the evil within, the singular personal weakness that results in strife and conflict among members of a community, but it is also a moral principle. Jealousy is to be feared above all since it leads to conflicts which spread through all other social organisations and networks and threaten the wealth of a community or of an individual.

Jealousy often leads to violence. This is due in part to the principle of equivalence, since no man can command another (equivalent) man successfully without eliciting jealousy ('He thinks he is better!') and, frequently, violence. Violence can often not be controlled once it starts and every effort is made to prevent its outbreak. Jealousy, therefore, is more than just 'a bad feeling' or emotional manifestation at the local level. Because it can lead to violence, and because there are so few resources to control violence at the local level, jealousy is a political threat and therefore a political (rather than psychological) concept.

Jealousy is often communicated through gossip and veiled threats or deliberate silence and is a potent force for maintaining equivalence of

TABLE 1. The structure of feeling in the politics of interpersonal relations

Evaluative ⟍ Sociological	Negative	Positive
Personal	Jealousy	Respect
Communal	Suffering	Equivalence

persons. It regulates any unexplained or untoward distinction and ensures an outward show of equivalence among members of the community. Since everyone is potentially exposed to the jealousies of others, it can be compared with formal systems of discipline or shaming in other types of political order.

The relationship among these four principles is expressed in Table 1. The four categories of feeling can be analysed further into two binary principles, negative and positive, and personal/communal.

These categories of political judgement or of political values can be further analysed in terms of two dimensions or components of meaning: the (morally) *evaluative* (positive and negative) and *sociological* (person as exposed being and community as moral entity). In these terms, jealousy is a negative property of a person. Ontologically unreal persons such as the 'spirits' of the ancestors do not feel jealousy for the living but may demand recognition and sacrifice. Equivalence is a positive value of a communal entity, while respect is a positive value associated with a real person.

The evaluative dimension is a judgement of positive or negative value. In the cosmology of the Lowveld all events and persons have a positive and a negative side. This is especially true of political events and of political actors. Respect that is given to the chief, to the father, or to the mother, or to whomever is seen to deserve it, is reflected negatively in the jealousy that other people might feel for the person who is respected. All people want to be respected and if they are not they may become jealous, or may be construed by their fellow members of the political community to be jealous. Respect is due also to the person, although it is bestowed by the community. The same is true of jealousy, except that jealousy comes from 'within' while respect comes from without. Indeed, the negative qualities of persons are generally believed to come from within that person. It is not a characteristic of the community, which is generally held to represent positive values of support and empathy for those who suffer, and which maintains the positive value of a commune among equal – even 'equivalent' – persons.

The sociological dimension complements the evaluative aspect of value (positive or negative). This dimension expresses the distinctions between the community and the personal as different forms of being, or different sociological realities. This distinction is already well rehearsed in studies of African political systems and, indeed, in the daily press and popular writing.

Healing community

Few people talk about being African without mentioning the community as the source of the most positive of values, of which equality/equivalence is the most important. Since all things have negative and positive aspects, this is true of this distinction as well. The personal is the source of evil – a witch is a person, not a community; a criminal is an individual, not a group that one lives with, even though the criminal or witch may be part of that group. As Magodweni put it: 'Is there not filth inside the body? When it comes out it is evil. We know it and deal with it. It comes from inside us.'

Healing practices that seek to deal with evil do so by cleansing the body of its evil substance. The intestines are cleaned through herbally-induced vomiting, or through herbal tea emetic enemas. Blood is purified through the steam bath in which the sweat is made to pour out before the patient is washed in a cooling bath of herbs that stay on the body as the subject dries in the air. Cuts through the skin allow medicines to be introduced to cleanse the blood directly. Additional herbal teas and liquids are drunk to ensure that the spirit is pure. Smoke baths are also prescribed to purify the person's 'air' (*umoya*, also 'spirit'), chest and mucus. In this procedure selected pieces of bark are roasted in a cauldron over a hot fire to give thick, rich-smelling smoke that is inhaled deeply through straws inserted into the smoke plume. The smoke is also allowed to circulate around the body. It penetrates the mouth, the nose, the eyes and lungs as well as the throat and pharynx. It rids the body of potentially evil conditions associated with the recesses of the lungs and mouth, the mucus and saliva of the mouth and upper respiratory tract.

In other rituals, such as the *kufemba* (the 'smelling out' of witch familiars that have been placed inside the body), different kinds of potentially evil 'substances' are identified and removed from the body. These are evil 'objects' (perhaps a stone, a piece of glass, or poison) and witch familiars. The 'familiars' are usually animals – some of which have never been seen (but are, in principle, tangible and could be seen someday) or are invisible in principle – that cannot be traced back to their malevolent source but which have been placed in the body by those who may wish us ill, or who merely want to control one's actions for someone else's benefit. The *kufemba* technique is directed to the person and, most especially, to the evil substances that lie *within* the person. These internal evil substances include bad blood (from the ancestors) and the bad air *(umoya)*, that we breathe, but also the intangible 'spirits' of others and other person, living and dead, who influence our very being. A good, 'clean' induced vomit – especially for the fourth time in a series of purges – is an indication of moral goodness as well as an empty stomach. The colourless stream that issues from the patient's anus after a proper emetic and enema cleansing indicates that the soul is pure. Sucking out and dealing with witches, their familiars and their intangible instructions leads to a purer, better individual, less likely to be led astray by these false voices.

Thus, the postulated potential evil of a person in the context of communal politics is also a 'medical' **and** a 'religious' problem. Medical practitioners – and sangomas – deal with the physical manifestation of this as physical quantities and qualities. The physical qualities – blood, menstrual blood, urine, mucus, saliva, tears and sweat – are physical indices of the presence of evil. Without (real) 'bad blood', there is no jealousy, without (real) shit, people don't act 'like shits'. Thus the physical context of the person is the access point for the healer in healing the danger of evil in the personal, and evil has this substantial presence in everyone.

Thus, the healer's statement that the 'shit' in a person is an indication of potential evil is a metaphor. On the other hand, in the observed practices of persons who attempt to deal with the evil they fear within themselves, these substances and their quantities and locations are fundamental and concrete proof of the proposition.

The same is not true of the community. According to the notion of ubuntu, the community is the source of goodness, a bulwark against pain and suffering. Though individuals suffer in their persons, they do so within a community. Those who suffer alone are likely to be evil themselves, or their lonely suffering is likely to make them so. As 'good' as the community might be, however, it also includes dangerous or polluted persons. Witches, those who have some quality of impurity associated with death or menstruation, violent people and criminals all live within the community too. Like the body, then, the community 'contains' evil. Ideally, when this 'evil' is identified, evil-doers in the community, like the bad blood or witches' familiars in the body, are driven out in order to cleanse the community. In practice, however, this is often impossible. While one may 'know' that one's neighbour is a witch and is responsible for one's misfortune, it is rarely possible to confirm such a suspicion. Thus one must continue to live with the people who wish to do harm, or who cannot help doing so. The enemies of The Good in the community are always part of the community. The 'body politic' (the 'community'), like the person's body, contains evil within it. The enemy is always within the gates at the local level.

The scale of healing: Personal to communal

For the reasons cited above the distinction between the personal and the communal can be understood as another version of the distinction between the positive and the negative. The personal-communal distinction, however, is a judgement in the moral key of good versus evil. The person is not necessarily evil, of course, but is the potential source of evil. The same is true of the community. The personal tendency to evil is countered and balanced by the community since the community disciplines and shapes the person into a moral being and exiles from itself those who persist in evil or who manifest it in their malevolent jealousy of others.

There is often a fine balance struck between communal forgiveness and condemnation and thus between salvation and damnation, or liberation from and captivity by the dark side of the spiritual realm. Religion, especially the Zionist and other African syncretic churches, or in the form of African traditional beliefs, often sets the terms according to which these judgements are made, and prescribes the means whereby the potential evil within the person is transformed by the goodness of the community.

In this sense, evil is also individualised, not generalised, while goodness, like life, is generalised and not personalised. Respect is not necessarily equated with goodness. A feared gangster or a corrupt politician may be respected at the same time as he or she is feared. People who are feared because of their physical prowess or cleverness are said to be 'respected'. In this sense, respect may also indicate fear. Nevertheless, because it is bestowed by the community, even fear of known criminals or dangerously corrupt individuals may be translated as 'respect'. The evil – murder, theft, assault, fraud – that may have helped them achieve the position they hold is not thought to be a general characteristic of the community, but rather of the individual.

The sociological imagination that seeks to understand the 'causes' of evil – that is, a tendency to crime or corruption – in the general condition of the community (such as its poverty, its marginalisation, its lack of jobs, its broken families) is not often generalised in this way to account for people who are known as fearsome and thus respected out of fear. Rather, their tendencies to evil are understood as coming from within their spiritual and bodily constitution, what they possess by virtue of being persons, rather than as the result of their community. What they possess as persons may be evil spirits, or they may suffer from curses that have been placed on them individually for some crime. Evil people, then, are ultimately sanctioned by rejection by the community, either in the form of *exile* or in the form of *exit*. Exile is the forced exclusion of the petty criminal who has stolen from his neighbours one too many times and is thus excluded from the community of good. Exit is a *choice* that is exercised by those who are both feared and respected because of their wealth, their power and their ability to commit violence or fraud and get away with it.

Exile is applied to criminals who offend against the community itself. They are 'excreted', just as the 'evil' of the person is cleansed through vomiting and induced diarrhoea. The apparent simile that likens evil to shit, blood, menstruation fluid, and vomit (among other bodily fluids and excretions) is rather more real. They are not laughable tropes, but rather the means by which evil may be expressed – or suppressed through careful removal by expert sangomas, *tinyanga*, and the practitioners of exorcisms within the Christian churches.

The shifting boundaries of political community

One way of dealing with the problems of evil within, and with a politics that lacks formal rules, institutions, contracts and the ability to enforce them, is to constantly adjust the definition of the boundaries of the polity itself.

Under the assumption of equivalence there is no legitimate criterion by which decisions can be made for the distribution of political goods except membership in the local political community (local citizenship). The goods of the community belong to all who are members of the community, but if the community is too large and the amount of goods too small no individual receives enough. If there is only a very weakly developed hierarchy, and little other way to differentiate among members of the political community, it is necessary to adjust the boundaries of the community itself to regulate the division of political goods. Thus the boundaries of the community – who is in and who is out – are negotiated and negotiable in all instances.

Exile and exit are the two principles that regulate the control of the community of equality. Exit is the route out of the community for those who succeed and who accumulate more wealth or respect than the community allows. Exile is the route out of the community for criminals and witches. The leader exits while the criminal is exiled. Both leave a community that is constituted as a group of equals who 'respect' one another and whose jealousy is limited by the equality of results and distribution of goods.

This act also re-defines the political community as a group exclusive of those of whom one is jealous and those who are not respected or who have no claim to respect. In effect, however, since both the exiled and those who have exited often also remain part of the community, though not part of its political identity, the enemies of the political community are still inside the community, not beyond its borders.

The pressure to conform to the principles of equivalence, jealousy, respect and suffering make ubuntu, or the notion of 'African community', unbearable. We might call this the 'unbearable burden of ubuntu'.

Ironically, the life and vocation of a sangoma offers an escape from the pressure of daily life. Many sangomas cite 'stress' as one of the chief causes of the suffering that led them to become sangomas in the first place.

CHAPTER 6

Marginal utilities and the 'hidden hand' of zombies

The theory of moral sentiments and zombies

One of the most puzzling of the 'occult' entities with which sangomas have to deal is the zombie. The zombie figure may be a new type of entity. It is not 'traditional', although it resembles, in some ways, a witch's familiars and witches who take the form of animals. It has, however, become fully part of the cultural universe in Umjindi, as in most other small towns (Niehaus 2005, 2013).

Any market, including the market for healing, exists for the utilities and values that can be realised from it. The price for 'divination' (*kupengula*) varies according to the value the patient believes she or he can realise from it. Divination, one of the healing processes that involves an exchange between the persons of patient and sangoma, acts to clothe patients with knowledge of possible threats and opportunities and of areas where they show weakness or strength. These values may be further transacted, not just for 'healing' but for most other endeavours, including economic. People often consult a sangoma before a job interview or when they encounter problems at work or during a business transaction. Together with other 'magical' methods, the assistance of a zombie is also possible. The 'use' of a zombie, however, requires a fine calibration of belief and scepticism, knowledge (how to do it) and credulity.

The zombie is part of the work of the healer because the logic of the zombie is part of the same moral universe in which the sangoma works. Sangomas know about zombies, and most claim to know how to capture one, but they all also believe that if they do so they will lose their own power to heal. Commercial herbalists, known also as *tinyanga*, also often claim to be able to create zombies. But most people I discussed the subject with were sceptical about whether zombies could, in fact, be real. The condition for that possibility, however, is the same as the condition for the possibility of being afflicted by witches or ancestors, attacked by others with magical means, or, indeed, for being healed: the person is existentially exposed and vulnerable to the force and will of others, for good or ill.

Healing creates a market for healing, that is, a market for the value of health transacted in terms of what can be exchanged for health. The same is true of wealth: it creates a market, just as the market creates wealth, and sets the terms of what can be exchanged for what: currencies for commodities, commodities for power, power for legitimacy and, in turn, legitimate power for wealth.

One value or valuable state can be exchanged for other values: health for belief, church membership for new cars and objects (or the more or less object-like things such as blood or smoke for the ancestor's spirit) can be exchanged for many kinds of tangible and intangible valued things, or desired states of being. This is the underlying logic of the market, as I use the term here, that permits humans to transform one kind of value into another, and to transact with each other in terms of these values. The terms in which these values are transacted – their relative value or 'price' – are dynamically created. This also sets up the conditions of the possibility of many kinds of transformation. One of these, in the context of the South African small town, is the zombie, a person whose exposure to the will of others allows his own will to be transacted by others in terms of a 'market-related' currency of body parts, blood, ritual, magical words and objects.

In the imaginations of those who transact with 'zombies', the zombie is real because its effects are real. While the zombie, like many other person-like entities such as witches or other enemies, is believed to be a flesh-and-blood being, people do not seem to be entirely certain that they have ever seen one, even though they say they might well have done. Those who 'believe in' zombies, however, are certain they have seen the effects of having a zombie. The evidence is wealth. The mystery is not that zombies exist but rather how and why wealth exists and how it comes about. The logic of the zombie, then, is an economic logic just as economics is a theory about how wealth comes about and how it is transformed and transacted.

The zombie cannot, therefore, be described as the 'lurid, even salacious episodes' of 'moral panic' or be ascribed to the 'contradictory effects of millennial capitalism and the culture of neoliberalism' (Comaroff and Comaroff 1999: 279, 281–282) but can rather be seen as an intrinsic outcome of a local moral logic of exposed being in an ontological system where persons and things interact with each other directly. Ideas about the zombie can be seen as an economic theory of the nature of wealth, especially of the wealth of others. This does not mean that the figure of the zombie is not also consistent with the logic of resistance to 'late capitalism' that the Comaroffs suggest, or that it does not also 'link local realities to global forces' (Niehaus 2013: 6). With respect to 'making' zombies, I agree, rather, with Isak Niehaus's claim that these acts are, as people who say that they use them insist, 'actual exercises in constructing, rather than merely representing, social realities' (2013: 5).

Zombies as inverted ancestors

In southern Africa the notion of the zombie can be understood as the inversion of the ancestor figure. While the 'ancestor' controls the one who is subject to it, the zombie is subject to another agent, the zombie 'owner'. Where the *indloti* is an intangible person with agency, capable of motivated and meaningful social action, the zombie is a tangible person that lacks autonomous agency and whose actions are controlled by another's intentions.

While 'ancestors', luck and the influence of witches is capricious and unpredictable, the zombie is entirely predictable, possessing an animal-like temperament. No one but the owner can have knowledge of the zombie, and the zombie itself has no knowledge of itself. No knowledge is possible in the case of the zombie, while, for the healer and patient working with the intangible persons of *emadloti* and other influences, knowledge is not only possible, it is everything. The healer provides a path to knowledge as the basic element of healing. The patient gains control over the self again and achieves the capacity to protect him or herself against the threats and vulnerabilities that healing makes known. This is not possible for the zombie.

According to Magodweni, the training of a sangoma aims to allow patients/initiates to gain control over the *emadloti*, or other intangible agents that afflict them. Unlike the zombie, however, these entities retain their own intentions and agency. The initiated sangoma, however, would never assist a client to capture a zombie, because seeking control over another is illegitimate. The healer's job is to heal. The capture of a zombie involves one person achieving control over another person. A sangoma only helps people establish control over themselves. Similarly, a witch takes advantage of the vulnerability of persons around her or him, but those afflicted have the ability, ultimately, to identify the source of their problems and to take action by protecting themselves, or by disposing of the witch. The zombie-as-victim, by contrast, has lost the ability to perceive its surroundings, and thus lacks knowledge of what afflicts it.

According to John and Jean Comaroff (1999), however, the figure of the zombie is simply a fraud, a misunderstanding of how modern neoliberal economies work. People who seek zombies in what they call an 'occult economy' seek 'unattainable ends' because they are deluded by their own greed; by false consciousness that makes them ignorant of economic 'reality'. The Comaroffs (1999: 284) claim that

> the essential paradox of occult economies, [is] the fact that they operate on two inimical fronts at once. The first is the constant pursuit of new, magical means for otherwise unattainable ends. The second is the effort to eradicate people held to enrich themselves by those very means; through the illegitimate appropriation, that is, not just of the bodies and things of others, but also of the forces of production and reproduction themselves.

In the Comaroffs' approach to the figure of the zombie, witchcraft, pyramid schemes, murder for 'muti' using body parts, along with many other forms of fraud, malfeasance, crime and moral panics, are confused. Such an approach also reintroduces the deficit theory of African culture by attributing a 'false consciousness' as a deficient mode of thought rather than taking seriously the reasons people give for the convictions they hold. By contrast, I attempt here to show that the zombie figure in its appropriate cultural context is the extreme instance of a more general local theory of social relations founded in the notion of the exposed being. In so doing, I compare it with other theories of how wealth, economy, and personal value work.

The 'essential paradox' for Christians and traditionalists is based on their common practical, intellectual and spiritual problem: how do things and persons, including the world of spirits, interact? This problem underlies the relationship between Christian Pentecostal belief about the nature and sources of God's gifts and the sangoma's belief about how luck and wealth come about.

The connections between ideas of ancestors, zombies and witches may be understood as an indigenous theory of the 'hidden hand' – that is, as the 'hidden' or 'occult' mechanisms of the economy and of wealth – since both the market for things and the circulation of spiritual presences (zombies, *muti*, powers) are similarly occult, mysterious and unseen by those who deal in them. For this reason, zombies and witches are understood not so much as 'fearful fantasies' but as ways of thinking about the mysterious-seeming vagaries and complexities of wealth and poverty, entrepreneurship and the jealousies that economic success usually engenders.

The connection between religion and economy is not new. Isaac Newton, Gottfried Leibniz and Adam Smith all pursued the issue of how money and evil might be linked. Their viewpoint pre-dates modern economic theory even as it provides the basic framework for contemporary macro-economic thinking and methodology. But as pre-modern thinkers their views can be usefully compared to the way people in Barberton think about the sources and nature of wealth and evil.

Economic and religious thought were closely integrated in European philosophy until the late eighteenth century. Newton, for instance, combined his mathematical and physical investigation with alchemy and biblical prophecy. He was also Master of the Mint in England from 1690 to his death in 1727. Leibniz's logical investigation of the origin of evil in his book *Theodicy* (Leibniz 1951 [1710]) began to explore the relationship between his emerging ideas about the mathematics of change, now known as 'the calculus', and European ethical and moral ideas about the nature of evil, pain and misfortune. Adam Smith developed the essentially deist notion of the 'hidden hand' in his *An Inquiry into the Nature and Causes of the Wealth of Nations* (Smith 1904 [1776–1789]) as a way of explaining 'market forces', but also used similar metaphors of the hand in his much earlier *Theory of Moral Sentiments* (Smith 1984 [1759]). He noted that people are 'led by an invisible hand' (Smith 1984 [1759]: 273) and that humanity, moreover,

> seems to imagine that he can arrange the different members of a great society with as much ease as the hand arranges the different pieces upon a chess-board ... [but] does not consider that the pieces upon the [actual] chess-board have no other principle of motion besides that which the hand impresses upon them (Smith 1984 [1759]: 233–234).

Smith's famous 'hidden hand' analogy was, for him, first, and primarily, a moral rather than an economic principle. His formulation of the nature of economic forces, then, could stand for the sangoma's understanding of how persons control other persons. The extreme instance is represented by the zombie, but everyone, according to the principles of *bungoma*, is, metaphorically, a piece on a chess board.

Another economist, William Stanley Jevons (1888 [1871]: 163) used Leibniz's and Newton's calculus in the late nineteenth century to create a new mathematical economics based on the notion of the 'marginal' (that is *final*) utility of the last slice of a loaf of bread.

> Bread has the almost infinite utility of maintaining life, and when it becomes a question of life or death, a small quantity of food exceeds in value all other things. But when we enjoy our ordinary supplies of food, a loaf of bread has little value, because the utility of an additional loaf is small.

His formulation is today an essential assumption for macro-economic theory. Jevons was especially concerned to convert the 'moral basis' of mid-nineteenth-century economics to a mathematical science, arguing that 'economics, if it is to be a science at all, must be a mathematical science ... simply because it deals with quantities' (Jevons 1888 [1871]: 3). As long as it feeds the family, the loaf of bread has *minimal* utility in and of itself. However, once there is nothing else left, the last slice of bread is the difference between life and death, and therefore of *maximum* utility. This is also a moral parable, but, since it uses the concepts of maximum and minimum utility, it is possible to construct a differential equation of utility as a function of time and as a function of supply and demand. Jevons's metaphor become calculable with the mathematical techniques of Newton's and Leibniz's calculus. This, in turn, makes contemporary mathematical economics possible.

The zombie figure in the southern African moral imagination, then, acts as if it were guided by the 'invisible' or 'hidden' hand of its owner, the agent that controls it in order to maximise his or her own utility. Assuming that the zombie is also human makes it possible to calculate its cost and to manipulate it as if it were another source of labour. Since it is dead to its own motives and possible agency, the zombie is a non-moral agent-at-a-distance, and thus absolves its animator, or owner, of moral responsibility for his or her own accumulation of wealth.

The morality of wealth

Entrepreneurship in contemporary South Africa is strongly linked to Pentecostal and evangelical Christianity, but the relationship between the new business elites in post-apartheid South Africa and Christianity is complicated and complex. There has long been awareness that South Africa has been the site of so-called religious 'syncretism', fusions of Christianity and pagan or African traditional practices and beliefs. This is indeed the case. The largest part of African Christianity in South Africa is of this type.

This syncretism has often been treated as a form of 'protest' against the originally mission-based Christianity of the 'main stream' churches (West 1975; Sundkler 1948; Comaroff 1985, Comaroff and Comaroff 1991), or as a political variant of southern African Christianity, inspired largely by the exclusion of black Christians from missionary churches.

Little of this approach resonates with today's reality, however, since the political landscape has changed radically. Instead, South Africa and southern Africa more generally are entrenched in a new neoliberal political regime that gives state backing to entrepreneurship and in no way interferes with religious freedom. This regime authorises wealth and wealth creation for black South Africans. Economic power and the political power of the state are also accessible to these new elites.

Seeing this as a form of political 'resistance', or a form of foolishness, then, no longer makes sense. Neither does it make sense to see it as merely authorising or legitimating political power or economic success. This is no longer necessary for many South Africans due to the very real and rapid shift in access both to the state and to markets. Finally, a view that takes witchcraft and belief in 'zombies' to be something like 'the standardised nightmare of the group'(Bank and Bank 2013: 249; Wilson 1951: 313), that is, the consequence of 'discord and jealousy' (Wilson 1936: 308) no longer holds much explanatory power because these beliefs are now often seen as a convincing explanation for a rapidly changing reality.

The emerging and very strong connection between evangelical and Pentecostal Christianity and entrepreneurship is increasingly understood today as a religious and quasi-political legitimation of wealth (for example, Van Wyk 2014). As such, it is part of an African intellectual tradition that seeks to understand the often occult operation of economic 'forces', processes and institutions as problems of the spiritual 'occult' – that which is 'not seen'. The economic 'occult' lies somewhere on the same intellectual terrain, generating similar problems for those who are economically successful. Whether they seek wealth through employment, especially by the state, or deploy wealth in new ways or create new forms of wealth, members of the new black entrepreneur class are not particularly anxious about their wealth.

Members of this new 'class' – so called 'black diamonds', 'black middle class' and often corrupt political elites in the ANC – are, however, anxious about the jealousy of those who have not ascended the ladder with them, those who are left behind in 'townships' and who are jealous of their new success. This is also not new. As I show in Chapter 5, jealousy, its companion, fear of jealousy, and its consequences in sorcery and witchcraft, have long been dominant political themes in southern African life. The concern of entrepreneurs in this environment, then, is not the legitimacy of wealth but rather escape from the constraints of jealousy and suspicion.

Nor are they particularly knowledgeable about or comfortable with where wealth comes from and where it goes. Many new entrepreneurs and those in the new middle class are operating in new terrains in which wealth and happiness are as mysterious as poverty and illness. The money often disappears as rapidly as it comes in. Spending habits are often not disciplined by social norms and high-spending lifestyles are admired…until they collapse. When they collapse this is often seen as being as mysterious as the source of the money and success in the first place: a consequence of 'bad luck'. Most people owe debts to their neighbours and to their in-laws, especially as marriage payments (White 2016), while the many other sources of debt cause anxiety, conflict, illness and even violence (Bähre 2007, 2012; James 2014a, 2014b; Rodima-Taylor and Bähre 2014). Thus 'bringing money' is a constant theme from many healers and their clients.

Money, its sources and sinks seem mysterious to many South Africans. With new opportunities come many new risks and uncertainties. Unlike in the Middle East or in the Middle American Bible Belt, these are not seen as uncertainties about the society losing its moral compass, or as social degeneracy. Quite the contrary, the acquisition of money is seen as social liberation and a reflection of personal success. What is problematic, however, is understanding what it means in the broader context of 'tradition' and the South African regional cultural frameworks and belief systems. This is an intellectual problem, or, depending on orientation, a spiritual problem, that existed before the current expansion of wealth in the national economies of southern Africa.

This approach is possible because religion in southern Africa has always had a more material dimension, especially in forms of Christian worship. Prayer circles in the bush (or any relatively uninhabited area in urban locations) and the use of clothing, beads, drums, candles, water and other substances all serve to interpret the Christian service and message in a distinctively southern African idiom where spiritual aims are often achieved through material means. This, however, presents – as it always has for Christianity – a particular conundrum based on the theological relationship between 'things of this world' (as *things*, material objects) and things of the other world (as spiritual forces or presences, that is, non-*things*, the immaterial).

For a religious tradition that, according to Matthew Arnold (1869: Chapter 4) adopted the 'Hellenic' *reason* of Plato and grafted it onto the 'Semitic' *legalism* of the Old Testament Bible, this poses a special problem. He claimed (1869: 142) that 'the uppermost idea with Hellenism is to see things as they really are; [while] the uppermost idea with Hebraism is conduct and obedience'. He did not comment on the fact that the material culture of the Church was largely modelled on the Imperial Roman styles, while the church structure itself was pagan Greek and, more generally, Mediterranean Bronze Age. This problem is fundamental, too, to African Christianity in southern Africa because the 'spirit' of Christian teaching is set against the materialism of African traditional religion and its fusion of bodily healing and spiritual salvation.

The question arises, too, since virtually no religious practices and beliefs are entirely 'pure', free from the African traditional ideas that pre-existed them and that inform much religious thought in all denominations in the region. This 'syncretism' is part of a much broader cultural fusion within a vibrant market for religious ideas, spiritual methods and techniques and religious leadership. Everything, literally, is available in the religious market of southern Africa and almost every religious person is 'shopping'. As is the case with other markets, all religious practice and belief in southern Africa takes place in a cultural environment where many forms of religious belief compete with one another and where few people are effectively 'mono-religious', belonging to only one religious group or church, or professing belief in only one set of spiritual institutions.

In so far as religious belief is materialist and 'this worldly' it is also effectively a discourse on things and how they are acquired. In other words, it is a discourse about wealth. This contradiction is also present in the core teaching of Christianity and it is this resonance that brings Christianity in touch both with economic thinking and with the parallel religious thought of the traditional African spirituality and ritual practices with which, in practice, it is blended.

The businessman and his zombie

Sipho (not his real name) is a prince of the Swazi royal line, a wealthy businessman and a born-again Christian. He chose to be 'born again', he says, to ensure his 'long-term' prospects in business. Previously he had relied on the guidance of 'witchdoctors'. At a table in a holiday resort he explained in lurid detail how he had gone to Mozambique to acquire a zombie to help him in 'business'. He said: 'You go to where there is a flat plain (*mhlaba uyalingana*, literally earth/ground that is 'equal', 'same as', 'equivalent'), very flat, and set a snare, and there you meet a most powerful witchdoctor [his term].'

The snare catches a goat or antelope and this is sacrificed by driving nails into it that are attached to a piece of paper carrying the name of the person he intends to capture as a zombie. 'The person must be someone you love very dearly,' he sighed. In fact, it emerged later that Sipho's first wife had died and many people suspected that she had been a zombie, a suspicion that was never confirmed.

In the morning the animal has been replaced by the human victim, who is now a zombie. The zombie's tongue tip is cut off so that it cannot speak normally. At home, nothing actually changes for the victim/zombie except that unknown to all it now works hard all night to create wealth. The problem that this businessman faced was not a moral one. 'Many people have zombies,' he said matter of factly. Rather, he was concerned that zombies only work in the short term. They cannot ensure long-term profits; only God can do that.

He explained the concept in business terms:

> It's like outsourcing. The zombie is a kind of delegate or consultant. That's in business terms. There is someone... [personal name, not disclosed]... who has used powers to get a high position. He has lots of cars and money. But he was not trained for it. He does not know what to do in his position, so the organisation hires other people to do the work. It is like the company outsources the skills that are needed. The man with the high office is always worried, however, that he will be found out and that he will lose his wealth. He will no longer have what he craves. He will fall from power because he has used *muti* to get his position. Only God can truly help him.

This discourse on zombies as outsourced consultants might have come from a highly paid business consultant from a prominent auditing firm. But it did not. He was explaining the notion of the zombie *in the same language the business consultant would use* to talk about the advantages of outsourcing, for instance, the cleaning staff at a business in the city.

As he continued talking he tried to make it clear that having zombies is an experience that cannot be described, it can only be experienced by the one who has carried out the rituals. Without the ritual, the *muti* has no effect. Only those who have actually carried out the ritual and experienced it physically can be fully aware of what it means. For all others it is a mystery; they will never be able to perceive a zombie directly. In other words, only through knowing the technique of making a zombie and by having participated bodily in the rituals and practices of zombie-making can one truly possess a zombie. The owner of the zombie, the 'witchdoctor' intermediary and the zombie are inextricably tied together in their own strange universe to which no one else has access. Others may suspect that the zombie exists and that it is working for the master, but only the master can truly perceive this relationship. Others who are not party to the relationship may see other things, but not the reality. 'If you are protected by zombies, if your enemies stop you, all they will see is you surrounded by soldiers; you will be protected. But they do not know how or why', explained Sipho.

Sipho and Christina (not her real name), the businesswoman friend who had accompanied him, continued to develop their explanation in explicitly Christian religious terms. Christina owned and ran a highly profitable trucking and transport business. She gave very generously to her Pentecostal church and credited this 'sacrifice' for her success in business. According to them, the devil is the true source of the power to create and to interact with a zombie. God, however, does not *will* this, and it is God who is more powerful *in the long run*. The devil, on the other hand, has a short attention span: he sees what he has accomplished and is satisfied; he goes on to do something else and loses interest. God is the only one who remains vigilant. Therefore, God is the only one that can achieve good in the long run, and can ensure longer-term success. The devil can only achieve short-term success with an act or a single transaction. The success is not permanent because the devil moves on to create more evil elsewhere. Christina's theodicy was contingent and circumstantial, not cosmological and universal.

The problem Sipho was dealing with was not a moral one, or even a social one, but rather a simple practical problem. The man he was speaking about got his new position through 'powers' which were not specified. It may have been his 'struggle credentials' (short-hand for saying that he had been appointed by the ruling ANC), or it may have been his use of *muti*. It is clear, however, that these 'powers' were not his personal skills or knowledge since he was struggling to cope with the new job. Nevertheless, the job was bringing in lots of money – and cars! – that he did not want to lose.

He feared losing them because he feared that he was incompetent. He was 'always worried' about being found out, Sipho said, and appeared not to know what was going on. However, because he already had a position of power he covered up his own lack of skills by 'outsourcing', according to Sipho, using contemporary management-speak. This story can be read as a metaphor for current problems in government in South Africa (which uses a great deal of 'outsourcing' and many consultants to cover for often-incompetent civil servants). It can also be read as a metaphor for why one might wish to acquire and keep a zombie.

There is a moral to the story: 'Only God can help him,' both Christina and Sipho told me. In the context, it is clear that this God is the Christian God and, in particular, the God that is imagined by Pentecostal Christianity in southern Africa. What God is meant to do in this case is to secure a person's economic prospects in the long term. The zombie, like outsourcing, often turns out to be more trouble and cost than it is worth. Zombies, like outsourced workers, have no loyalty and cannot secure the future. They are a short-term solution.

Sipho had solved his problem about the future prospects of his business ventures through baptism into a new life. Witches and 'witch-doctors' disgust him now, but God and his regular attendance at a Pentecostal church, he believes, give him the power to create wealth. Using the political-economic rhetoric of development and the Oprah Winfreyesque jargon of self-realisation, he says: 'We do what we can to develop ourselves.'

To ensure God's help, however, he has had to get rid of his zombies, a process, he maintains, that is more emotionally taxing than acquiring the zombies in the first place. Sipho says his zombies were kept in calabashes that spoke to him. When he converted to Christianity, when he was born again, he had to kill the zombies. They begged and pleaded with him not to kill them, but he had to destroy them in order to become a Christian. It was very hard for him to do this, he said, but he did it in order to end the evil. Ending the evil also secured him better business prospects for the long run.

Christina supported his story, saying that she had seen and heard talking calabashes, though they were not hers. She said: 'We entered a hut, and the calabashes were against the opposite wall, and one of them spoke with a deep male voice. The voice was coming from the calabash like there was a hole under the calabash and someone was in there speaking.'

She seemed to be suggesting that there might have been some trickery involved in the calabashes she had seen, but went on to describe a number of other apparently inexplicable visions and experiences in her own search for business success. She had ultimately found both success and a spiritual home in Pentecostal religion. In her home there is large plasma television set on which she watches almost nothing but religious programmes, especially South African religious programmes that involve long sermons and healing events. Several Pentecostal churches and organisations have dedicated subscription TV channels.

Christina was adamant that she had never sought nor possessed zombies. She was clearly uncomfortable with the entire idea, but did not dismiss it out of hand. Indeed, she told a number of other stories that supported the general possibility that zombies might exist, even though she herself was sceptical.

She said, for instance, that she had seen a snake on the roof of her grandmother's house. The snake was not killed but was said to have 'something to do with the ancestors'. No one had explained this to her and it remained a mystery. The snake was left on the roof.

She went on to say that her grandmother, who was originally from Mozambique, had eventually 'disappeared'. No other kin of hers were known to the family. She developed some kind of 'madness' in later life and became convinced that her daughter was trying to kill her. She would be found hiding in the wardrobes. She would try to wander away or to escape. Children would see her and call out and she would be brought back. Eventually she escaped and disappeared in 1993. 'No one knows what happened to her,' Christina concluded.

The thrust of these stories is more than just storytelling; they are taken seriously. Our discussion that afternoon was not entirely a religious discourse, nor entirely a business discourse. It was both. Religion, magic and doing business were all part of a somewhat magical universe – or at least of a universe with the possibility of magic – in which people's fortunes and fates more often than not unfolded mysteriously and precariously and of which neither precedent nor outcome was known.

Magic and the religion of business

Why, then, are religion, magic and business so closely linked in this case? It seems to me that the answer does not lie in a functionalist explanation of magic as 'failed science' (Frazer 1922), or religion as a 'disease of language' (Muller 1866: 12), or even as 'delusion' (Dawkins 2006). Neither Sipho nor Christina seems particularly concerned with the legitimacy of what they are doing and do not use religious ideas to support their activities. Rather, it is a practical choice, in their eyes, that simply ensures a longer run of success. It is a kind of magic, but it is a magic we are already familiar with in business.

What is the relationship, for instance, between the 'magic' that is attributed to Alan Greenspan as chairman of the US Federal Reserve Bank and Sipho's magic? J M Keynes called Isaac Newton, erstwhile Master of the Mint, in charge of coinage of the realm, 'the last of the magicians' (Gleick 2003). Nailing a paper bearing the victim's name to the head of a sacrificial animal, as Sipho did to create his zombie, recreates the routines of bureaucratic paperwork. Many attribute a kind of 'magic' to the market, including the father of economics, Adam Smith, who said the market acts 'as if led by an invisible hand' (Smith: 293). This is surely a magical explanation, even though it is couched in the counterfactual 'as if' locution.

Sipho's choice, he tells me, was a rational business decision. There was no spiritual revelation of truth; merely an informed choice in pursuit of longer-term profits. All exchange is a temporal process. The nature of economic transactions is, itself, determined by the time the transactions take and the intervals between them (Sahlins 1972). This economic process is necessarily part of both the short-range past and near future, as well as of the long run in both 'directions' of time. It depends on what kind of business one is doing. In as much as time exists at all, we suppose it has a beginning and an end: hence its religious significance in terms of creation and death, soul, sin and salvation. The Abrahamic religions all tell us that sins are counted: God, too, lives in an audit culture. Economics and religion, material and spiritual values, transactions between man and man and between man and God are, and have always been, closely related.

In the case of African entrepreneurs, however, the range of time is both 'compressed' because of their attention to close-range networks of exchange rather than to experientially distant bureaucratic and state-regulated economic institutions, and 'expanded' because of their attention to a time of salvation and theodicy. This both creates and constrains a close relationship between the value of business and the ultimate values of religion. At the same time, ideas of ancestors, witches, zombies and other spiritual or 'occult' influences provide both a cosmological justification for and a theoretical understanding of where wealth 'comes from' and where it goes. This cannot be fully understood without reference to the particular structures of local-level African business and to cosmological belief systems, both with reference to their process in time and the structures of social organisations that make such business possible.

A 'reaction' to Christianity?

Religious discourse in South Africa has been treated as a structural conflict between two cultural forms (Comaroff 1985; Comaroff and Comaroff 1991, 1993; Wilson 1936) and as a political response or resistance to 'colonialism' or domination during the cultural assimilation of Christianity. It might be better, however, to see the relationship between Christian and African traditional discourses as *parallel* attempts to 'solve' a central cultural or intellectual question about the relationship between matter of 'technique' or 'art/artifice' on the one hand and matters of spirit/mind on the other.

Both southern African traditional and (Euro-Mediterranean) Christian philosophies are concerned with what appears to be a fundamental contradiction in their philosophical systems. That they have looked to each other for the solution cannot be fully understood as assimilation, cultural contact or opposition/resistance because it is also the consequence of being engaged in a common philosophical project. The fact that southern African Christianity cannot get 'tradition' out of its system any more than the 'traditional' can ignore the Christian theology signals their fundamental *similarity*.

This similarity has to do with the proper relationship between technique ('sorcery' or *muti* or zombies) and knowledge. As Plato tells us in the last chapter of *The Republic*, art is always 'merely artifice' and imitation (*mimesis*). It can never be fully real. This precept has been taken up fully into Catholic Christianity, most notably by Saint Augustine, the African saint and founder of much of what we know today as Christian thought. In southern African 'religion' this same dichotomy is expressed in the conflict that exists between solving a problem through resort to *muti*/magic and solving it by resorting to true knowledge of the ancestors and their immaterial presence. As we shall see, this draws the two forms of religion closer together; it does not keep them apart or oppose them to each other.

The problem of the relationship between techniques, involving things or implements, and knowledge, involving spirit or spiritual insight, is integral to both Christianity and to the philosophy of traditional healing or 'traditional African religion'. The working out of this common problem is responsible for their continuing relationship of integration and conflict within a similar philosophical framework. The solution to the problem has implications for both systems of exchange, or economy, and systems of time. Since the details of the relationship between technique and spiritual knowledge must be worked out over time, this has implications for the destiny of the soul/spirit and therefore for salvation; the questions drive philosophical enquiry in both domains.

The zombie as *technē* or *epistēmē*

How do Christian cults and indigenous religious beliefs interact?

For people like Christina and Sipho, who are perplexed by the relationship between witchcraft and Christianity, the move from 'pagan darkness' to Christian 'light' is a useful metaphor for transformation, that is, an authorised metaphor of movement from bodily transformation of things to rhetorical and spiritual transformation of bodies. They are engaging deeply with the text of biblical revelation as text – not its 'thing-ness' or objectivity but its meaningfulness-as-read. The act of reading provides and achieves the desired end rather than magical manipulation of objects. Reading the Bible provides the rhetorical and spiritual means of acquiring deep inner knowledge through the 'gift'. It is newly and richly protestant in the way of Martin Luther: it insists on a reading of the Bible – of having knowledge of it, as opposed to mere technical manipulation of the means for ritual regulation. This is a tension present in Christianity, from its pagan and Jewish roots right through to the tension between *bungoma* and Christianity in the South African Lowveld.

Witchcraft, sorcery (the deliberately evil use of *muti*) and pollution can scarcely be distinguished from one another. All involve the influence, usually malevolent, of one person over another, with concrete and real illness or damage caused by some relatively insubstantial influence emanating from one person and directed, intentionally, at another. In the case of witchcraft, this malevolent influence emanates from an insubstantial part of the substantial person, such as from the 'snake' in the belly, his/her spirit that is bitter or distressed, or from some inherent but non-physical propensity to cause ill or harm to those around him or her. This is the case of the insubstantial interior influence. In the case of sorcery, *muti* is a substance that is directed by some person's will (or 'spirits') against another person, usually for some gain, or out of jealousy or the need for revenge.

The case of pollution also involves the influence of one person over another, often, but not necessarily, with direct intent. Influence in all cases is exercised through some interior state of being of the material body, or through contact with some other substance, especially blood, or the event of death. It affects another person, however, through interpersonal influence. In this respect the issue is the premise of the interpersonal influence of one person by another by any number of means. In these cases, witchcraft, sorcery and pollution cannot be properly divided from one another.

The zombie and *muti* are τέχνη (*technē*), 'know-how', as opposed to επηστημη (*epistēmē*), abstract knowledge, or 'knowledge-that' *something is true*. For that reason, they carry the stigma of being a technique – not just an art, but an *artifice*, or an *un*natural intervention – rather than a simple common-sense knowledge. Michel Foucault (Gordon 1980: 197) used the word 'episteme' to refer to his notion of

> the total set of relations that unite, at a given period the discursive practices that give rise to epistemological figures, sciences, and possibly formalised systems...the totality of relations that can be discovered...between the sciences when one analyses them at the level of the discursive regularities (Foucault 1972: 191).

We cannot understand the figure of the zombie outside of the 'discursive regularities' of *bungoma* that links persons, witches, the 'science' of medical plants and the magical empiricism (Chapter 10) of the total healing endeavour.

But the epitome of *bungoma* is, perhaps, more appropriate to the sense in which Plato used it to refer to abstract knowledge as opposed to the technical arts. Plato's 'idealism' was translated into Christian doctrine as Holy Spirit, the immaterial or incorporeal substance of God in the doctrine of the Trinity. The Holy Spirit, according to Christian belief, was bestowed on the first Christians at the Pentecost. The notion of spirit, *umoya*, whether the Holy Spirit (*Umoya oNgcwele*) or spirit(s) of a more ordinary sort, is fundamental to both Christianity and to *bungoma*.

The Pentecost is the coming of the Holy Spirit, discussed by Paul in 1 Corinthians 12. Paul of Tarsus's first letter to the Christians of Corinth is the seventh book of the New Testament after the four Gospels, Acts and Romans, or the third book that is not one of the four gospels. It is therefore of special significance. As Paul had founded the Church in Corinth, his epistle to his followers there is necessarily one of the foundational documents of the new faith. It is included in all canonical versions of the Christian Bible. In it, famously, Paul spells out his views of sexuality – that it is better to marry than to burn in hell, but it is better still not to marry at all and thus to please God as a man would please his wife – and, above all, insists upon the principle of bodily resurrection and the gifts of spirit. It is, therefore, especially concerned with the body and the spiritual implications of bodily actions and health. Other parts of it focus on ritual and the politics of the new church, but its focus on bodily technique stands out.

In this passage he reminds his flock that they were once pagans. This resonates strongly with virtually all people in Barberton who also agree that they were once pagans and that it is only by virtue of their knowledge of the Holy Spirit that they came to and maintain their faith in Christ. It is a crucial passage, also, to those who continue to practise 'paganism' despite their knowledge of Christ, since in this letter Paul mentions prophecy and 'speaking in tongues' as well as 'interpretation of tongues' (languages) as among the various gifts of the Holy Spirit.

Debates are frequent among both Christians and 'pagans' (traditionalists) about whether this authorises 'traditional healing' by spirits (the

Holy Spirit or the 'spirit' of the ancestors). Since the sangoma specifically speaks in the 'tongues' of the ancestors – and, in the case of the *emandzawe*, in their own distinct language or dialect – this passage in the Bible also seems to validate their claim to spiritual gifts that are spoken of by Paul in this foundational letter. Most agree that the letter does indeed authorise prophecy, whether by sangoma or by those who are inspired by the Holy Spirit specifically – the *emaprofeti*. In many cases prophets are sangomas and sangomas are prophets, although often in different contexts.

Let us look at the content of Paul's message:

1 Corinthians 12:1–11

1 Now about spiritual gifts, brothers, I do not want you to be ignorant.

2 You know that **when you were pagans**, somehow or other you were influenced and led astray to **mute idols**.

3 Therefore, I tell you that no one who is speaking by the Spirit of God says, 'Jesus be cursed,' and no one can say, 'Jesus is Lord,' except by the Holy Spirit.

4 There are different kinds of gifts, but the same Spirit.

5 There are different kinds of service, but the same Lord.

6 There are different kinds of working, but the same God works all of them in all men.

7 Now to each one the manifestation of the Spirit is given for the common good.

8 To one there is given through the Spirit the message of wisdom, to another the message of **knowledge** by means of the same Spirit,

9 to another **faith** by the same Spirit, to another gifts of **healing** by that one Spirit,

10 to another **miraculous powers**, to another **prophecy**, to another **distinguishing between spirits**, to another **speaking in different kinds of tongues**, and to still another the **interpretation of tongues**.

11 All these are the work of one and the same Spirit, and he gives them to each one, just as he determines (New International Version, www.biblegateway.com).

Here Paul is speaking to *pagans*, not Jews. The previously Jewish cult had now been founded solidly among the gentiles, where it would continue to grow vigorously, in opposition to and in protest against the Jews and to the magical cults of the Middle East and Mediterranean. This has deep resonance for religious people and pagans in the Lowveld, too.

The Pentecost in Christianity is *Shavuot* in the Jewish calendar, and takes place fifty days (7 weeks, plus 1 day, (or $7^2 + 1$) after Easter/The Resurrection or after *Pesach* (Passover) (Leviticus 23:15). This was the moment, according to the Gospel of John, that the Holy Spirit descended from God, presenting for the first time the possibility for the foundation of a new church, or a new heaven and new earth (as in Revelations). According to John 14:26, as Jesus sat with his disciples at the Last Supper (the *Pesach* meal) he told them, mysteriously, that he was going 'where they could not follow', although they would 'already know the way'. In this crucial passage Jesus also tells them that 'I am the way and the truth and the life. No one comes to the Father except through me.' Near the end of the meal, after Judas Iscariot has left to 'do quickly' what it is he must do according to prophecy, Jesus tells his assembly,

26 But the Counsellor [the King James Version uses 'Comforter'], the Holy Spirit, whom the Father will send in my name, will teach you all things and will remind you of everything I have said to you.

27 Peace I leave with you; my peace I give you. I do not give to you as the world gives. Do not let your hearts be troubled and do not be afraid.

28 You heard me say, 'I am going away and I am coming back to you.' If you loved me, you would be glad that I am going to the Father, for the Father is greater than I.

29 I have told you now before it happens, so that when it does happen you will believe.

30 I will not speak with you much longer, for the prince of this world is coming. He has no hold on me,

31 but the world must learn that I love the Father and that I do exactly what my Father has commanded me.
'Come now; let us leave' (New International Version, www.bible-gateway.com).

The Book of Acts 2 tells us:

1   When the day of Pentecost came, they were all together in one place.
2   Suddenly a sound like the blowing of a violent wind [Hebrew *ruah*] came from heaven and filled the whole house where they were sitting.
3   They saw what seemed to be tongues of fire that separated and came to rest on each of them.
4   All of them were filled with the Holy Spirit and began to speak in other tongues as the Spirit enabled them.

The 'one place' in which this group of believers sat that day is usually equated with the 'upper room' in which the Last Supper was celebrated. The 'rushing of wind' is the *ruah* of Hebrew scripture, that is, 'wind', 'breath' and 'spirit'. The same set of connotations is found in many Bantu languages, including siSwati, in which *-moya* is '1. Wind, air, breath … 2. Spirit, soul, life …' (Doke et al. 1990).

Thus the Pentecost event is taken as fulfilment of Jesus's prophecy immediately before his crucifixion, and as the origin of the Holy Spirit in the Church as the 'body of Christ'. It is this aspect that is most salient in the Pentecostalism of the Lowveld societies. The events of the Pentecost are easily assimilated to the experiences of spiritual 'upliftment', '*kuthwasa*', or revelation through the suffering of the sangoma, the healer, and his students, the *emathwasana*.

These acts, described in the Christian Bible and fundamental to the practice of Pentecostal Christianity, critically involve the central paradox that has been suggested. The realisation of Spirit is achieved through material means, through a kind of magic. A process of exchange is also involved: Christ gives his bread as his body; the body becomes bread, or vice versa, in the act of exchange; Judas is paid. In other words, the traffic between magical things and spiritual outcomes is embedded in a process of exchange that forms a fundamental philosophical paradigm for understanding all these transactions equally. No one type of transaction is hegemonic or dominant, and thus no single part of the exchange, essentially magical, can be said to legitimate or justify the other. They are part of a ritual package.

Similarly, the 'occult' in economic exchanges can be understood in terms of the unseen, or behind the scenes, magic of religion, witches and zombies. They form a coherent intellectual system.

The zombie and its marginal utility

It is tempting to see formal economics as fully rational, and therefore opposed to this 'philosophy', but consider the grounds on which contemporary mathematical economics is based. An example from William Jevons illustrates this.

William Stanley Jevons, together with Alfred Marshall and Léon Walras, was responsible for developing the method and concepts of 'marginal utility' in economics, what was called the 'Marginalist Revolution'. This concept is only *apparently* mathematical, but it is ultimately responsible for the wholesale shift in economics from the discursive analytical and narrative practices of political economy to the heavily mathematical approach that is entirely dominant today. This shift was in some ways similar to the shift after the publication of Darwin's works from 'natural history' in the biological sciences to modern scientific biology. But, there is more than a hint of mystery in the formulation of this important concept.

Jevons's derivation, in the late nineteenth century, of a calculus of economic 'value' from a 'time experiment' allows us to see in a uniquely visual way how classical mathematical economics derived its formulae for a mathematical economics. It also allows us to see how the mathematics of economics is uniquely and closely linked to issues of ultimate values, particularly to the notion of the 'end of time' (Jevons 1888 [1871]: Chapter 3). Jevons uses the metaphor of the loaf of bread to represent economic goods and their utility. With a surplus of bread (symbolic of life itself), its value is negligible. When the *final* slice of bread is cut, its value becomes limitless; until then, 'every act of exchange thus presents itself to us in the form of *a ratio between two numbers*' (Jevons 1876: Chapter 2.6). In other words, the end of (economic) history for Jevons was symbolised by the last slice of bread, the final or 'marginal' utility. This can be interpreted through the mathematics of calculus as a function relating bread to value as a continuous demand curve from zero ('a three-pound loaf') to infinity (the last slice).

As mathematical economics emerged and grew a debate arose as to whether economic functions were continuous – in which case the calculus could be legitimately applied – or (as is actually the case) discrete, that is, 'punctuated' or nominal – in which case, the calculus does not strictly apply (it is 'undefined'). Strictly speaking, mathematical economics is merely a metaphor of economic value, rather than, as in physics, a genuine description. We should not be surprised, then, that macro-economics and prophecy have much in common.

Thus marginal (*final*) utility and the biblical 'end of days' are intrinsically related. The 'final slice of bread' metaphor reflects the parable of the loaves and fishes in the Christian New Testament in which Jesus creates surplus from scarcity (presumably the market value of bread and fish fell immediately in response to the miracle), but at the same time translates the economic into the spiritual since the feeding of the masses, taken as gift, boosts the Saviour's spiritual value by an immeasurable amount: it proves he is God. The mathematicisation of economic value, however, is the condition for the possibility of a mathematical macro-economics. This, in turn, depends on the notion of the ratio and the infinite series that converges to a limit (or value) that is the foundation of the calculus.

The religious notion of the infinity of God and convergence with His 'will' and person are not distant concepts, as both Leibniz and Newton knew very well. When they invented the calculus to solve problems in mathematics, navigation and physics they thought they were discovering God's mysteries. Leibniz's theodicy and Newton's varied studies in physics, alchemy and biblical prophecy were rooted in similar ideas of transcendent infinitude and the mysterious convergence of stars, numbers and mathematical reason.

Newton had a major impact on practical economics when, as Master of the Mint, he redefined English currency, standardising the strange ratios of 20 shillings to the pound and 12 pence to the shilling (not to mention farthings, ha'pennies, thruppence, guineas and sovereigns, among other coins). Using his theory of gravity and planetary motion Newton 'proved' that the prophet Daniel had predicted Christ's crucifixion precisely (Gleick 2003: 108; Newton 2004 [ca. 1670s-1680s]; Pratt 2004). Leibniz's principle problem in his theodicy is also 'the conformity of faith with reason' – in terms that echo our own problems today of theodicy and philosophy and their relation to science, economics or biology (see, for instance, Dawkins 2006).

Leibniz 1951 [1710]: para 77) distinguishes between types of reason:

> [T]here is often some confusion in the expressions of those who set at variance philosophy and theology, or faith and reason: they confuse the terms 'explain', 'comprehend', 'prove', 'uphold'...Mysteries may be *explained* sufficiently to justify belief in them; but one cannot *comprehend* them, nor give understanding of how they come to pass. Thus even in natural philosophy we explain up to a certain point sundry perceptible qualities, but in an imperfect manner, for we do not comprehend them.

This is as true today as it was in 1710 when Leibniz wrote it. The 'big bang', quantum mechanics, gravity, mind and consciousness can be explained, but few would contend that they have been fully *comprehended*.

Prophecy, macro-economics (both capitalist and Marxist) and evangelical time all depend on a notion of the end of time when prophecies are proven (or exposed as fake), when final or 'marginal' utilities can be calculated and/or the saviour returns. Marshall, Jevons and Walras wrote at a time of profound economic and religious transition. Of course their ideas resonate with these currents. Classical economics was conjoined with biblical tradition at birth.

Marginal utilities and the economy of zombies

The remarkable fusion of business, witchcraft (or zombie-making) and religion that we see in Sipho's narrative is reflected more generally in fundamental theological problems in Christianity involving the nature of the relationship between body and spirit, and in the theoretical discourse of economics involving the 'end of time' and the creation of value. In this philosophical context we can see that the discourses of Christianity, traditional African religion (or philosophy) and economics are all attempts to solve a problem that confronts everyone. This problem concerns the nature of wealth, its sources, its uses and its consumption or loss. Wealth, and the mechanisms of economy that produce it, are generally mysterious.

From the beginning of economic life, it is likely that people have faced these same problems. In Umjindi, however, there are, more or less, two main sources of philosophical knowledge: Christianity and tradition. These two systems of thought interact to provide an explanation of the mysteries of wealth.

The parallel problems in *bungoma* and religious thought of this region cannot be characterised as a 'reaction' to conquest, colonialism or threatening external hegemonies of this sort. The problem is how to account for the nature of new wealth in the midst of pervasive and chronic poverty. This is 'solved' through a religious discourse that is best understood as an intellectual effort – either 'spiritual' or 'economic' – to solve fundamental problems of the nature of being, its risks and pleasures. It is remarkably free of moral or ethical reasoning.

The zombie, the witch, the ancestor and the Holy Spirit are all factors in the equations that result. While this is not economics in the conventional sense, it is an economic discourse built on alternative cultural assumptions. As we see from the work of Newton in alchemy and economy, religion and mathematics, this is not new, nor is it foreign to Western thought. Jevons's thought experiment with a loaf of bread shows us, similarly, that deeply penetrating philosophical ideas can emerge from a kind of 'savage thought' that deploys the materiality of a loaf of bread in order to derive a system as abstract as mathematical economics.

CHAPTER 7

The market for healing and the elasticity of belief

If economic logic can be used to understand the use of zombies then the idea of the market for healing is a useful means for understanding how people choose healers, modes of healing and therapies. In this chapter I use the abstract idea of 'the market' as a way of thinking about how people conceive and transact values relating to health and healing in this small town. The market for healing described here includes a range of options. Some degree of informed choice is required. It is possible, then, to understand healing not so much as a 'search' or 'quest' for 'therapy' (Janzen 1978) but as the 'infrastructures of information' (Özden-Schilling 2016) where every kind of cure, therapy or healing is, as Julie Livingstone says, 'improvised' (2012). Richard Werbner (2015: 169) speaks of diviners' clients in the small village of Moremi in the Tswapong Hills, Central District, Botswana, 'shopping' or even 'jockeying' for their desired outcomes. 'Clients go back and forth from one diviner to another' or 'turn to distant diviners, not merely for a special occasion or a crisis, but sometimes routinely'.

This market is governed less by price than by a parallel market for belief, for while healing and being healed are values that have a market, it is not always possible to evaluate the effectiveness, utility or economic efficiency (value for money) of any healing process. Thus it is difficult to establish a price for healing where 'price' can be defined as what sufferers are willing to trade for what they *believe* might help them. The efficacy of healing is partly contingent upon knowledge and belief that contribute to the placebo (or its negative twin, nocebo) effect; therefore, the efficiency of this 'market' is uncertain. But, as Livingstone writes in *Improvising Medicine*, her study of a cancer ward in Botswana, 'care proceeds amid uncertainty in contexts of relative scarcity' (2012: 6). Livingstone uses the cancer ward as 'a metaphor for and an instantiation of the constellation of bureaucracy, vulnerability, power, biomedical science, mortality and hope that shape the early twenty-first-century experience in southern Africa' (2012: 8).

David Livingstone, the nineteenth-century missionary and explorer of southern Africa, wrote about the practice of medicine in the very different historical context of nineteenth-century Bechuanaland (Botswana): 'we must place ourselves in [the Tswana person's] position, and believe, as they do, that all medicines act by a mysterious charm' (Livingstone 1857: 25). Livingstone, like his father-in-law, Robert Moffat, contended mightily with traditional healers and what he called 'rain makers' or 'rain charmers' (1857: 176, 638). He noted that the term for 'cure' could just as easily be translated as 'charm', an observation reflected more recently by Paul Landau (1993, 2010: 76–84).

This is what we might call a *non*-economic market, albeit with a range of choices, costs, prices, inputs and outcomes. Choices are made on the basis of belief, even though belief itself is not stable. People may change their beliefs to access a particular therapy and abandon them again if it fails. It is as though the economic rationality of the market changes the premises of its reason with each purchase. Thus, judgements are not made on the basis of relative utility, or value for money, but nevertheless involve calculations of supply, demand, cost and benefit (Callon 1998).

Despite having the abstract character of a market, there is no market-*place*. There is no public or openly accessible social space in which pricing or goods are discussed. Instead, people gossip and share information in relatively closed networks of person-to-person relations.

For the economist, the notion of 'elasticity' typically refers to the responsiveness of price to demand, and vice versa. If price changes little with respect to changes in demand price is said to be 'inelastic'; if it changes in response to changing demand it is said to be elastic. In a well-functioning market price, supply and demand should change in close step with each other, ideally in a one-to-one relationship. In this 'market' price elasticity is almost zero since prices do not respond to supply, demand or the perceived efficiency or effectiveness of the product. In effect, the 'price' of healing is the cost of membership in a community, be it a church or a network of knowledgeable people who can refer a potential patient/client to a healer. The effectiveness of any particular healer is not a foregone conclusion and relying on one or another, or a combination, generally depends on what the patient/client believes. Importantly, belief is elastic: it changes to accommodate the need for healing.

Belief, therefore, is frequently the most 'elastic' factor in the local economy of healing since it allows some people to assume, independently of any evidence, that it is true, that is, that it will work for them and will be personally, if not generally, effective *as long as they continue to believe*. It is as though all therapies and medical interventions are acknowledged as placebos, that is, as 'mysterious charms'. Since few therapies in this market, including the biomedical itself, produce reliable or measurable results, belief enables clients to evaluate moral states of being rather than, or in addition to, evidence of efficacy as they search for healing. Belief in a therapy allows clients to evaluate their choices and participate in healing with a greater sense of certainty, but their evaluations entail a careful titration of cultural values, risks, empirical evidence and personal experience. There is, consequently, a market *for* belief.

Belief and the market for healing

People who experience illness, and even those who do not, seek healing in a way similar to the way they might shop for goods in a market: they seek knowledge about what is available, evaluate the goods on the basis of particular criteria, make selections and pay a price. I use the term 'market' in its most general sense, as a social space in which many kinds of healers offer an array of medicines and therapies to potential clients, who shop for these goods for protection, or to seek relief from suffering, disease, misfortune or loss. In the healing market, however, the value of the commodity is determined largely by the client's belief in the efficacy of the therapy – its ability to address the complaint and promote healing, health, success or protection, as the case may be. It is as though this were a double market: a market for healing and a market for belief. In practice the economic price of these goods is relatively inelastic since medical doctors and healers charge a fixed price. But since belief is the condition for the efficacy of healing, and vice versa, it is the quantity and quality of belief itself that is elastic, rather than the market price. An 'elastic' belief amounts to scepticism. Scepticism, based on the choice the market offers, is therefore as important a force in this market as belief.

In this sense, the market of healing is not so much an *economic* market because choices are not made on the basis of an economic rationality of 'value for money' or price per efficacious result. Instead, *belief* in the efficacy of a particular therapy functions in this market as the primary criterion for selecting it.

Therapies also have prices, but differentials of price are usually very small. A traditional healer, prophet (faith healer), massage therapist or herbalist sets his or her price according to what a biomedical general practitioner would charge for a first consultation or visit to the surgery. Specialists supply services in response to demand, with some risk to both client and practitioner. Many types of medical and healing systems are available to all or most patients/clients. While the therapies are owned by specific practitioners, and knowledge is jealously guarded, there is little or no formal regulation of this market, no legally binding contracts or means to enforce them. It is, therefore, an incomplete or partial market that does not fully conform to the economist's theoretical ideal of a place in which knowledge and goods circulate freely, regulated by 'laws' of supply, demand, cost of production, and price.

It is, however, a space in which choices are made and information circulated and where few political or institutional constraints interfere with the client's choice of therapies. Prospective clients spend a good deal of time discussing their beliefs, going to church, attending healing sessions – whether Christian, traditional African, New Age or others such as spas, self-help groups, 'seminars', 'healing workshops' and so on – in which knowledge circulates and options are discussed. People clearly invest a great deal in the maintenance of their beliefs, in convincing others or in being persuaded themselves. In this way it is a 'free market' and transaction costs are low: everyone has some knowledge of most therapies and therapeutic systems and information is not difficult to obtain. Indeed, the centrality of belief in this market ensures the accessibility of information, since to subscribe to a therapy one must believe in it, and to believe requires having at least some knowledge of it.

'Healing' can mean many things. As a category it is only definable in terms of what Ludwig Wittgenstein (1952: para 65) called a 'family resemblance' category. In the context of Mpumalanga, I use this to mean that categories within the broad field of healing have overlapping resemblances, as do the features of members of a family: no element exhibits all features and each element shares only some features with others. Elements of such categories are nevertheless recognised as being 'of the same sort'. Bodies and minds are healed in different ways by different means, including rituals, song, prayer, dance, massage and medication. Herbal or pharmaceutical methods are used to 'heal', but the ways in which they heal have little in common. Healing may consist of correcting the balances of forces or energies within the patient; it may result from the elimination or attenuation of disease or a reduction in pain or discomfort or it may simply make suffering more bearable. Healing takes many pathways, but not all of them lead to a 'cure'. It is also rarely clear whether it is mind, body, or both that is healed since it is still not entirely clear how mind and body interact in the healing process. Indeed, ambiguity is a necessary and unavoidable property of healing (Waldram 2000).

Medical anthropologists often treat ethno-medical systems as if they were internally coherent structures of meaning within the definable boundaries of the community of practice. But people in Umjindi, and often in South Africa more generally, do not insist on – and one rarely finds – formal consistency in belief systems, especially as these relate to health and healing. By viewing healing as a market I am moving away from widely used metaphors of healing as a search, a gift, or as the receipt of specialised services. A search has a goal, a gift is received as such and a service is expected and rendered, all with a degree of internal consistency of rights and obligations or rules. A market, on the other hand, has options and risks, gains and losses; outcomes are not guaranteed. In the case of therapeutic or medical interventions there is also no guarantee that they will necessarily lead to better health, or to a cure, or even to reduced suffering.

Biomedical practitioners in Umjindi are almost all African, trained in South Africa or elsewhere in Africa. They are, however, believed to be little better than the many other non-biomedical options, including traditional healers. Each type of healing, however, is not entirely independent of the others. Many types of therapies implicate or entail each other. Thus, the unpleasant side effects of antiretroviral (ARV) or TB medication are frequently mitigated by 'traditional' medicine consisting of herbs and teas, or the 'magic' of *muti*. People spread the risk of relying on one therapy by initiating others. A more or less elastic belief system permits this: beliefs change to fit the therapy, and thereby enable it. For instance, one might seek Christian faith healing just in case traditional healing or patent medicines do not work. People who go to biomedical doctors may also seek to heal themselves with other 'New Age' systems such as Reiki, reflexology, crystals, patent medicines, 'home cures' and other options.

Medical parallelism in Umjindi

The social diversity of Umjindi municipality is matched by a diversity of options for healing the many illnesses and diseases that afflict those who live there. For instance, Doctor Mukasa, who runs a main-street shop in central Barberton, advertises healing or cures for 'Court case, Drop (Gonorrhoea), Bring back lost love and Tuberculosis', as well as offering 'penis enlargement'. Dr Mukasa's menu of services, while seeming at first sight to be a random list, is a good indicator of what ails Barberton: TB, HIV/AIDS, sexually transmitted infections and violence arising from jealousy over 'lost love' and lovers' quarrels. The protection he offers in the case of 'court case' often has to do with issues of violence arising from 'lost love', as well as from accusations of witchcraft or other 'undue influence' among 'co-wives' (usually a mix of girlfriends and/or wife/wives), or competing boyfriends/husbands, as well as conflict between generations over rights and obligations of kinship. Gonorrhoea is a consequence of the complex sexual networks in Barberton, as is the desire for a bigger penis. Dr Mukasa's treatments are symptoms of Barberton's Zeitgeist.

Most Barberton medical doctors have a favourable attitude to traditional healers (Green, Thornton and Sliep 2003). Within half a kilometre of the city centre one can consult several healers like Dr Mukasa, five or six medical doctors and a similar number of sangomas. There are psychologists and dentists, chiropractors and homeopaths. There are also seven

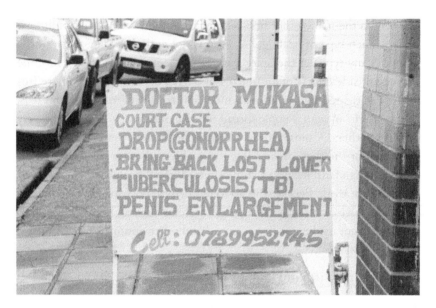

FIGURE 7.1: Sandwiched between a beauty shop and a furniture repair shop on a Barberton main street, Doctor Mukasa offers a range of healing services attuned to the people's needs.

centrally-located churches in the municipality and about 40 formally-constituted churches, with buildings and staff. All churches offer healing services of various kinds. Flint (2008: 7), describing a similar situation in neighbouring KwaZulu-Natal, calls it a 'multitherapeutic society'.

In addition to pharmaceuticals, South African pharmacies sell a wide range of 'traditional' and 'natural' or homeopathic medicines and substances. Some, such as 'blue stone' (copper sulphate crystals) and oils (almond, olive, glycerine and so on) are used by sangomas and other healers such as massage therapists and aroma therapists. Packaged herbs such as Echinacea, St John's Wort, and dietary supplements are also sold in large volumes. Patent medicines such as 'Lennon's Dutch Medicines' are an important retail item in South African pharmacies and in most small general dealer and *spaza* (informal) shops in the townships. A range of 'natural,' packaged, 'cure anything' remedies such as Borsdruppels, Witdulsies, Behoedmiddel, Haarlemensis, and Duiwelsdrek is marketed by Aspen Pharmacare, South Africa's largest producer of generic antiretroviral medications.

In addition, Chinese merchants offer Chinese traditional medicines, and shops owned mostly by immigrants from Pakistan offer a range of Pakistani and Indian Ayurvedic, Unani and home remedies. Flyers, offering healing services including aromatherapy, energy therapy, massage, reflexology and many others, are available in hairdressers, on the street and in advertisements in local newspapers. Almost everyone seems to be aware of the healing power of crystals, of water and candles, of prayer and holy water, among other practices such as eating clay, fasting, marijuana-smoking and so on. Finally, there is a reasonably well-equipped and staffed government hospital and private and public clinics.

While there are many options for healing in this broad market and a steady demand due to the relatively high disease burden in this reasonably prosperous community, not all efforts are aimed at healing. Much attention is directed at 'protection'. Christian churches vigilantly guard their members against witches and evil spirits (on the authority of Leviticus 23:6). In this time of 'immune deficiency' – everyone knows the phrase, even those who do not listen to the rest of the HIV/AIDS prevention messages – and co-infections, people talk constantly of 'building the immune system' and do so by means of drugs such as antiretrovirals, chemicals such as table salt, or 'blue stone' (copper sulphate), commercial herbs (Echinacea), baths using herb-infused water, steam or smoke, body rubs and by consulting with sangomas and the many other types of healers.

Thieves, smugglers and illegal miners (young men who work old or disused stopes in the many old and abandoned gold mines – a major source of income for large numbers of young men in the area) guard themselves similarly because they are exposed to danger in their work, or wish to avoid being seen. People talk of increasing their 'immunity' to witches in ways similar to the way they talk about protecting themselves from theft. They often point to white people in the community who appear to suffer fewer deaths from AIDS or witchcraft, for instance, believing that whites are better protected from witches, or even do not suffer from witches at all. In this context, healing is also protection, since disease is always 'sent' from some other source and to heal is also to protect from such influence. But protection is also healing, since failure to protect (from evil or viruses) brings illness. Health improves as one's 'defences' improve. Even as almost everyone refuses to admit the huge prevalence of HIV, or to say when someone has it or has died from it, the idea that AIDS is the failure of 'protection' ('immunodeficiency') accords as well with local theories of illness as it does with biomedical ones, while not being wholly true of either.

Exploring the options for healing

When Susan (not her real name), one of my research collaborators in Barberton, fell ill, she entered the local market for healing. At first she consulted widely among traditional healers, but eschewed clinics and Christian faith healers. She was concerned that we (she and I) had not yet done a *pahla* for Magodweni, who had committed suicide a year previously. *Pahla* is a ceremony in which a spirit is formally called and recognised and an offering of beer and snuff, or, as in this case, a goat, is made to it. Susan said frequently that she was afraid her health would be affected by this neglected duty, but I continued to neglect it due to pressures of other work. I was not aware of how ill she had become, or how ill she feared herself to be, until she began a serious and rapid decline. She lost weight precipitously and eventually became too weak to stand. Her two sons had come to visit her from Johannesburg in order to carry out a healing ritual with her that involved the sacrifice of a goat followed by cleansing rituals for all of them, including vomiting, emetics and, especially, reconciliation among all kin and friends who attended the ritual.

By the time I came to assist her she had been in and out of the local government hospital but had refused treatment. She feared that the hospital drip would cause her further illness. I took her back to hospital, where a government-employed Tunisian doctor saw her. His English was poor, but eventually we understood his diagnosis to be active TB. She was sent for HIV testing and counselling in a separate facility and was diagnosed as HIV positive. The night she was admitted to hospital her body temperature was over 40°C according to her chart, and her blood pressure was 95/65; she was dehydrated and close to death.

It emerged that she had also been to see several local biomedical practitioners and had been self-medicating with a range of drugs that she had acquired from a range of practitioners. These included a number of TB-specific antibiotics, other antibiotics and antiprotozoal agents and a range of herbal and other commercial products. Some, such as Ilvitrim, are widely used in South Africa for treating opportunistic infections, especially TB, among AIDS patients and others, such as Flagyl/metronidazole, for treating other infections commonly associated with AIDS.

She had also taken anti-inflammatories including Naproxen (a.k.a. 'Aleve', 'Midol') and other strong painkillers, probably acquired from local pharmacies but not under prescription. She had taken Ciprofloxacin, too, which is considered to be 'second-line' TB treatment and should only be used where drug resistance is beginning to manifest. Using it inappropriately, as she had done, is likely to increase drug resistance. Indeed, the efficacy of this drug has decreased so much due to abuse of this sort that it is no longer used in many cases (Andrews, Shah, Gandhi, Moll, Friedland 2007; Grimaldo, Rivera, Quelapio, Cardaño, Derilo and Belen 2001). Local general practitioners had given her vitamins such as Pyridoxine (vitamin B6), which is used in TB and AIDS treatment to alleviate neuropathy, and other substances such as sea salt. She told me that one general practitioner had diagnosed high blood pressure, even though her blood pressure on admission was consistently and dangerously low. Despite telling her that she had 'high blood' the GP had not prescribed any appropriate hypertension medications.

Susan had been prescribed, or acquired for self-medication, more than 16 medications including the following:

- From government clinics, but not prescribed for Susan:
  Ilvitrim (sulphamethoxazole 400mg and Trimethoprim 80mg), prescribed for 'J Ngobeni';
  Metronidazole [brand name: Flagyl] 200mg, prescribed for 'J. Ngobeni', Mpumalanga Provincial Clinics 'Pre-pack';
  Flagyl tablets [generic: metronidazole], large white, scored, no other identifying marks; '1 tablet 2 times a day', in generic prescription plastic packet, neither patient nor issuer identified;
  Ciploxx 500 (Ciprofloxacin 500mg), in trade marked box with package insert, 'Cipla Live Sciences', expiry 06/2012 (it had expired); 10 tablets in original package, all but one used; and
  Naproxen 200, in generic plastic packet from pharmacy, but no identification of pharmacy, patient or prescribing doctor.

- Other pharmaceuticals:
  Nucotrim tablets (co-trimoxazole 480mg), Gulf Drug Company,
  in blister pack, not otherwise identified.
- From Dr 'A', MBChB (Wits):
  Multivitamin (small bi-convex orange tablets);
  Salterpyn (large light green tablets);
  Vit-B-Complex (small bi-convex black tablets); and
  Betacin (small yellow gelatine capsules).
- From Dr 'B', MBChB (NUI) [National University of Ireland],
  LRCS and PI (Eire) [Licentiate of the Royal College of Surgeons]:
  Sea salt;
  'UHC 20';
  B6 [pyridoxine, one of the B vitamins];
  Folic 15 (small yellow scored tablets);
  [unreadable writing on packet], 10 small green gelatine cap-
  sules; and
  Voltrol (?) 15 (small yellow tablets without markings).

Thus, although it is probable that Susan was aware that she might have
TB and/or HIV and/or AIDS, she had resisted formal diagnosis and had
refused hospitalisation. She had also refused to follow suggestions that she
go to a government clinic, possibly because she feared – or already strongly
suspected – the diagnosis. It is significant that although both GPs she consulted apparently held biomedical degrees – at least according to their
stationery and printed medication packets – their diagnoses were entirely
incorrect and their treatment inappropriate and ineffective. Kate Wood
and Helen Lambert (2008: 220–221) document a similar case of a private
doctor's incompetence in the Eastern Cape, South Africa.

Susan had felt that she was getting better on traditional medication,
with prescribed rituals and with herbal concoctions from local street ven-
dors and pharmacies. She had initially refused the option of the government hospital but ultimately I insisted, going as far as to carry her in my
arms, almost against her will. Emaciated and dehydrated, she was light
enough to pick up easily. Six months later, after treatment for TB, but prior
to starting ARV treatment, her weight had increased from 34kg to 54kg
and she felt better despite still being quite ill. She consulted traditional

healers more as her condition improved, however, seeking purification from the polluting effects of 'Western medicine'. She frequently expressed uncertainty about whether she was better or not. She never discussed the HIV positive diagnosis that she had been given (for what she told me was the first time) while in hospital. As the TB improved she started to smoke and drink again, effectively denying the threat that HIV still posed.

Susan's case is far from unusual. Even in life-threatening situations such as this one, people continue to shop around and often select ineffective and dangerous healing treatments while refusing those that might be effective. It is clear, too, that the biomedical GPs in Susan's case were no more effective than the other practitioners she consulted outside the government hospital. Moreover, these practitioners were among the best known and most widely consulted in Barberton. There was, in fact, little difference in effectiveness, real or perceived, between practitioners. Scepticism is thus an essential skill for shoppers in Barberton's health market.

The role of belief in assessing healing efficacy

However we understand or define healing it is clearly a 'good' that all humans desire and for which most are willing to pay. The cost of healing – the amount people are willing to pay – is extraordinarily difficult to assess, and 'payment' almost never takes the form of a single 'price'. There is a universal and stable demand for healing, in Barberton, as elsewhere, and there are myriad specialists who provide myriad services. Unlike in the economic market the costs of healing, its benefits, the nature of supply and demand and their relation to price are not measurable in ordinary currencies of trade. The 'supply' of ancestors who can be supplicated, or the demand by ancestors to inhabit a living body, or the quantum of evil in a spirit, cannot be measured. And yet, given the diversity of therapies and healing available in this multitherapeutic environment, choices must be made, and costs and benefits assessed.

Research has shown only recently how the so called 'placebo effects' – the quantum of healing achieved by physiologically ineffective or inefficient therapies – 'are genuine psychobiological events attributable to the overall therapeutic context, and that these effects can be robust in both laboratory and clinical settings' (Amanzio, Corazzini, Vase and Benedetti

2009; Finniss, Kaptchuk, Miller and Benedetti 2010). While belief might account for a placebo effect the placebo effect is not sufficient to account for the complex interaction of belief and therapy.

The placebo effect is the measure of the effect of belief – or 'perceptions' – on healing. The chemical or physiological effects of a medication are established by randomised controlled trials that test them against that of the placebo. The effect of the drug under test, then, is the amount of healing that can be accomplished over and above what can be achieved by belief alone. But if medicine is only as effective as the placebo, then placebos may be held to be as effective as the medication and the net effect of healing is due to belief, its symbolic efficacy. Belief, in this case, may achieve what an economic rationality would fail to do. With limited exception this appears to be the case in Barberton. The 'market' for healing is a market for belief.

People seek healing whether they are ill or not. They continue to do so even after being healed and even if they have *not* been healed. When a client pays a biomedical doctor for a treatment, or purchases pharmaceuticals, or when actuaries assess risk and demand for health, biomedicine has a price. Hospitals, pharmaceuticals, equipment, doctors, adjunct personnel and the patients are all highly regulated and bureaucratically controlled, even though the medical outcome – its 'value for money' – is not entirely controllable and is never guaranteed. The primary challenge, then, for a client such as Susan, is to find ways to assess the effectiveness of these methods of healing, given that none of them is obviously or clearly superior in practice and that all have both a price and a risk attached to them.

A young sangoma stated this quandary succinctly. She had followed her mother into the profession and was not fully comfortable with her decision. She had been discussing how many traditional healers, along with the general public, often suspect or declare that 'healing is fake'. She believed that only 'the mind', as she put it in English, could heal the body. '[Biomedical] doctors have a lot to fear from us, and that is why they do not like us,' she said. Up to this point she had been engaged in a diatribe against both traditional healers and medical doctors. I asked her what she meant. How could traditional healers be a threat to doctors even as she was telling me that most of them were 'fakes'? 'Because most of them are no better than we [sangomas] are,' she concluded. 'Haven't you noticed?' ('Gogo A', 4 April 2010).

Healing as spiritual protection and cultural revival

When talking of healing, people often speak of 'boosting their immune systems' in the same breath as they mention how best to protect against witches. Both are elements of healing either as response or prophylaxis. AIDS, understood as a failure of the immune system, is taken to be both *evidence for* and a complex *metaphor of* a more general need for protection of all kinds. Thus, healing is protection and vice versa, as the AIDS campaigns attest.

It is October 2009 and a large congregation of Members of the Zion Christian Church (ZCC) has gathered in the garden of Chief Kenneth Dlamini of the Emjindini Tribal Trust in order to bless the community's *ummemo*. This celebration takes the form of a cultural festival, with danc- ing troupes, traditional costumes, food stalls and speeches. Formerly, it was the occasion at which the chief's followers performed services for the chief, for which they were rewarded with beer and meat.

The *ummemo* is the traditional Swazi chief's labour levy and village event, at which members of the community, having rendered service to the chief, congregate. The community of the Emjindini Tribal Trust is com- prised of families that have received grants of land from the chief. The legally mandated Tribal Trust is only a small section of a farm that was granted to some members of this community as part of a land redistri- bution and restitution process. There are also many people attending the ceremonies from town and other chiefdoms. The *ummemo*, however, is an important element of the re-traditionalisation of the landscape and society in this increasingly densely settled rural area to the west of the town of Barberton.

The re-traditionalisation of land and landscape and of cultural life and society in parts of rural South Africa, exemplified by the *ummemo*, is an important reference point in the shifting grounds of traditional healing. It opens space for traditional healers to dig wild herbs in the bush and to dance and drum in public. While it allows them to be more publicly visible in the mix of healing options, despite obvious conflict with Christians and biomedicine, it does not necessarily give them wider public acceptance or more paying clientele.

While the organisation of the *ummemo* takes some effort, the Traditional Authority and the chief himself will make a fair amount of money renting spaces from which people can sell food and drinks, homemade and commercial beer and traditional and craft items, among other goods and services. It is a local village fair with traditional dancing. Maidens are dressed in traditional attire that leaves their breasts bare, and men with bare chests and big bellies dance solemnly in loincloths of duiker skins. Cattle are slaughtered, people feast and drink. It is a fine time and a high event that marks an emerging new traditionalism in South Africa.

The ZCC is one of the biggest churches in South Africa, with three to four million members throughout that country and the southern African region. The church has its headquarters in the town of Moria, in neighbouring Limpopo province. Up to two million people converge on Moria each year during mass pilgrimages at Easter. Healing is understood to be one of the church's primary strengths. The healing theology of the church traces its origins to John Alexander Dowie (1847–1907), a Scottish faith healer who founded and built his widely influential Christian Catholic Apostolic Church in Zion, Illinois, in the USA, after being a pastor in Australia. Missions from this church were sent to the old Transvaal Republic as early as 1895 and the church became established in the region over the next decade. The ZCC eventually emerged out of this Apostolic and Pentecostal background and became the dominant 'healing church' in the region. While members of the church often condemn African 'witchcraft', lumping it together with sangomas' healing practices, there are significant crossovers. Many sangomas who profess Christianity are also members of the ZCC or related churches.

This was the third *ummemo* Chief Kenneth had hosted at the Royal Kraal of Emjindini since the chiefdom was re-established on land restored to the community in the late 1990s. In the past, members of the chiefship had gathered on this day to offer service to the chief and to be seen and blessed by him. Today the *ummemo* is part of a movement to revitalise older Swazi traditions. As with medicine, modernity and tradition compete without a clear hierarchy of values, mirroring the inchoate and emerging political culture of this region.

Chief Kenneth wants the *ummemo* to be a success. He has invited the members of the local ZCC to hold weekend services at his place. Local membership is greatly augmented by ZCC members from many churches, some from as far away as Bushbuckridge in the neighbouring Limpopo province, or from Elukwatini and Nelspruit in neighbouring municipalities and districts. They come from within a radius of perhaps 150km and all have been summoned by the regional elders to participate in the blessing of Emjindini, Chief Kenneth and the *ummemo* that will take place in two weeks' time.

The congregation is divided into male and female sections. All wear variations of the ZCC uniform. The elder males are dressed in what looks to be a version of the uniform of the South African Police Service, circa 1950 – cotton drill khaki jackets, black ties, brown trousers. Their shoes are highly-polished black. Over their shoulders they wear a 'Sam Brown' brown leather belt and bandolier. The younger women are dressed in uniforms of green and yellow. The men in the choir and those seated in a row of plastic chairs behind a high table wear dark suits. All the clothes are home-made. They drink only tea that is grown and marketed by the church. They have brought several sheep and a cow from ZCC-owned farms for slaughter, paid for by the chief. They are a costly lot to host, but they are skilled in the arts of protection from evil, for themselves and for others. The chief's belief in their belief makes them worth the price.

The chief complains that he has had to 'pop out' several more goats and a cow as well. He has also had to 'pop out' money for maize meal and other foods because the members of the congregation are very strict about food taboos and what they can and cannot eat or drink. And then there are the contributions he must make to the church to give thanks for its blessing. The congregation stays for three days and has to be accommodated. Chief Kenneth is not a member of the church, and is sceptical about the effectiveness of the blessing, but he does not want to leave such important protection to chance.

The rituals the ZCC carries out are designed to protect their members and clients (such as Chief Kenneth) from the bad influence of sorcerers, including traditional healers such as sangomas. But Chief Kenneth seeks healing and protective services from other healers as well as from the ZCC. Thus, tradition and re-traditionalisation in this context do not imply a *return* to a coherent or logically consistent culture. Rather, revaluing some elements of it further complicates an already complex cultural environment.

A few weeks after the gathering of the congregation of Zionists I find myself shopping for 'traditional attire' that I will dare to wear for the first time at this year's *ummemo*. Sandile, my friend, needs an item that has gone missing from his traditional clothing. Nokuzola (not her real name), a woman in the Emjindini community who has just been nominated for the Traditional Music Award of South Africa, is known to make this item and offers to sell us one. A month before she had urged me to send as many cellphone messages to the Traditional Music competition voting for her as I could possibly afford. She had done well with her performances, CD sales and cellphone campaign and was due to leave that afternoon for Durban, where the awards would be announced, so we had to rush over to see the collection of traditional gear she makes and sells as part of her business of tradition.

Sandile was not impressed with the fluorescent green beads she thought he would like. He bought the garish beads but decided he also needed to shop around for something more 'traditional'. (Later, he bought a bandolier of pink beads.) Adding her voice to the rising chorus of people who wanted to see me in traditional attire that year, she lent me a set of front and back aprons of duiker skin, telling me that I would have to buy them if I wanted to use them again.

By acting out tradition according to its precepts, we make manifest its growing power, a power traditional healers also use. Tradition is augmented, not diminished, by contemporary technology, since cellphones and cameras amplify the visual displays of power and carry the voices of those who act in the name and spirit of tradition. Duiker-skin aprons and fluorescent orange-beaded bandoliers are worn over bare chests by men using the latest digital cameras to document their participation in the chief's cultural revival. Similarly, bracelets of skin from sacrificial goats worn on the wrists of young illegal miners protect them from danger and arrest, while they use cellphones and lithium batteries to plan and prolong their raids on gold mines, feeding global markets from this out-of-the-way spot.

Tradition in the global market and the work of healing

Healing, tradition, and traditional healing have many other purposes and roles. Any person or activity that might require protection can be protected using much the same methods as protection from illness, bad luck, spirits or disgruntled ancestors. The tools are multi-purpose and flexible. On the way to Nokuzola's house, which is less than a kilometre from the chief's, we pass four churches. We also pass two young men in the blue overalls that are almost universally worn by labourers throughout South Africa. They are both wearing fresh strips of goat skin on their wrists and ankles. One of them is carrying plastic knee guards under one arm, while the other sports a massive gold chain around his neck. The knee pads and display of gold mark them immediately: they are illegal miners. Despite looking like ordinary labourers, signs of wealth such as the gold chain, indicate they have struck gold.

The economy of healing is linked in surprising ways to other economic activities. Most of the beads and paraphernalia used by traditional healers, for instance, come from Indian-owned shops. Many of the items local healers require, such as cowrie and other seashells, come from the Indian Ocean, while fabrics come from India, Mozambique and Swaziland. Healers' practices link the local economy to a regional and transnational economy, while the illegal gold trade – protected by healers – links it to global markets. Indian-owned shops typically sell the various items of the sangoma's kit, including beads, shells, the items in the divination kit and clothes.

One of these shops in the Barberton Indian quarter sells traditional regalia and requirements for rituals and religious groups. It also sells uniforms for the Zionists and other Christian groups, for Swazi traditionalists and for sangomas. The Muslim owner of the shop, Mr M, came to Barberton 30 years ago with his father, who was a trader. Mr M, who has been running the shop for many years, speaks fluent siSwati. He is also deeply versed in the requirements and material culture of Swazi ritual and healing culture, both Christian and traditional, while being a deeply religious Muslim man. On one occasion in the shop I had heard a Muslim cleric on the radio giving a sermon in English, with frequent passages from the Quran in Arabic. The message of the sermon was that, in paraphrase, 'the Jews and the Christians will steal your faith. You must be constantly vigilant against them because they will do you wrong. You can be kind to them, and treat them as if they were friends, but they have only one intention in mind, and that is to undermine Islam and to destroy it' (from field notes).

Mr M was suspicious of us and although after I explained my research and interests he began to tell me the prices of the items, he seemed to want us to leave the shop as soon as possible, even though there was no one else there. The reason was the radio. The imam delivering the radio sermon went on to consider whether it was the duty of, or merely an option for Muslims to kill Jews and Christians. Eventually, the sermon came to an end and as it did we all relaxed. While the ordinary news was read on the radio, Mr M was much more willing to take time to chat.

Powerful international religious and ritual discourses meet and blend in this little shop on the corner that sells what appears to be a mix of odd-ments in the old style of southern African rural shops. The material par-ticulars of rituals and powers to heal in Islam, Christianity and African traditional medicine, among others, are sourced from all over the world and arrayed here under the counter glass and on the walls. The local mar-ket for healing is closely tied to specialised global markets. Against a back-ground of global conflict and local suspicion the business of supplying the material necessities of 'tradition' goes on as it has for centuries.

When we arrive on the day of the *ummemo*, Mr M was instructing his shop assistant, the husband of a sangoma I had interviewed and whom I knew in other contexts, on how to put price labels on tubes of rose-scented incense.

'You must do this with PRECISION! The way Germans do it, with precision,' he says to the bemused assistant. Looking up, he greets Sandile in siSwati. '*Sawubona, unjane?...Yebo, sikhona*' (how are you?...yes, we are fine). Literally: 'We see you...Yes, we are here', then turns to me and asks, 'Are you German?'. I say no, and he tries 'French? Canadian?' I think per-haps I should opt for one of these, but kept him guessing.

Sandile, still not satisfied with the beads he has bought, asks to see the bandoliers. While looking for them, the shopkeeper, determined to pin me down with an identity, asks, 'What's your surname?'

'Thornton,' I say.

'Oh, English.'

'No,' I say.

Turning to ask Sandile his *isibongo* (family name, surname), he quickly places my friend among Barberton's black elite of landowners, business-men and politicians.

As I examine the *mahiya*, the cloths that are part of Swazi traditional attire, he began to proselytise.

'You know, when we go on the hajj...you know the rituals of the hajj?'

'Yes,' I say.

'On the hajj, we wear only an upper and a lower cloth, like the Swazis, like the Africans.' I do not contradict his bold generalisation.

'Only ours are all white...only white. Very pure.' He goes on to explain that men wear only the white cloths and, dropping his voice for emphasis, adds, 'they don't wear underwear! They are all natural!' He looks at me to gauge my reaction; I remain blank faced.

'Of course, the women are fully dressed,' he explains, perhaps in case I feel ill at ease over this revelation.

Since we are buying traditional attire he begins to develop his theory that the Africans must have adopted their own traditional attire from the Arabs because Arabs, during the hajj, wear only a top and bottom cloth wrap. This means, he concludes, that 'the Arabs are much more ancient. They came first!'

Religious differences could not have been starker, yet his business was built entirely on his trade in goods and materials for religious observances of all kinds (except his own).

Sandile watches me with one eyebrow raised. Turning to our friendly shopkeeper I tell him that I do not agree with him on that point. 'How much is that cloth?' I choose a cloth and pay and we head for home as the first heavy rain of the summer hits the dust on the roads and washes it down the gutters in a red torrent. As much as the healers I worked with wondered whether white people 'had ancestors', the ethnic and religious identities queried and exposed in this commercial interaction suggest the complexity of the market for the material culture of healing.

Competition in the market for healing

In most respects the traditional healers in Barberton are not particularly 'traditional', nor are they concerned simply with healing medical conditions. They compete intensely with one another and with a wide range of other healing systems and methods: religious, biomedical, quasi-technical (for example, 'healing' technologies such as weight loss machines), New Age, Chinese traditional medicine and many others. When they use herbs in healing it is rarely for their biomedical or pharmacological properties – supposed or actual. Instead, herbs are used to smoke the whole body in smoke baths, or are burnt and rubbed into the skin, or into cuts in the skin, or used in enemas and emetics, in baths and steam baths and as packets of magical substance or charms. In the vast majority of cases there is little opportunity for pharmacological substances to enter the body. These substances index the healing power of 'the bush', nature, the uninhabited wild that is devoid of witches (because it is not inhabited). The term *muti* can be translated as 'medicine', or 'charm', but also as 'bush'.

One such application is the use of *muti* in crime, especially theft. One day, the house that served as my research base in Barberton was burgled. I had just arrived and had unpacked my computer, camera gear and notes. Before going to bed I had been working on my laptop on the table in the lounge. The computer and camera were visible from the window, but not thinking, I went to bed and did not wake as the thief bent burglar bars away from the window, crawled through the gap and took the computer and camera. The next morning, when I told the story to local friends one immediately nodded his head and said, 'I'm sure what tipped you off was the smell'. 'What smell?' I asked. 'The thieves use a kind of *muti* to make sure that you don't wake up. It's made from the hair of hyenas, snake fat and other parts of animals. If they burn it by the window you will not wake up and they can do what they like,' he told me.

In fact, I had not smelled anything and there was no evidence of burning by the window or anywhere else, but most people believed that I had slept through the burglary because a magic sleeping potion had been used. I did find that the thief had injured himself and I followed the blood trail into the bush towards the squatter camp nearby. I tracked him only far enough to convince myself that the theft had been merely opportunistic; others believed strongly that magic had been used.

Such 'disappearing' medicine is attested to historically in the Cape region. Olfert Dapper, in an account published in 1668, mentions the use of 'amulets', as does J G Grevenbroek in 1695, who writes, 'superstition makes them suppose that this piece of wood will avert all dangers if darkness should surprise them in open country infested with lions and snakes'

(Dapper, Ten Rhyne and De Grevenbroek 1933 [1688]: 187). This usage is pervasive today among healers and their clients.

Since theft of all kinds – together with other kinds of crime – is a significant part of the economy in most South African towns, including Barberton, it is unsurprising that thieves pay significant amounts of money for magic of this sort. Although not a matter of healing, it contributes to the income of quite a few *emagedla* and *tinyanga* (types of non-initiated healers and herbalists, not sangomas) and helps to sustain their healing activities. However, the majority of initiated healers do not practise magic of this sort since if they do so they risk losing the powers bequeathed to them by the *emadloti*.

Belief, the 'placebo effect' and the market for healing

Does the quality of belief influence the quality of the healing, therapy or cure? Belief, like rational thought, allows us to assess our relationship to the world and to evaluate our internal and external states. While rational or economic judgements allow us to evaluate evidence and reach conclusions based on the idea of cause and effect, belief permits us to evaluate moral states of being and to underpin knowledge and action with a sense of right-eous certainty. This is all part of the 'placebo effect'.

The centrality of belief in this market is manifested in two ways. First, it is widely understood that no therapy is entirely effective unless one *believes* in its moral value. On learning that I study 'witches' many white people in Barberton have asked me specifically whether I can tell them if witchcraft can affect them. Their question implies a belief that witchcraft is an objective fact and only its sphere of influence is in question. A vital part of the race discourse in Umjindi, for instance, is the belief among many black people that whites do not suffer from witches or witchcraft. Whites themselves seem to be divided about whether this is true or not, and whether witches exist or not. There are also different Christian and New Age ideas about what witches are and how they act. This is predicated on the notion that a witch has no power over those who do not believe in witches.

Second, people also believe there is a reason why a therapy is chosen, and that reason is not necessarily rational. Ancestors may guide a person to a particular traditional healer, for instance, without regard to whether or not the therapy the healer offers is effective. Similarly, someone who believes he or she has been healed by crystals, for example, may understand this in terms of larger systems of belief about the (mystical) power of nature. Similarly, someone who attends a doctor's surgery is likely to have made a decision to believe that this will be an effective healing route. The point is that evidence of effectiveness after the fact is less important than prior belief.

Belief provides a structure for the 'market'. Belief is reinforced when black people say that witchcraft does not work on white people. Some whites, on the other hand, are often not entirely certain that witchcraft does not work on them, and fear it, even as they tell black people that it can have no effect on them 'because we don't believe in it'. White people, however, are often strong believers in many other kinds of spiritual influence, including witches, but most confine their beliefs to issues of Christian spiritualism and its dark twin, Satanism. They are comforted by a kind of hopeful relativism.

Each system of belief has a set of practices and boundaries and divides the demand for therapy into different markets. Since they are flexible, shaped to the occasion and deployed for specific reasons, practices range from active therapies for medical and psychological (spiritual) complaints, or for passive comfort and protection, to active aggression. As in any segmented market where boundaries limit knowledge and thus efficiency, there is ample opportunity for arbitrage and insider trading, fraud, schemes, gaming, double-dealing and, of course, for dealing across the borders of belief communities. The notion that only Christians can practise Satanism, for instance, or that African witchcraft cannot directly affect white people, places limits on the effectiveness of these practices. These limits are the boundaries, albeit porous, of belief that structure the market.

This abundance of diversity is puzzling. Carol Legg (2010: 230–231) provides an ethnographic account of responses to aphasia in a largely black but polyglot suburb of Cape Town. She notes:

> [T]here is no evidence of a discrete cultural account of aphasia [due to stroke] but rather a wide variation in causal notions that included

biomedical causes, social and behavioural determinants, transgression of social rules, and the influences of supernatural powers such as witches and ancestors…[T]raditional, biomedical and religious cures…were obscured by a burgeoning and not always ethical open market offering miracle cures. Uncertainty prevailed.

People were uncertain about the trajectory of stroke and aphasia, about the possibility of treatment and about the integrity of healers and healthcare workers. People were also uncertain about their own alignments in this setting where Christianity, indigenous culture, biomedicine and western thought wrestle for hegemony (Legg 2010: 238).

Although Legg was writing about a suburb or 'township' located in a very different part of South Africa, two thousand kilometres away, similar problems exist. Not all therapies are effective in all cases and some are completely ineffective in all cases. Despite this, each therapy, however improbable, still manages to secure some part of the overall market. People may be spreading their bets, but few have sufficient resources to gamble in the market for healing and there are strong emotional and social limits placed on the degree of risk a person is likely to take with an illness by betting on the wrong therapy for the condition.

Diversity, doubt and uncertainty prevail and make it impossible to characterise the patient's anxious predicament as a true 'quest' in a cultural 'tradition'. Rather, it seems more like a shopping trip without a shopping list, with limited funds and no guarantees.

Choice in the 'market' for belief

All forays into markets, or quests for healing, raise a question in two parts: 'what counts as healing (or, how do I know that I am healed)?' and 'what do I need to believe in order to believe that I am healed?' The endeavour is, therefore, a search for a set of beliefs that would constitute valid conditions for healing to take place and for its efficacy to be assessed. In other words, healing is not merely conditional on the biological or physiological state of the person, but on states of belief that provide cognitive and emotional conditions conducive to believing that healing is possible and to assessing the outcome.

There are also many types of illness and disease, some of which resolve themselves (heal spontaneously), some of which proceed to morbidity and death and some of which come and go (like malarial fevers, TB coughs or AIDS symptoms) or maintain themselves at moderate, survivable levels for a long time. There is also a continuum of states of health that might be judged to be 'healthy', 'relatively healthy' or 'healthy enough'. Illnesses and disease range from tolerable to intolerable and from something you can live with to something you die from. For instance, 'people *living* with HIV/AIDS' (PLWA) is a formalised category of people with a recognised disease who may or may not display symptoms of being ill.

Thus, it is not entirely adequate to speak of the 'social causes' of disease and illness (Comaroff 1981; Farmer 2006; Kleinman 1973b; Kleinman, Das and Lock 1997; Lindenbaum and Lock 1993) and to isolate the illness from its appropriate therapy or social response. Both an illness and a therapy may be assessed as having a cause and a cultural context that helps to determine whether the illness is amenable to therapy and which therapy is appropriate to the illness.

In order to solve this problem the patient must ask what would count as 'being healed'. A first order question is 'how do I become healed?' In systems where there is only one answer to this question the first order question is all that is necessary. Having received an adequate reply the patient will go to the doctor or the healer and request to be healed. The question of how to evaluate not just the effectiveness of the therapy but how to know how such an evaluation might be conducted, and on what terms, is a *second order* question about the cultural frameworks that constitute the multi-therapeutic social field in southern Africa.

Many of the illnesses that afflict people in South Africa are complex, of long duration and display a variety of symptoms. High blood pressure, diabetes, TB, diarrhoea, dehydration and malnutrition, HIV/AIDS and malaria manifest in many ways; symptoms come and go. Other disorders, such as generalised anxiety and depression or undiagnosed sexually transmitted diseases and other common viral infections are often also vague and hard to diagnose. Many of these are poorly treated in southern

African medical systems and some of them are simply untreatable given the technology and resources available. Others, such as HIV and TB, often involve co-infection and drug resistance. When, and often if, they are treated, a long treatment regime may be involved, with many opportunities for failure. Thus the question of what would constitute 'being healed' is one that most people are forced to ask. It is often far from obvious.

Part of this evaluative process involves a question about what kind of cure is on offer. A spiritual cure might mean that a patient is at least at ease with his or her impending death. Thus, healing in an environment of such medical parallelism involves more than the diagnostic categories of healing itself. Implicit in this is a set of cultural categories of disease and illness as well as of what constitutes a cure. The question resolves into what is at its core a question of the sort a cultural anthropologist asks: in what context does belief X make sense? Is there a cultural explanation for the belief?

FIGURE 7.2: Price list posted by the healer Magodweni in his *indumba*, Emjindini.

It becomes evident that there is a constant conversation going on about who believes what, and with what consequence. When the newspapers print a story about a worker at a funeral business who has sold the fresh hand and breast of a white woman to a sangoma in Green Valley in the Lowveld, a typical question is: 'Why do these people believe that this will give them power?' People of all 'races', colours, classes, religions and occupations ask this question. Similarly, if one hears about a miraculous incident of AIDS being cured at a Christian church, or how Mohammed, a healer from 'Africa' (South African's locution for anyone who is African but not South African) has healed a man in his surgery in Barberton's main street, most people who feel inclined to discuss such things eventually come to the question of belief: What must one believe for such a cure to work? Virtually everyone I have known in my years of fieldwork in Barberton links belief and healing in such discussions and few question the fundamental premise that appropriate beliefs can cure certain illnesses and that belief can be acquired and discarded as necessary. What they seem to want to know is not whether some *belief* is valid or not, testable or not, or 'true', but rather, *what is required for a belief to be effective?*

CHAPTER 8

Apotropaic magic and the sangoma's patient

Apotropaic magic

The problem of witches and witchcraft has been central to anthropology throughout the twentieth century. The anthropological literature is not about whether witches exist but rather about how to account for their purported existence: a cultural question of belief rather than an ontological question of under what conditions their existence can be taken for granted. These are simply the wrong questions. According to *bungoma* philosophy, witchcraft, like the healer's craft, is predicated on interpersonal exposure to the 'power' or 'shadow/presence' (*isithunzi*) of others (see Werbner 2015: 2–3 on the similar concept of *seriti* in Sesotho/Setswana). Witchcraft derives from a radical theory of the person as inherently infectious and vulnerable. Person-like agents cause illness, but not all agents of this sort are human, and not all are tangible; thus, their agency cannot be given a 'social causation' account in all cases.

From the perspective of the sangoma's patient, if not from that of most contemporary social theory, witches are person-like agents, either tangible or intangible. They are not mere 'representations' of what could be interpreted as imagined harm triggered by social distress. To be vulnerable to witchcraft, however, one must understand oneself as an 'exposed being', exposed to a range of influences that can damage health or prevent 'good luck'. These influences include other *tangible* persons, some of whom may be 'witches', but also other *intangible persons* such as 'ancestors' and 'spirits'. The fundamental premise of healing in the southern African healer's paradigm is that if patients/clients can be given protection through apotropaic magics their 'natural' health and luck will be able to continue. The 'exposed being' – an existential condition of personhood as 'patient' rather than 'agent' – is vulnerable unless protected from illness, witchcraft and misfortune. In terms of this concept all persons are assumed to be well unless protection fails.

This approach helps us to understand the pragmatic efficacy of logically incompatible medical beliefs in conditions of medical parallelism. Protection, or apotropaic magic, is more significant than therapy in traditional 'medical' practice.

These concepts – 'exposed being', 'protection', '(in)tangible persons' – also help to explain the relative non-specificity, or generic quality, of most traditional 'therapies', since they are understood less as specific treatments of disease ('therapy') and more as protection from illness and misfortune, that is, as apotropaic magic. In protecting the patient, the healer effectively seeks to add *something* to the person of the sufferer/patient. Rather than seeking to adjust therapeutically some internal system of the patient, the southern African healer *augments the person* of the sufferer to prevent further attack and attempts to create the *augmented self* – the 'immune system'.

The sangoma's patient as person

I was frequently asked, while doing fieldwork, whether white people, *abelungu*, 'have *emadloti*', 'ancestors', and whether they, like black people, are subject to witches and the demands of these ancestors. As a white anthropologist I give an anthropological answer: 'Yes, they do. They just deal with it and think of it in a different way.' This chapter develops a way to answer that question.

Once called 'rainmakers' or 'witchdoctors', especially by nineteenth-century missionaries such as Robert Moffat and David Livingstone (Livingstone 1857: 16, 85, 176, 638, 666; Moffat 1846: e.g., 34, 65, 80–88, 152) these designations continue to cast a shadow of misunderstanding and stigma over both practitioners and their patients.

The 'rainmaker' term is still used in the work of many contemporary archaeologists and historians such as Thomas Huffman (2007), while 'witchdoctor' continues to be used in the popular press and imagination, and especially by Christians. The term *shaman* has also been used in reference to the distinctive practices of the southern African healer, especially in the work of David Lewis-Williams (1981, 1996, 2002) and his students, in the study of rock art.

In fact, sangomas spend a good deal of time hunting, gathering and preparing *muti* – vegetable, animal and mineral substances – from the bush or from markets and from other healers. In this, the sangomas in Bantu-speaking contexts are as much hunter-gatherers as the healers among the 'Bushmen' (San). The 'Bushmen' are the 'classic' hunter-gatherers of southern Africa, whose healing practices have been widely studied. They share many aspects of healing practice, including trance, trance dance and the use of magic from the 'bush' that is collected and hunted. The healing and gathering of the sangomas, and their distinctive styles in the societies in which they live, suggest that these sodalities constitute cultural enclaves or 'sub-cultures' that originally derived from the autochthonous 'Bushman' who were incorporated over time into the Bantu-speaking villages. Indeed, elsewhere in Africa, healers frequently come from autochthonous communities that were incorporated into the societies of invading settler peoples.

While virtually all southern African people accord sangomas some respect for many reasons, there is also widespread fear of and scepticism about them. Magodweni spoke to this in response to an anthropology undergraduate student's question at a class session at the University of the Witwatersrand on 4 October 2005:

> I believe and know witchcraft exists. It depends on what kind of witchcraft. It may happen that in your family they have always practised witchcraft, so when you are born they perform certain rituals in you (*bafaka imicikilisho yokusebenza kuwe*). They put certain *muti* in you growing up practising witchcraft; that is the inheritance of your family. Then there are those who have bad hearts. They go and buy these medicinal herbs. There are places where they sell these herbs. [But] like I said, healing is different. There are those who have learnt to heal.

In response to another student's question on the same occasion about whether witches could be 'uprooted' entirely, Magodweni replied:

> We are fighting witchcraft but we can never conquer it, so if the witches can be finished, then I can lose my job. No one will be bewitched and fall sick. The problem with witches is that they never have meetings so we can never know who the witches are. So if we fight, it's is a kind of a losing battle for us because they keep on fighting and we are fighting back.

The South African government has long attempted to 'suppress witchcraft', while also attempting to bring sangomas into formal government-regulated organisations (Chavanduka 1978; Last and Chavanduka 1986; Flint 2008; Last 1986; World Health Organization 2002). However, healers I have interviewed in this regard take very seriously the Suppression of Witchcraft Act of 1957 (amended 1970) and refuse to actually identify a witch by a personal name or anything other than the most general characteristics. There have been prosecutions under the Act, which identifies as criminal any person who:

> (a) imputes to any other person the causing, by supernatural means, of any disease in or injury or damage to any person or thing, or who names or indicates any other person as a wizard; (b) in circumstances indicating that he professes or pretends to use any supernatural power, witchcraft, sorcery, enchantment or conjuration, imputes the cause of death of, injury or grief to, disease in, damage to or disappearance of any person or thing to any other person,

among a number of other acts, including professing 'any knowledge of witchcraft', or any action on the 'advice of a witchdoctor' (Government of the Republic of South Africa 1957).

Nevertheless, the practice of witchcraft and the existence of witches is held to be a fact of South African life (see especially Ashforth 2005; Geschiere 1997; Niehaus 1998, 2005; Niehaus, Mohlala and Shokane 2001). These authors seek to understand the political and economic contexts and causes of witchcraft accusations. Niehaus (2005: 206) remarks that while it is 'essential to interpret occult beliefs in the framework of political-economic changes', it is not sufficient to do so because of the multidimensionality of meanings, practices and subjective experience associated with them. All agree, more or less, that witchcraft can be understood in terms of the 'social causation of illness' model, in which broadly social causes – political change, social stress, globalisation, capitalism, and social change – create the context in which believers-in-witches interpret their misfortune *as if they were caused by witches*, while, in terms of social theory, *their misfortune or illness is actually caused* by social and political forces they are unable to conceive of or to perceive (Hammond-Tooke 1989; Kleinman 1973a, 1973b, 2010; Kleinman, Eisenberg and Good 2006 [1978]). In other words, the figure of the witch as social imaginary and discursively-determined subjective experience is the central concern of most current and contemporary studies.

Adam Ashforth (2005: 12–13), for instance, notes:

> In the course of everyday life in Soweto, witchcraft accusations are the exception rather than the rule. When gossiping about other people's misfortunes…Sowetans rarely find it necessary to utter the words 'witch' or 'witchcraft'. Witchcraft discourse…serves primarily as subtext – that which is not spoken but without which one cannot comprehend what is spoken. To say 'the wife is to blame' when a husband dies, for example, is automatically to invoke witchcraft…Everyday life in Soweto – as in most of Africa, most of the time – is lived more in a mode of suspicion and fear of occult assault rather than open accusation and persecution of witches…[T]he sense that life is continually exposed to people deploying evil forces to harm and kill is palpable, the fear of occult assault is real, and the enterprise of healing devoted to protection from evil forces is enormous.

Ashforth believed that the 'forces' that led to this 'subtext' of witchcraft were largely political, especially the sense of injustice in South Africa. In a blurb on the jacket of the book *Witchcraft, violence and democracy in South Africa*, Achille Mbembe claims that Ashforth 'inscribes' the study of witchcraft 'in political science'. Ashforth (2005: 153), however, radically misconceives witchcraft as the 'antithesis' of 'healing', largely because he confuses the power of witches with political power and believes healing to be a deficient medicine. Both conclusions are wrong, at least with respect to the *bungoma* tradition.

For the sangoma it is the nature of the *person*, or *personhood* of the patient in southern African health beliefs that deserves attention. It is the cultural understanding of the person who suffers that is at issue, not the sociological 'forces' as cause of suffering. Paradoxically, both healer and client are effectively 'patients' in this system, since the healer feels, smells, or otherwise receives a diagnosis by experiencing the pain of the patient. Healer and patient are co-sufferers rather than in a political relationship of 'therapeutic citizenship' or of the 'biopolitics' of Foucault. They are not mere elements of a biological population, alike in their 'species being', as medicine would have it. This is a kinship of suffering as existential condition.

By taking the *personhood* of the sufferer as the primary anthropological issue, we are able to ask useful empirical questions about the nature of healing and protective magic or *muti* that is used to protect against witch-craft and to heal those who believe themselves to be suffering from sorcery or witchcraft. Asking questions about the 'existence' of witches or witch-craft is misleading, since this cannot ever be a valid empirical question. By exploring concepts of personhood, however, we are able to ask useful – that is answerable – questions about the cultural construction of the person who is vulnerable to and can suffer from witches and witchcraft.

This intellectual strategy shifts attention away from evaluative questions about why 'Africans' believe in witches (which do not exist) and towards the phenomenology of personhood, that is, towards an enquiry into the kind of person who is vulnerable and suffers. This is a valid question in medical anthropology, whereas the question of witches is not. It also allows us to account for the similarity of effect attributed to 'ancestors', 'spirits', 'medicine'/*muti*, and magic/sorcery. In other words, it is not the unseen 'cause' that is in question but the visible effect on actual people.

The person, as *exposed being*, is vulnerable to witches and also to other intangible but similarly *socially constituted forces*. The role of healing in southern African cultural systems is, therefore, to protect the exposed being – the vulnerable person, as culturally constructed – from the range of threats that such a person experiences. The ritual and practical processes of protection constitute a type of magic, that is, a symbolic intervention that is primarily intended to augment the person-as-exposed-being. This form of 'healing' can be called apotropaic magic, that is, magic that is intended to ward off, or turn away, bad influences or causes of illness, ill luck and disease. These interventions are often realised through ritual, but also through the use of materials and objects such as beads, amulets, ingested substances, scarification or other forms of injection (enema, rubbing into cuts, vaginal insertions and so on), but can also be accomplished through invocation, song, prayers and other linguistic or conceptual means.

Most academic discussions present 'witches' and 'ancestors' as causal agents, while at the same time arguing – explicitly or implicitly – that the precise logical concept of causation was at fault for those who 'believed' in witches and other intangible agents of good or ill (for example, Ashforth 2005; Comaroff and Comaroff 2006; Evans-Pritchard 1937; Geschiere 1997; Niehaus 1998, 2005; Niehaus, Mohlala and Shokane 2001). According to Max Gluckman, Evans-Pritchard had shown 'how the belief in witchcraft as a theory of causation works', and thus the question was closed (1960: 86; Werbner 2015: 40). But the influence of these agents can also be thwarted, turned back against them, delayed, or otherwise transformed either into forces that could do no harm or could not harm *yet*, or whose harm was reflected back in a form of automatic reciprocity (one harm automatically returns another). Thus, the power or force of any agent can be neutralised, blocked or returned. This applies to the powers (*emandla*) of the witch, the sorcerer and the intangible person-like agents such as spirits and ancestors, as much as it does to *muti*. These agents, like their targets, are *vulnerable to their own powers* and to the powers of other agents. If this were not the case, healing would be impossible in so far as it is caused – as it usually is – by one kind of agent or another (cf. Werbner 2015: 34).

This amounts to a kind of ergative grammar of healing, rather than the more common agentive or 'subject-object' grammar in which a 'medical practitioner' as active subject/agent *practises on* (as transitive verb) a *patient* (as passive object-of-action). Instead, the sangoma practises healing in the mode of 'bad things happen' ergativity rather than 'someone did [evil] to me'. An 'agentive' framework explains suffering in terms of a grammar that has an active subject (the agent) that does something (the act) to an object (the patient or sufferer). This can be stated as '*S* did *V* to O' ([subject] did [verb] to [object]) in SVO (subject-verb-object) grammars that express action and its 'agents' and 'objects' in agentive or nominative-accusative languages. For sangomas and their patients both are simultaneously subjects and objects of misfortune. In ergative grammars, or ergative constructions, the subject and the direct object are not grammatically distinguishable. For instance, we could say, in English, 'the cook boils the soup', but equally, using an ergative construction, 'the soup boils'. The healer's magic is an 'ergative construction' in a way similar to language. Both the healer and the patient are sufferers and healers are healed because of their juxtaposition and ritual work.

This is why, in ordinary language, people say that it is necessary to 'believe' in a medicine to make it work. But in terms of the conceptual framework outlined here, 'belief' is equivalent to 'exposure' to influence. It is the conscious act of accepting the influence of the healer and the medicine, including the sense of connection (an 'intersubjectivity', but without the prejudice of a 'subjective' position) between the healer and the healed and the sources of the medicine. Indeed, the healer may become the healed and vice versa, as in the 'wounded healer' paradigm advanced by Carl Jung (1981 [1959]) and Paul Radin (1972 [1956]: 255). For Radin and Jung, the healer/healed, wounding/wounded dichotomy is likened to a trick of the trickster:

> There is something of the trickster in the character of the shaman and medicine-man, for he, too, often plays malicious jokes on people, only to fall victim in his turn to the vengeance of those whom he has injured. For this reason, his profession sometimes puts him in peril of his life. Besides that, the shamanistic techniques in themselves often cause the medicine man a good deal of discomfort, if not actual pain. At all events the 'making of a medicine-man' involves, in many parts of the world, so much agony of body and soul that permanent psychic injuries may result. His 'approximation to the saviour' is an obvious consequence of this, in confirmation of the mythological truth that the wounded wounder is the agent of healing, and that the sufferer takes away suffering.

And, Jung reminds his readers, the ancient Greek word that we today take to mean 'medicine', especially the substances and herbs used in healing, had the original meaning of substances that could both harm and heal. In other words, the substances were powerful or active and their valence, qualitative or quantitative effect could be manipulated by a skilled healer. 'The primitive medicine man is a healer and a helper and also the dreaded concocter of poisons. The very word φαρμακον [pharmakon] means "poison" as well as "antidote", and poison can in fact be both' (Jung 1981 [1959]: 227).

Exposure and the 'exposed being'

Emblematic of the exposed being is the practice of what I call 'exposure' in the healing-trance or *bungoma* ceremonies. To be healed, pollution and polluting activities, secrets and 'harmful' emotions must be exposed. This is similar to confession, except that what must be confessed is not 'sin', but rather conditions that will block effective healing or that will affect other people. I give an example of this sort of exposure in Chapter 3.

This bears some similarity to the Christian rite of confession, as developed by Augustine, Bishop of Hippo, but reflects much more strongly the idea expressed in the suppressed Gnostic gospel of Thomas. This 'gospel', which is among those that did not become part of the Christian canonical texts of the life of Jesus, may reflect religious beliefs that were current in early Syrian Christianity, but, since it is written in Coptic, it may also reflect a more 'African' belief system. It attributes the following words ('saying' or logia) to Jesus: 'Logia 70, Jesus says, "If you bring forth what is within you, what you bring forth will save you. If you do not bring forth what is within you, what you do not bring forth will destroy you"' (Didymos Judas Thomas, known as 'Thomas', Gospel, saying 70).

The primary value of confession in the southern African healing tradition, like that attributed to Jesus by Thomas in this non-canonical 'gospel', treats the secret within as something that can cause harm by harming the person. It is the concept of the 'secret within' or of 'secret' and therefore hidden power that was the primary concern of the ancient philosophy known as 'Gnosic'. In Gnosticism, like other related traditions such as Manichaeism, the religion of the Persian prophet known as Mani, the belief is that 'the kingdom of god is within [you]'.

In the apocryphal Christian tradition displayed in the Thomas gospel, possibly once widespread in Syriac and Coptic Christianity, 'what is within' is the cause of harm and to 'bring it forth', that is, to expel it, is like expelling a witch, or expelling what in southern African 'traditional' healing are today widely called 'toxins' or poisons. Similar effects can be achieved through emetics that cause vomiting, or diarrhoea, or through other forms of physical cleansing such as 'steaming' or sweat baths. Like the witch, or like substances that have been placed inside the person by evil agents, 'that within you' can be expelled through either confession or cleansing.

The exposure clears the way for other interventions, allowing the 'ancestors' to enter and healing to take place. This act is held to affect the entire assembly or congregation at the session. But it is also involuntary. All those who attend the gathering take the risk that they will be exposed in this way. But to the extent that the revelation is forced, or revealed by the ancestors through trance performance, no one is held responsible. The exposure contributes to the group's well-being by revealing a secret that should not be held. It is the exposure of the unspoken social reality. The secret threads of social and sexual relations that link people together below the public surface are made visible, almost tangible. The 'ancestors', as well as absent lovers, spouses, kin, family and others, are all part of this otherwise-invisible web that 'exposure' makes visible.

Divination (*kupengula*, v.) with the bones (*tinhlolo*) has a similar rationale and form. In this form of divination a collection of objects – including astragalus bones, dice, dominoes, seashells, seeds, coins and other objects – is thrown on a mat between the healer and the client. Each breathes across the 'bones' before they are 'thrown' from the cupped hands of the healer. They fall in a pattern that is held to reveal – or expose – the unspoken secrets of *both* healer and client. (Indeed, there is always a token in the collection that represents the healer.)

Divination is, in itself, an act of healing, because it exposes what is hidden and permits flows of energy (*emandla*). While it is also diagnostic, divination in the southern African *bungoma* tradition is not merely a diagnostic technique for which subsequent therapy is prescribed. It has, however, been widely misinterpreted in this way, analogous with Western diagnosis or with other divinatory systems. Divination, like the trance performances of the healer, exposes the secret fabric of relations that include good and evil, witches and the well-intentioned and the intentions of those whose motives are unknown.

Like the confessions and exposures of participants in public performances, the act of divination opens the way for 'luck', or 'goodness' to enter, either directly or through the mediation of the ancestors and medicines/*muti*. Divination names specific illnesses, or sources of suffering, and therefore 'diagnoses' these, but it is not the specific diagnosis (as named illness) that is relevant in most cases. The aim of divination is, instead, to identify the sets of relations that are held to cause a state of increased exposure to evil, and therefore to illness. The 'pieces' of the divination set represent three things: sources of danger, points of concern where protections may be lacking and types of gifts by which sources of danger can be mollified, or indications of ritual objects by which protection can be increased. For instance, a large Indian Ocean cowrie – always part of the divination set – may represent 'women talking' when the mouth of the cowrie is uppermost, or pregnancy when the shiny top is exposed. Both indicate a weakness, but can also indicate a source of danger. Sharp-pointed whelk shells are 'spears' that can point towards the client or away, indicating degrees of danger. A red stone (red carnelian, for example) can represent blood, indicating that a sacrifice is required, while a coin in a certain position may indicate that an ancestor can be bought off easily with a five-cent piece. Red, white and black pieces may indicate the colour of cloth that should be worn to strengthen the self. In short, the display of divination pieces presents a complex picture of threats, weaknesses and magic (rituals, medicines, gifts, *muti*) that can be used to deal with these.

Illness, ill luck, or misfortune is not, therefore, the direct consequence of dysfunctional relationships, social 'stresses' and 'strains' or social 'forces'. It is, rather, the consequence of a reduced ability to protect oneself against other persons (tangible and intangible) and the powers of plant, animal or mineral magical ('medicinal') substances. The effect of the 'witch' (*mtsakatsi*) in the *bungoma* tradition of southern Africa, like that of other sources of danger, is not in any simple sense a reflex of political or community conflict – or, as Monica Hunter Wilson declared in *Reaction to Conquest* (Wilson 1936), 'the standardized nightmare of the group' (Bank 2013; Wilson 1951) – but rather one among several types of relations between persons and persons and objects and persons.

After divination, 'throwing the bones', if the patient can be protected in ways that are specific to the relationships thus revealed rather than to the specifics of the diagnosed illnesses, healing can take place without respect to the specific illness or loss of luck. Herbs (*umuthi*, 'muti') and ritual (*sebenta*, 'work') may be prescribed for specific illnesses, or may be sought elsewhere, but the diagnosis is not the primary effect of divination by throwing bones, it heals by exposing the patient to the unseen, forceful reality that exists around him or her.

Through exposure patients become subjectively aware of their own condition and of their relations with others. While confession, involuntary exposure or divination reveal the previously unseen lineaments of a relevant social order, they also give access to these relations. Patients' illnesses are the result of being subject to the unseen intentions of others but once those intentions are revealed patients can become the subject of their own social action. They are no longer the passive targets of others, but can 'take control of their life'. With a renewed sense of agency, or even autonomy, patients can now act with intention to heal themselves.

The beginning of a divination/healing seance frequently goes something like this:

> Sangoma (S): I can sense that you are not well/and put your stick in the middle (are seeking healing)/it has fallen (happened in this way). [*ngiyabona kutsi awusikahle/induku yakho kufuneka uyibeke emakhatsini/atikho tiwile.*]
> Patient/client (P): We agree. [*Siyavuma.*]
> S: They have fallen with dirt/filth.
> P: We agree, we agree [with what you say]. [*Siyavuma, siyavuma.*]
> S: The head aches, the shoulders are too heavy.
> P: We agree, we agree.
> S: Also an abnormal heartbeat. Just there, inside your stomach.
> P: We agree, we agree.
> S: Both the feet and knees are infected.
> P: We agree, we agree.
> S: When you try fixing this side, another side is ruined; you didn't do it on purpose.
> P: We agree, we agree.
> S: And then you also will have pains. I feel [hear] them inside my uterus.

P: We agree, we agree.

S: Your knees and feet are also affected; something done purposely.

P: We agree, we agree.

S: Wherever you are, you are living an uncomfortable life. Surely, it is painful on the path you take/they say that you are the biggest witch.

[*Vele, kubuhlungu ngalendlela kwenteka ngayo/batsti ungumtstakatsi lomkhulu*]

P: We agree, we agree.

S: But it is not like that.

P: We agree, we agree.

S: You have to be very careful now/your doors are closed/things are not good for you/your heart is broken/you are worried because of your shoulders, your headache/and the heartbeat you have been getting/it makes you tired.

Suddenly both see something in the 'bones' on the mat.

P: [How] can you see the man?

[*Uwumbona njani lobabe!?*]

S: The one that belongs to you?/Here he is [*pointing to one of the bones on the mat representing the 'man'*]. They have put you into a corner outside/you are not allowed to stand next to him/look where you came from/they have put a spell on you/to make sure you two lovers are separated.

[*labakukhipele ekhoneni ngaphandle akufuneki wena ufole ukubeleni kwalo babela angitis niyatsandzana kufunka ubelakubeleni naye manje buka kutsi usukaphi, bakufaka nesicintfo kutsi vele nihlukane nalobabe.*]

P: Go with it, Healer.

[*Hamba naso, Gogo.*]

S: They have cursed you.

[*Usivumise, kutsi bakuloyile.*]

P: We agree, we agree.

[*Siyavuma, siyavuma.*]

S: It is that woman that has bewitched you.

[*Uloye ngalomsikatsi.*]

The sequence of revelations by the sangoma is rhythmic and antiphonal, each statement followed by *siyavuma*, 'we agree', from the client/patient, until the rhythm is broken by something remarkable. Here, 'the man' suddenly catches the attention of both the healer and client. Quite rapidly it is revealed that a man (the lover) and another woman (the man's other lover and the patient's rival) are involved in the woman's problems. It is also revealed that while the client has been accused of being a 'big witch' another woman, who wishes to separate her from the man, has also bewitched her. It is these relationships that take up the rest of the consultation in this case, and the specific somatic symptoms (pain, knees, shoulders, heartbeat) are never mentioned again.

In the southern African healing process, being exposed – that is, being vulnerable and acknowledging vulnerability – is to act the part of the exposed being. While the exposed being is vulnerable to harm it is also the only condition in which healing can be effected since one must also be vulnerable to the healing process itself, and to the healer.

Both healer and healed are 'exposed' and vulnerable. Whether they are healed or wounded, or perhaps both, depends on the actions of other persons, tangible (real human beings, but also other tangible objects or animal 'familiars') and intangible persons. The 'ancestors' influence this outcome together with other intangible persons such as witches and tangible non-persons such as plants or 'herbs'. In Chapter 9, for instance, the herb *Boophone disticha* is used by both healer and patient to induce a trance in which they can investigate what is ordinarily not visible. In this case, the plant allows the patient to 'see' the witch. But this is a very dangerous act since, in the dreamscape that one inhabits during trance, the witch can see the patient (the one who drinks the *B. disticha* concoction) and possibly also the healer. If the healer is not equipped with stronger protection, healer and patient are exposed to possible death at the hands of the witch. Since many patients do, in fact, die from this treatment, it is used only as a last resort, and their possible death is already fully comprehended.

In southern African healing traditions, across all ethnicities, healers often cite sexual contact as a source of danger. Sex is hardly taboo, but it can be a conduit of danger emanating from other sources, especially death or other forms of pollution. Thus, sex with a woman who has had an abortion or a still-birth, or who recently attended a funeral, can cause a man a generalised illness, *fufunyane*, characterised by coughing and swelling. Notably, it does not cause sexual illnesses but rather illnesses and weakness in other parts of the body. Sex itself is not held to cause illness but is a point of weakness through which other dangers can exert their influence.

Similarly, the practice of 'virginity testing' presents another example of exposure. In Limpopo province, especially among tshiVenda speakers, girls were secluded for up to two weeks while 'grannies' or 'aunties' cooked for them and 'spoiled them', but also subjected them to daily 'tests'. While in seclusion the girls were forbidden to dress. They went to school, but returned to the house where they were secluded and lay down with their legs spread 'to see if anything had happened' that day. The older women separated their labia, and probed them with their fingers to 'check' their status. According to my informant, Singo, a Venda woman of the 'royal family', what the girls feared most was not the digital penetration – they had been prepared for that – but that the elder female leaders of the traditional school could put 'medicine' secretly into their vaginas. This medicine could cause them to fall ill but, above all, could prevent conception or block the birth of a child, causing the mother to die.

Witchcraft, subjectivity and rationality

Evans-Pritchard wrote in *Witchcraft, Oracle and Magic among the Azande* (1937) that he believed he had solved the problem of the rationality of witchcraft beliefs by distinguishing between the social or moral power of witchcraft and otherwise 'rational' or scientific explanations of events that were ascribed to witches. He discussed the case of a granary that had fallen on a man, killing him. He noted that the Azande were perfectly aware that termites had weakened the support posts so that the granary could fall at any time. However, the Azande people with whom he discussed this matter insisted that it was a witch or sorcerer that had caused the granary to fall at that moment on that man. A moral or social cause was therefore cognitively compatible with a scientific one. This, he said, was how witchcraft worked: it was a supplemental causal system functioning as a sort of moral parallel to the physical, natural world in which termites, not witches, caused granaries to fall. This truncated logic is not necessarily wrong; rather, it is incomplete.

But there is another way to understand the relationship between the 'natural powers' of ants, the quality of the timbers supporting the granary, the unfortunate man who was killed and the 'social' powers of the witch. In southern African healing systems – and probably others as well – the ants, the timbers and the humans are all active agents in the constitution of the situation. This is not to say that 'nature' or science and human agency are confused. Human agency or 'power' is equivalent to, and influenced by, the 'power' of other substances, other persons, natural agents, unconscious or consciously intending human agents and even intangible persons such as ancestors or witches.

The 'witch', then, gets too much attention in the Western theoretical framework, largely because, for the most part, it is only possible to think in terms of what Max Weber, in his canonical work on social theory called 'social action', or agency (Weber 1978: 24). There is also a heavy overlay of Christian thought in Africa deriving especially from Augustine, Bishop of Hippo, in which wholly immaterial agents – God, Jesus or Holy Spirit – are held to be the ultimate cause of all things. The djinns, spirits, angels and other immaterial, transcendental agents of a 'spiritual' realm are strong characteristics of the Abrahamic, Judeo-Christian-Islamic religions that derive ultimately from the Mediterranean Neolithic. For both Weber and Augustine these entities are versions of an abstract immaterial agency. For Weber this amounts to a means-ends rationality (*Zweckrationaliteit*), while for Augustine it was the transcendent reason of 'spirit', whose ultimate purpose was unfathomable. In southern African healing systems, by contrast, all agents, whether tangible or intangible, are held to have presence (*isithunzi*) or 'shadow' and determinable intentions.

By shifting attention to the 'patient', or victim, it is possible to see that the witch's magical power is equally the victim's exposure to this power. A witch is not a witch without a victim or target. Neither may have conscious knowledge of being either a witch or a victim. In effect, this is because everyone could, or might, be either. The fundamental issue is their vulnerability to each other and the understanding of personhood that this implies.

By contrast, in practice in the cases I have observed, the healer and the patient do not focus on the witch but rather on the ways in which 'the witch' can be identified, and the means by which one can be protected from its influence. Whether or not they actually *believe* in witches people are concerned with protection from witchcraft among a number of other non-agentive 'scenarios' of vulnerability or 'spiritual insecurity' (Ashforth 2005: 7ff). Witches, moreover, are only one type of danger. Ancestors, colleagues, family members, neighbours, 'spirits', god/God, objects, medicines, places (such as crossroads, behind the house, at a gate, in the bush), sexual substances, death and many other tangible and intangible influences can all affect the patient.

Apotropaic magic and the therapeutic process

Apotropaic magic is not a therapeutic process. Therapy involves a set of linked procedures, some of them ritual or 'magical', but each of them consequent upon the other in discrete, controllable steps. Therapy starts with a known condition – a diagnosis – and proceeds towards a 'cure'. In this it may be entirely ineffective or somewhat unpredictably efficacious, but it is a process that promises a better state of being rather than the prevention of one that could be much worse.

The classic apotropaic acts and rituals, on the other hand, are those of the Mediterranean, where 'the hand of Fatima', an *oculus* on the prow of a ship, a gesture such as spitting, among many others, are designed to prevent harm from the 'evil eye', the jealousy of others, or from the hidden dangers of *shetani*/satans, spirits, sprites and other sources of harm. Women, children and those with madness or illness or in ritual states of impurity are especially vulnerable and Mediterranean cultures, probably from as early as the Neolithic revolution through antiquity and up to modern times, exemplify apotropaic magic in these settings. In southern Africa the reliance on apotropaic rituals and gestures is less formalised and stylised and specifics vary. This is primarily because, unlike those in the Mediterranean region with up to 20 000 years of stable settlement, southern African cultures can often boast at most only 2 000 years.

This apotropaism in traditional health practices is much more important than therapeutic process. In other words, the outcome of a session with a traditional healer is far more likely to be an attempt to protect against harm than therapy. This is often articulated in terms of 'treating the root causes'. The 'root causes', the source of illness, are often not a disease that can be treated, but rather a condition of life that can only be mediated by avoiding what might be worse.

Unlike the notions in many Western European cultures of the unpredictability of 'luck', in the southern African culture luck (*inhlanhla*) is not distributed randomly. It may be unexpected, but it is not random. Luck favours the lucky, and being lucky, that is, having good fortune, depends on the luck of others, and especially the luck they see others having. This sets up 'unlucky-ness' that can affect the luck of others.

The contrast can also be represented, to a degree, as prevention versus cure, or as avoidance versus acceptance, or as a focus on the external 'social' context (as in 'social causation of illness') versus a focus on the internal functionality of the organism. We might contrast these two approaches in approximate terms as apotropaic magic versus therapeutic process. But none of these distinctions should be understood as simple opposites, or 'binary oppositions' since the apotropaic magic of the healer is not an 'opposite' to medical therapy, or even to therapeutic 'magic'. Each involves a complex cultural framework in which both healer and healed, agent and patient, doctor and client are differently represented.

A system of medical beliefs that relies primarily on apotropaism rather than therapy (including remediation and cure, or hope of cure) does not tend towards any sense of 'therapeutic citizenship' as Vinh-Kim Nguyen (2010) has used this phrase. His notion of 'therapeutic citizenship' is constituted by the patient's belief that rights and obligations are dependent on certain kinds of illness and entrance into the 'republic of therapy' involves the right to be treated and, ultimately, cured, if possible. This confers a kind of citizenship on a disease, especially for those diseases, like HIV/AIDS, that are heavily and disproportionately funded by international donors and international medical research.

The public health practitioner, by contrast, works with less than the person – in the sense that an abstract person is less than the reality – and begins with a generalisation concerning the bodies of persons. The healer's 'public' is not the political public as either citizens of the state or as subjects of a king or chief, but rather the generalisation of his or her patient(s). This public is not an abstract entity and is not enumerable by census or treatable by a generalised intervention.

The medical system of the sangomas creates only networks of healers and patients – many of whom carry both roles – and does not lead to the institutionalisation of specific forms of suffering. Patients do not suffer as a population and are not treated as 'republics of therapy' because they suffer with and through each other, as related persons rather than as categories.

The sangoma's public

Clearly then, traditional healers are not and can never be public health practitioners (Thornton 2003). They are often recruited as public health auxiliaries, for instance to assist in diagnosing TB and recruiting patients, but to the extent that they fulfil this function they are simply participating in a different game. This is not and can never be 'healing' in the traditional, *bungoma*, sense of the word. The healer's patient, is not an element of a population, a subject of a state and 'effect' of power/discourse or a citizen of a (re)public.

Curiously, this different theorisation of the suffering patient and the healer does not imply 'holism', or 'holistic' health. A healthy person in the traditional African sense in southern Africa does not require wholeness but rather a regulated partiality, or controlled partibility, in which the person acquires strength, or goodness (*ubuhle*), or health (*imphilo*) and 'fortune' (*inhlanhla*) and can be said to possess well-being (*inhlala kahle*) as the result of balancing the parts of his or her person, both integral and external, tangible and intangible.

The concept of the person, then, is not so much a subject to an abstract 'society' in Mauss's or Durkheim's sense (Carrithers, Collins and Lukes 1985; Mauss 1985 [1938]), or as subject to the state as an element of a public, but rather as a variably partible person. The *person is a process* in which each human entity is continuous in time and across other persons and social contexts. In terms of this assumption a public that might have 'health' as one of its attributes – as in the notion of 'public health', the health of a population composed of persons whose 'bare life' is primarily at stake – does not hold. This is because there is no concept in southern African *bungoma* that fully parallels the Western notion of 'the public'.

In the world of southern African small towns, villages, townships, squatter camps and informal settlements people are especially vulnerable to each other. The state – as police, public health practitioners, state hospitals and clinics, and even water supply and other services – is often quite distant. In many ways the state even disavows its claim to these citizens.

Under the apartheid policy of 'separate development' several large parcels of South Africa were given 'independence'. There is no more effective disavowal of the state's claim to a people than this. The post-apartheid state has continued to shirk responsibility for the marginal, the poor and the rural by allocating them unserviced 'farms' (in South African land affairs these may be tens of thousands of hectares in extent), placing them under 'traditional authority' or simply ignoring them. The lack of public protection and effective public health means that people are most at risk from other people. The political conditions for a 'biopolitics' in the Foucauldian sense are, therefore, largely lacking.

But more than this, the clients of traditional healers and complementary and alternative medicine practitioners in these circumstances also experience what they call witchcraft (*butsakatsi*) and the call or influence of the ancestors. They also acknowledge – sometimes with fear, sometimes with gratitude and trust – the influence of current and previous lovers, family members, neighbours, political associates, bosses and subordinates, among others. In fact, each person involved in a social relationship involving property, kinship, love, power or trust is believed to have a more or less direct, but intangible and 'spiritual', power over another. Each human being is exposed to every other in a radical way. This is not understood as a co-mingling of substances, as has been claimed for the 'dividual' person in Hindu religious practice, nor a concept of pollution, as is evident in the Judeo-Christian traditions and other earlier Mediterranean religious beliefs. It is also not necessarily a concept of contagion or of infection as understood by biomedical sciences. It is a sense of mutual participation that may be more or less beneficial, but is also necessary and inescapable. It is a sense of deeply persistent bonds that make each human being vulnerable to others. Each person in search of healing is also searching for protection from excessive exposure to others. The patient of the healer in this context comes as an 'exposed being', not merely (or even) ill, but *susceptible* to the other.

But a patient must also be vulnerable to healing and 'in the market' for healing. As people are vulnerable to the influence of witches, other tangible persons (that is, other human beings with whom they have social relationships) and to intangible person-like agents ('ancestors', 'spirits'), so must the client of a healer, as patient and sufferer, be vulnerable to the healing practices that are offered. To be healed, in other words, means being exposed, and acknowledging this exposure as one acknowledges one's exposure to spirits, to evil, to death and misfortune. It is only through this double-sided acknowledgement of vulnerability to good and evil, health and sickness, that one can be transformed into another. The healing that a sangoma offers (*kuphila*) is understood as a transformation, just as becoming a sangoma involves a transformation of consciousness called *ukuthwasa*.

In southern African concepts of healing and the sources of illness and evil causes are mutually vulnerable since they are all agents of one kind or another. The witch is vulnerable to protective medicine turned against him/her, the 'spirit' and ancestor can be thwarted, their influence barred, albeit perhaps only temporarily. The world in which a sangoma and his or her patient operate is conceived as a complex web of mutual causation and interacting *vulnerable* agents. Agency and its consequences (that is 'causes') can be blocked or reflected back, either permanently or temporarily.

The concept, then, of mutually vulnerable multiple agents, in which the patient and the healer are enmeshed as elements of a larger system of powers and protections or 'reflectors' can help us to understand how *magical empiricism* (Chapter 10) might work and how healing that uses 'magic' as a 'logically flawed' imaginary force works. But it also has huge implications for the way in which we understand how patients are recruited from the 'public' by both the healer and the biomedical or public-health practitioner.

These differences become especially relevant at the level of the person as a member of the public, as a subject of the state and as an anonymous biological element of a population.

The subject/patient of the traditional healer is never stripped of his or her social being like the subject of the modern medical and public health regime, who can be characterised as having only 'bare life' or 'biological life as such' and who can be 'killed but not sacrificed' (Agamben 1998: 10; cf. Caton 2006: 122) relative to the biopolitical sovereignty of the state (Foucault). Such a person is merely an element of the 'population'. Instead, the subject of the traditional healer possesses not 'bare life' but 'exposed being' and is never an element of a 'population':

> According to Foucault, a society's 'threshold of biological modernity' is situated at the point at which the species and the individual as

a simple living body become what is at stake in a society's political strategies...In any case, however, the entry of *zoē* into the sphere of the polis – the politicization of bare life as such – constitutes the decisive event of modernity and signals a radical transformation of the political-philosophical categories of classical thought. It is even likely that if politics today seems to be passing through a lasting eclipse, this is because politics has failed to reckon with this foundational event of modernity (Agamben 1998: 10).

The tragic events of the Holocaust and, indeed, of twentieth-century war, terrorism and genocide are understandable only if 'these decisive events of our [twentieth] century have their foundation in the unconditional assumption of a biopolitical task in which life and politics become one ("Politics, that is, giving form to the life of the people")' (Agamben 1998: 86).

If, as Giorgio Agamben argues, sovereignty claimed over 'bare life' is the beginning of biological modernity, might it be correct to understand the vulnerability of the exposed being as un-modern, 'primitive', or 'African'? Are the *zoē* and *bios* of Agamben and Foucault the 'modern' attributes of the human being as subject to the state, subject to 'discourse', while the exposed being is simply rooted in logical error and is therefore 'pre-modern'?

One way of answering this question is to look at the role of 'bare life' versus 'exposed being' in the constitution of human suffering and vulnerability at the *extreme*, at the margins of the system. This is an argument based on the limits of the system that seeks to lay bare the systematicity of its limiting cases.

Agamben, for instance, wonders why Hannah Arendt's work on totalitarianism never managed to take on the issues that Foucault highlighted so well, especially at the end of his life, those of the biological, the 'bare life', the *zoē*. Foucault, he also notes, fails to deal critically with the nature of the totalitarian state despite his concern with the pervasive power of the state – more or less trivialised in his metaphor of 'capillaries' of power in the pervasive networks of everyday life:

While both of these powers concern the domestic jurisdiction of the head of the family and therefore remain, in some way, within the sphere of the *domus*, the vitae *necisque potestas* attaches itself to every free male citizen from birth and thus seems to define the very model of political power in general, not simple natural life, but life exposed to death (bare life or sacred life) is the originary political element (italics in original) (Agamben 1998: 55).

For Agamben the *homo sacer* or 'sacred person' exists at the limits of what it is to be human. This is the person who possesses no more than a 'bare life', who can be killed without consequence. The *homines sacres* exist in a world that Victor Turner called the 'betwixt and between' and that Agamben (1998: 91) called the 'extratemporal and extraterritorial threshold', where the person is subject 'to the most extreme misfortunes'. For sangomas and their patients, however, all persons exist in this state, as sacred persons who are always susceptible to the most extreme misfortunes. This mutual exposure as both sacred and mundane, necessary and yet avoidable *for the time being*, allows an understanding of the appeal of healers' magic, their flawed logic and their surprising efficacy.

Healers and healed alike are exposed beings, always necessarily vulnerable to other tangible and intangible persons, including 'witches' and 'ancestors'. Thus, while life, *zoē*, is the natural and inalienable condition of all humans, our mutual exposure – vulnerability – as 'exposed beings' will eventually tell and misfortunes, including death itself, will inevitably come to pass.

CHAPTER 9

Magical weevils and amaryllis in southern African ritual landscapes

The healer is embedded in the southern African landscape and his or her world is not confined to the human, but is multi-species and trans-ethnic. The material logic of magic in healing uses parts of plants and animals and minerals such as ochre as intrinsically active agents. The sangoma feels – dreams (-*phupha* [isiZulu], -*toro* [Sesotho-Setswana]), senses, or 'hears', (-*zwa* [isiZulu], -*kwa* [Sesotho-Setswana]) – that things like animals, plants, stones and other parts of nature, including the landscape, have agency: they act and can be guided, but they are not inert 'ingredients' or tools. By contrast, in the popular imagination *muti* herbs and animal parts are inert substances, or materials, that healers use as a medical doctor uses pharmacological chemicals or prosthetic devices. Instead, in *bungoma*, these items *speak directly to the healers and their patients*, not through a biological or physiological process, but as an intangible presence. This is what connects the healer, the patient and nature and leads them to the therapeutic process.

A world beyond the human: The multi-species trans-ethnic world of the healer

A healer's use of a large beetle (*Brachycerus ornatus*, Red-spotted Lily Weevil) and the beetle's food plant, the poisonous bulb known as 'Bushman's poison bulb' (*Boophone disticha* or *Ammocharis coranica*) illustrates this transcendence of ethnic and even human boundaries. These cultural practices link a species of beetle, a plant and specialised healing practices that transcend the ethnic, political, racial, and linguistic boundaries of San (|Xam, among others), Khoe ('Koranna', 'Hottentot'), Bantu-speaking peoples and even southern Africans of European ancestry (see Watt and Breyer-Brandwijk 1962 for the variety of plants used across all ethnic groups). These relationships extend over considerable historical time and are embedded in a landscape that they help to shape and which, in turn, presents possibilities and constraints for human dwelling (Ingold 2011, 2012). The location and lifeways of plants and animals in the landscape and their relationships with human users exemplify what, in anthropology, has recently been called 'nature-culture' and opens a chapter in what is being called the new 'multispecies ethnography' (Kirksey 2010; Kirksey and Helmreich 2010; Langlitz 2011) that constitutes 'a growing body of research pointing to the importance of animals in processes of knowledge formation, social organisation and bodily regulation' (Porter 2013: 133).

These 'magic bundles' incorporate plant and animal materials in the context of cultural meanings of landscapes and other non-human lifeforms in order to offer protection against witches and evil and in hunting, trance and healing, practices that are regional rather than 'ethnic' or 'tribal' and span San (Bushman), Khoe, Bantu and Afrikaans cultures. The practices integrate sets of relations that link human, plant, animal and mineral elements in what has been called 'natureculture' and 'human-animal collectivities'. These include stone tools made from large stone flakes of local dolerite (diabase) that are made opportunistically on the spot – a contemporary reinvention, or in continuity with ancient lithic technologies – thus linking the mineral with plant and animal parts of the landscape. Landscape and culture are seen to be mutually productive.

Items of material culture belonging to this tradition have largely disappeared in southern Africa itself, partly because plastic or manufactured goods have replaced earlier materials and partly because a healer's kit is buried with the healer at his or her death. During the eighteenth and nineteenth centuries, however, missionaries, travellers, hunters, explorers, soldiers, police and civil officials collected (purchased, purloined or took by force or persuasion) many elements of this cultural heritage because healers, indigenous doctors and 'witchdoctors' were both a curiosity and a threat to Christianity, sometimes also to secular power and, above all, to 'modern' medicine, or even to 'modernity' itself. Today most early examples of this material exist primarily in European collections.

Beetles on a string

When I found a set of six dried beetles strung together on a leather thong in the Naprstek Ethnological Museum in Prague in 2011 I was intrigued. Some years earlier I had begun to try to piece together a history of what is called 'traditional healing' in southern Africa. From the healer's own perspective this effort is meaningless, since healing knowledge comes always from dreams, the ancestors, the bush and the landscape itself. Knowledge and practices thus have no history: from the sangoma's perspective they are always already there. From my anthropological perspective a complex history certainly existed, but archives and texts do not exist. Archaeology and the study of material culture were the only options. Since healers have

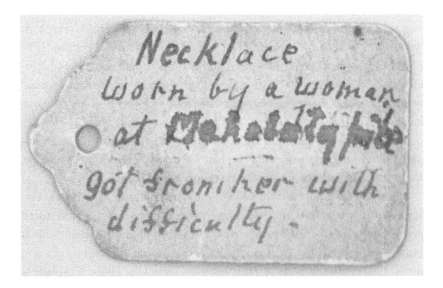

FIGURE 9.1: The label of the 'Bamangwato beetle amulet'. It reads 'Necklace worn by a woman at M[?, illegible], got from her with difficulty'. Naprstek Ethnological Museum, Prague (Photograph: Robert Thornton).

and use large collections of material culture, especially strings of beads and other objects, examination of these provided one way to solve the problem.

Glass beads have been used in southern Africa for well over 1 000 years (Wood 2000) and bead-like objects (small round objects with holes in them) appeared in the archaeological record approximately 42 000 years ago, and possibly as long ago as 75 000 years (D'Errico, Ten Rhyne and De Grevenbroek 2012). They form a large part of some of the earliest archaeological finds and are made of stone, shell, bone, teeth, ivory and probably other more perishable materials and appear to have been strung together. Placed in an interpretive context of southern African modes of healing and ritual protection these assemblages or bundles of objects seem to be stable over a very long period of southern African history.

But beads and beaded objects are generally included in catch-all categories of objects without obvious utility or nutritional use. Although they are usually labelled as 'decorative', 'ornament', 'jewellery' or as 'ritual objects' – and certainly have these functions too – they usually belong to the healing cults of the region and have many functions, including apotropaic magic, control of flows of blood, spirit and 'energy' in the body or as gifts and objects of value in exchanges.

Writing about minimally modified bead-like items of this sort in the archaeological record, Francesco d'Errico et al. (2009: 16055) remark that 'ornaments made of slightly modified natural objects establish a powerful symbolic link between the natural and cultural worlds in which humans lived and continue to live in southern Africa'. The objects are often also intrinsically beautiful, attractive, colourful, crafted and made of unusual materials, but they not merely decorative. They represent 'entanglements' across [animal and human] species (Porter 2013: 144), or 'the collective set of dependencies between humans and things … between things and other things, and between humans and other humans … [that] draws humans into the lives, interactions and uncertainties of things' (Hodder and Mol 2015: 2).

The beetle amulet was a case in point. It had been collected between 1875 and 1879 in what is today Botswana by Dr Emil Holub, a Czechoslovakian medical doctor who made extensive, even exhaustive collections of Tswana material culture. He attributed it to the region of the Bamangwato, the Tswana paramountcy under the chief Khama.

But why did people put dead beetles on a string?

Parts of plants and animals used in healing act directly not only as symbols standing for something else but as agents in and of themselves. Only if the patient and healer is open to these forces, as an 'exposed being', can therapy be effective (Thornton 2012a). This is why a beetle protects, why the holes from which herbs are dug are left open, why effective therapy must be dreamed and why hallucinations induced by plants such as *Boophone disticha (L. f.)* allow one to 'see' witches in their own landscapes, among other things.

Three of the beetle amulets in the museum collections are strung together with glass beads. Archaeological, historical and anthropological analysis of objects like glass beads often consider each element separately as a 'type' of artefact. Such approaches neglect the whole object of which beads are a part. Even considering the whole object is insufficient, since the object only has effect when it is part of a much larger social and natural context. This is why, for instance, most contemporary black African users of *muti* are very sceptical about whether such things 'work' on white people *out of context* and why magical items lose their effectiveness once 'collected' by police, or others, including anthropologists and museum collectors. It is worthwhile, then, to understand the objects not merely as wholes, but as parts of a living space, or, in short, a landscape.

Beads are almost always parts of other objects such as necklaces, dolls, dress, ritual regalia, votive, religious or other ritual objects. It is the whole object – the bundle, string or 'decorated' object – that has cultural significance, although each bead also carries meaning and value based on size and colour, among other features. Beads are also parts of strings of relationships.

Beads and beaded strings/things/bundles mediate social relations as they are given and received in reciprocal relationships involving love, marriage, healing and protection. They participate in exchanges across generations and between men and women and are given to the 'ancestors' or 'spirits'. The latter beings constitute a category of intangible persons, or agents, that involves a bundle of concepts including *umdlozi, ithongo, isithunzi, umoya* [isiZulu]; *moya, modimo, seriti* [Sesotho/Setswana], among others; terms which are usually translated as 'ancestor', 'spirit', 'shadow' or 'god'.

The land and landscape play a central role in southern African healing traditions. The distinction between settled ground or homestead

(*Umuzi/-sendle*, *hlathi* [isiZulu, Nguni]; *motse/naga* [Setswana]) and the 'bush' or the 'wild' is fundamental (Comaroff and Comaroff 1990: 198). People – and intangible persons called 'ancestors', among others – exercise power over one another in the settled area, while the power of earth and plant and animal life provides energies of a different kind. Often the power of earth, plants and animal parts to heal is called 'medicinal', or magical, or simply 'witchcraft'. Their power, however, derives from the fact that they are not part of people's powers over each other. They are not, and cannot be, witches, or any other kind of person, tangible and living, or intangible. These persons and presences inhabit the house, village or town. The power of plants to 'heal' depends first of all on their being from the wild and on their ability to connect living persons to their own *impersonal* power, that is, a power that is not connected to the power of other people; a power to heal or harm or to influence one another in other ways. Since most of the work and healing methods of southern Africa's healers concerns management of relationships, the use of elements of the bush – types of earth, plant and animal parts – plays a very large role. Thus, medicines are always mixed: earth, plant, animal and human are combined. Powdered herbs (plant) are combined with ochres (earth) and fats (animal); powerful objects are strung and worn with other, different objects. Shell and stone beads are strung

FIGURE 9.2: *Brachycerus ornatus.* This local variant has a rougher shell and variably-shaped red spots. University of the Witwatersrand Entomology Collection, School of Animal, Plant and Environmental Sciences (Photograph: Robert Thornton).

with wood, glass and metal on sinew, for instance. This achieves a balance that is not available in any other way.

Beetles: Unstable interfaces

The use of *B. ornatus* reveals the unstable interface between the human and the animal and between the settled zone of dwellings and the 'bush'. This relationship has been extensively explored first by the San (Bushman) artists in rock art (Rock Art Research Unit 2012) and then by David Lewis-Williams, Thomas Dowson and others who have revolutionised the study of rock art since the 1980s (Clottes and Lewis-Williams 1996; Dowson, Lewis-Williams and Annegarn 1994; Lewis-Williams 1981, 2002; Lewis-Williams and Challis 2011).

They have been able to show that southern African rock art reveals a 'spiritual' (intangible, imaginative, healing) world in which shamans change into animals and back again in order to harness their powers for healing. Drawing specifically on analogies with Siberian shamans they call southern African healers 'shamans' and link these practices specifically to the 'San' or 'Bushmen'.

As Rane Willerslev (2007) shows for the Siberian shamans of the Yukaghirs, animals, plants and humans are endless mimetic doubles of one another (see also Kirksey and Helmreich 2010). This appears to be the way in which the creators of southern African rock art see the plane on which this art is created: as a landscape in which human-animal mimetic doubles create and harness a space of powerful healing energies. Sangomas share a similar set of concepts and practices.

The beetle's food plants have been recorded since the eighteenth century as powerful poisons, medicines and charms against witchcraft among Bushman, Koranna and other Khoikhoin peoples, *trekboere* (early Afrikaans-speaking pastoralists) and among Bantu-speaking peoples. Use and knowledge of the plants extend across all southern African cultures over several centuries, revealing a long-standing cultural ecology involving humans, insects and plants.

The beetle is *Brachycerus ornatus* (Red-spotted Lily Weevil), a large, glossy black beetle with red spots. The plants are *Boophone disticha* and *Ammocharis coranica*. The beetle-plant-human nexus points to a close relationship between African indigenous knowledge systems – traditional healing and witchcraft, in particular – and southern African biogeographies and biodiversity. The plants are widely distributed across southern Africa, but populations are small and very local. Similarly, because the beetle is flightless and dependent on the plants, it is also regionally widespread, but only locally prevalent. The protective magic involved is therefore specific to a locale, but also pervasive across a variegated regional landscape.

A landscape is far more than just the surface properties of land (Árnason, Ellison, Vergunst and Whitehouse 2012; Thornton 1996b, 2000b). In this set of relations we see layer of a rarely-seen landscape that involves 'relations between people, animals, and plants – ultimately between beings and ways of being – in a variety of locales [in which] ... paths of relations serve to open up the complexity of landscape' (Árnason et al. 2012: 5). Healers, beetles and plants inhabit a landscape that is woven into culture, medicine, magic and dress. As Tim Ingold (2012: 206–207) remarks:

> We should not necessarily assume that the relation between land and scapes, identified as optical, is confined to the sensory modality of vision, nor conversely that the contrasting relation identified as haptic [touch, tangible] is confined to the modality of touch ... In recent years it has become fashionable to multiply sensory scapes. Thus we have soundscapes, touchscapes and smellscapes ... In every case, the scape is a formal mapping, in the mind, of the material of the world of sensory experiences.

In this way the beetles become 'good to string', linking landscape and patient, nature and culture: natureculture in healing bundles. This is a landscape that is visible only to those within it and whose plants bring specific visions of its possibilities, and dangers. By 'mapping' these points the healer connects the patient to earth and nation (*umhlaba* [isiZulu], *sechaba* [Sesotho-Setswana]) and creates a 'healing scape'.

The beetle 'amulet' is included among a large number of other artefacts collected by Holub in the 1870s. Holub's collection of Tswana artefacts eventually formed one of the core collections of the Naprstek Museum,

FIGURE 9.3: The 'Bamangwato beetle amulet' consisting of six beetle exoskeletons on a leather thong ©Naprstek Museum of Asian, African and American Cultures, Prague (Photograph: Robert Thornton).

although many other items were dispersed to other museums (Jiroušková, Kandert, Mlíkovský and Šámal 2011).

According to Emil Holub (1881), the items originate from the Ngwato 'tribe', one of the sections ('tribes') of the Tswana people that, since the nineteenth century, has held the paramountcy in what was then the Bechuanaland Protectorate. The centre of the Ngwato polity is the town of Serowe in Botswana, 260km north of Gaborone, the country's capital. Isaac Schapera's *Handbook of Tswana Law and Custom* is based partly on the 'law and custom' of the Ngwato and their neighbours but draws primarily from the Kgatla law. Holub's designation of this as 'Ngwato', however, designated a region more than an ethnic group, since it included people living in the Ngwato territory under the Ngwato paramount chief, including those who married in or were adopted or captured.

The San ('Bushmen', now often called 'Basarwa', though this name is recent), who were noted for the power of their healing rituals and protective magic, and the 'Koranna' (Khoe) were part of this polity. Most speak Afrikaans and/or Setswana today, although some speak Khoe languages. Contrary to widely held notions – both popular and academic – that southern Africans were 'perennial tribesmen', Paul Landau (2010: xi) shows convincingly that 'hybridity lay at the core of [Tswana and other] sub-continental political traditions'. This interpretation of the historical record is increasingly accepted (Morris 2002). It would be misleading to assign the beetle amulet to any specific group, 'Bushman', 'Khoe' or 'Bantu'/Tswana, especially since these categories may have been entirely meaningless when the artefact was made.

There are also three similar items in the British Museum, one consisting of a beaded necklace with a single beetle exoskeleton in the centre (Figures 9.4–9.6), the other two single beetle exoskeletons with two short strings of beads (Figure 9.4). One of these strings is made of blue and white beads, the other of white and pink beads. (In the distinctive colour palettes of southern African beads and beadwork, pink is distinguished from red and usually carries other meanings concerning identity, or the desires of a spirit: see Chapter 7.)

FIGURE 9.4: Two beetle amulets from the British Museum, London ©The Trustees of the British Museum, London.

FIGURE 9.5: Accession book with description of the single-beetle amulets, British Museum, London ©The Trustees of the British Museum, London.

FIGURE 9.6: *Brachycerus ornatus* exoskeleton (front and back) incorporated into a necklace/amulet from the Henry Wellcome Medical History Collection, now in the British Museum (British Museum Acc. No. Af1954,+23.159AN1165312001 and Af1954,+23.159AN1165314001) ©The Trustees of the British Museum, London.

Among the earliest records of beetles used in healing is Robert Jacob Gordon's description of 'beetles' taken out of the leg of a patient, which Gordon observed during travels in 1777 in what is now the Northern Cape. Gordon, then governor of the Cape under the Dutch East India Company, described a healing ritual that would be familiar today among most southern African healers. It is known as *kufemba* ('smelling out') among Nguni-speakers, and is 'barely distinguishable from those carried out by Khoisan in contemporary Namibia' (Low 2004: 68). Gordon (1988 in Low 2004: 68) reported

> an old Hottentot [Khoe] witchdoctor made the youth [the patient] come naked into his hut in the twilight…we went to sit beside the youth, who had a pain in his foot. He rubbed his thigh and his leg, and, holding his foot against his head, roared and growled like a lion and tiger. He then held his hands against the youth's head and heart and did this a few times, after which he sneezed three or four times in succession and, opening his hand, displayed some beetles which he said he had taken from the leg.

In this description beetles *represent* an illness or pain that has been identified by the healer and removed, but they are also active agents since 'someone' put them there in the first place.

The use of the beetle in healing in the nineteenth century is attested to in the records of ǀXam Bushman collected by Wilhelm Bleek and Lucy Lloyd in the late 1860s and early 1870s:

> We do this, to a very little child, we take an African ground weevil [!nu!nurru-ssi][5832 *verso*]. A black little handsome thing, rather round...shaped more like the shell of a tortoise.... [T]hey do (thus) to the little child, that the weevil may take out from [5839] it convulsions.... (Bleek Lloyd Collection, LL.VIII.21; ǀhan≠kass'o)[2] [Numbers in square brackets refer to page numbers in the original manuscript sources, here and *infra*, while comments in square brackets are those of Lucy Lloyd, not the direct speech of her informant.]

And:

> [7822]!nu!nurusi, *Brachycerus* [7821 *verso*] tied on the throat of a little child when the latter is ill with a cold, or with another illness.[3] The *Brachycerus* used as a means of cure for little children [7821' ǀhan≠kass'o from his mother ǀxabbi-an, and personal observation] the *Brachycerus* [7821' (very hard back to pierce)] is the one on account of whom a little child recovers; while it (the *Brachycerus*) is the one who eats the illness.[4]

---

2   Original material is in the Archives of the University of Cape Town but available online at: http://lloydbleekcollection.cs.uct.ac.za/books/ BC_151_A2_1_096/A2_1_96_07822.html

3   ǀhan≠kass'o later applies this term to *Brachycerus obesus* (LL.VIII.31.8790'), presumably after being shown a specimen; this identification is retained by Dorothea Bleek in the Bushman Dictionary (486) as 'the' meaning of the term (although ǀXam insect categorisation is generally more generic than species level) (pers. comm. Dr Mark McGranaghan, Rock Art Research Unit, University of the Witwatersrand, 8 January 2013).

4   Bleek-Lloyd Collection. Available online at: http://lloydbleekcollection. cs.uct.ac.za/books/BC_151_A2_1_044/A2_1_44_03479.html

The beaded objects in Figure 9.6 would hold the beetle at the throat of the person who wore it. It is likely that, when used in the context of the beads and stringing sinews that hold it in place, the beetle 'eats the illness' and its position helps to constitute its ability to heal. The strings of beetles from the Naprstek Museum may well be 'spares' for a similar purpose. Elsewhere in the archive, Ihan≠kass'o remarks that only one beetle is used for each application. Each beetle's ability to eat the illness, then, is individualised.

Khoe and San communities used a considerable number of plant, animal and insect species in healing rituals (De Prada-Samper 2007; Watt and Breyer-Brandwijk 1962). The !nu!nurussi, however, is explicitly defined in the Bleek-Lloyd archive as *Brachycerus* (see Figure 9.7).

The significance of the beetle in 'Bushman' culture is also indicated by a rock engraving of what appears to be a *B. ornatus* beetle. George Stow, a Victorian polymath, recorded the engraving in the 1870s in a pencil drawing. Stow classified these and other rock art and petroglyphs as 'Bushman' art (Rock Art Research Unit) and called them 'mystic symbols' of an ancient race whose 'ancient myths of times yet more remote, when, as they believed, men and animals consorted on more equal terms than they themselves, and used a kindred speech understood by all!' (Morris 2002: 60; Stow and Theal 1905: 398). Authorship is most often ascribed to 'Khoekhoe' (Smith and Ouzman 2004) or 'Bushman', but these labels are unlikely to have been meaningful 1 000 to 2 500 years ago when the engravings may have been made (Morris 2002).

George Stow found and drew these images (Figure 9.8) in what is today the Northern Cape province, on the Riet River some 75km south of Kimberley and more than 500km to the east of where the IXam texts were collected by Bleek and Lloyd. The site, now known as Driekopseiland, is a South African National Heritage Site (www.driekopseiland.itgo.com).

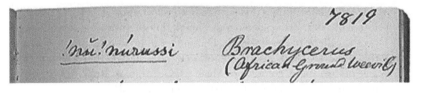

FIGURE 9.7: Definition of |Xam term !nu!nurussi as *'Brachycerus'* (African Ground Weevil).

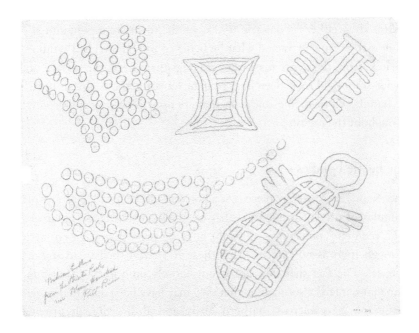

FIGURE 9.8: Drawing (ca. 1870s) by George Stow of 'Bushman' rock engravings showing a six-legged spotted creature that may represent *B. ornatus* (lower right), with other unidentified images – possibly patterns of beads and magical bundles (Source: http://lloydbleekcollection.cs.uct.ac.za/stow/STOW_022.html).

More than 3 500 engravings are pecked into the surface of a glaciated andesite pavement lying in the bed of the river. Although the 'geometric' engravings in Stow's drawing (Figure 9.8) are still visible at the site today (2013), the possible *B. ornatus* figure has been covered since Stow's time by the drifting sediments of the river and is no longer visible (pers. comm. David Morris, Kimberley Museum, Kimberley, Northern Cape, South Africa, 9 February 2013).

If the image does represent *B. ornatus* the rock engraving further demonstrates regional significance and historical depth for the beetle's magic and healing power. Stow's drawing (Figure 9.8), together with others like it, shows patterns of circles representing the original works that are composed of small cupules chipped into the rock. These patterns are strongly suggestive of the patterns of beads and objects that we see in the beaded magical bundles and amulets, although they have been previously described as either 'geometric' (90% of them) or 'representational'. In his drawings Stow extracted what he believed to be individual symbols or 'devices' from the dense mass of engravings that covers the surface of the glacier-smoothed rock. Seen in aggregate, however, these appear more like the bundles of 'medicine' and *muti* that are used in healing and protection throughout the region.

The beetle bundles

The Naprstek Museum piece does not include beads. There are many examples of other San material that use shells or horns as containers to hold 'cosmetic' powders – more likely to be protective than cosmetic – although there is no evidence that these *B. ornatus* shells held any other material. The fact that they are strung loosely on a leather thong in an even number (six) also suggests that they may have been used in divination. Divination pieces across southern Africa are all directionally orientable with a head/tail, right/left, top/bottom orientation so that they can be seen to be 'active' (when the top is showing), cancelled or inactive (bottom up), or to be directing their action to other elements of the divination patterns. Beetle shells, like other shells, and goat astragalus (*talus* or ankle) bones, all have these properties. These pieces are usually paired, too, with a male and female part of each pair. Sets of astragalus bones, widely used in divination sets, also have different roles or 'generations', with each pair representing youth, the middle-aged and elders. This is certainly possible with beetle shells of this sort, which is why the set may have been used in divination.

Divining pieces – seashells such as cowrie and *Conus*, dominoes, dice, ivory and bone pieces – all also have dots, like the beetles. These are interpreted both as numbers and as patterns, in different ways according to context. A large part of a typical full set of divining 'bones' (*amathambo*, [isiZulu]) has dots or markings like these.

The type of beads, or, in the Prague example, absence of beads, is indicative of 'Tswana' (Sotho-Tswana, or better, 'Highveld') cultural usage in the nineteenth century, when these items were collected. While Zulu and other Nguni groups used small 'seed' beads extensively from 1800 or so, Tswana and people in the northern Limpopo and southern

Zimbabwe areas where these items are likely to have been collected used glass beads. The beads they did use generally display colours such as yellow, black and red, like the beads in Figures 3.5 and 3.6, compared with the beads used further south in Nguni contexts where red, black and white are favoured.

Since these were collected as 'amulets' by Holub, a medical doctor, and by Henry Wellcome as part of his collection of medical artefacts, we may conclude that they were used for healing and protection. Although it is tempting to assign these pieces to a specific 'ethnic', 'tribal' or linguistic category, the healing cultures they represent were not restricted to ethnic, linguistic or kinship groupings. This cultural knowledge belonged to specialised healers, not to ethnic or political groups.

The beetle *Brachycerus ornatus*

The *Brachycerus ornatus* beetle belongs to the sub-order Polyphaga ('eat anything') of the Coleoptera ('covered wing') order of insects. This sub-order of beetles contains by far the largest number of species of Coleoptera. The *Curculionides* family of weevils, to which *Brachycerus ornatus* belongs, is one of the largest families within this grouping. The *Brachycerus* genus as a whole is widely distributed throughout Africa, the Mediterranean-Palaearctic and Madagascan ecozones. There are about 500 named and identified species, almost all of which are closely associated with particular food plants and are often endophytic. *B. ornatus* feeds exclusively on *B. disticha* and *A. coranica* (where 'coranica' refers to the Koranna ethnic group of the Khoe peoples). The *B. ornatus* and its food-plants are highly distinctive, prominent within short seasonal periods, endemic to the southern African region, and widely distributed in specific ecological niches.

B. ornatus is a large beetle with a hard-shelled body that reaches 4.5cm. The dried exoskeleton survives handling and can therefore be used in amulets. Though locally conspicuous it appears to have attracted little scientific attention (Louw 1990; Picker, Griffiths and Weaving 2004). It lives in burrows associated with one or two species of the amaryllis family and feeds exclusively on these plants. Describing it for the first time in 1887, Francis Pascoe (1887) noted that 'the number of described species of *Brachycerus* is about 260, by far the greater part being from South Africa and apparently south of the Tugela River'. *B. ornatus* appears to have a limited local prevalence but a wide regional distribution.

There are eight specimens in the collection of the University of the Witwatersrand (personal communication, James Harrison, Wits University) and 41 in the Transvaal Museum in Pretoria, which come from Mozambique (including two collected by the Swiss missionary and ethnographer of the Tsonga/Shangaan people, Henri-Alexandre Junod) and from Botswana (including the Kgalagadi/Kalahari region), Namibia, South Africa and Zimbabwe. Since the beetle is flightless, however, it is likely that all populations are local, perhaps limited to a few concentrations of *B. disticha* or *A. coranica*, its food plant.

The beetle is aposematically coloured, with bright red to red-ochre spots on the abdomen and on glossy black elytrons that are fused, forming a solid case. Aposematic colouring usually alerts potential predators that the insect is poisonous or at least unpalatable. In a multi-year study Schalk Louw (1990) reported no predators on the adult beetle.

It appears that its colouration wards off predators and this may play a role in the use of the beetle in amulets intended to ward off witchcraft (*butsakatsi*) and 'bad luck' (*umkhwazi*), or to bring 'luck' (*umhlanhla*). Black (*-mnyama* [isiZulu]) and red (*-mbomvu* [isiZulu]) are also two of the most significant colours in healing practice, in addition to white (*-mhlope* [isiZulu]).

It is not known whether the beetles are actually toxic, as their food plant, size and colour suggest. Toxins, if present in the beetles, may be acquired from the food plant since these contain poisons that are lethal to humans and cattle and probably also to other species.

The beetle's food plants, *Ammocharis coranica* and *Boophone disticha*

Boophone disticha and the closely related *Ammocharis coranica* figure prominently in all indigenous pharmacopoeias (San, Afrikaans, Khoe, Nguni, Sotho-Tswana and so on), and are used, among many other things, in protective magic against witches and to poison arrows (Nortje 2011: 27, 73; Van Wyk and Gericke 2007: 156, 240). The foliage of the plants, like the flowers, is conspicuous in certain veld environments (see Figures 9.9–9.13).

They are also highly poisonous, producing large numbers of physiologically harmful and psycho-active chemicals, including alkaloids, terpines, phytosteroids and other complex phyto-compounds. Naturalists, missionaries and travellers from the seventeenth to the twentieth century have commented on these plants, often in considerable detail, for both their beauty and their poisonous effect. Robert Jacob Gordon drew the plant he called *Boophone Haemanthoides* in around 1777, which is perhaps the first record of it.

Southern Africa's vast botanical endowment includes many species of the amaryllis family. Examples of these plants were grown in European gardens at least 100 years before the publication of Linnaeus's *Species Plantarum* of 1753 (Milne-Redhead and Schweickerdt 1939: 159), the book on which all modern botanical taxonomy is based. *Ammocharis coranica* and *Boophone disticha* are closely related members of the Amaryllidaceae (Nordal 1982).[5] They are widely distributed in relatively isolated open veld, often near rock outcrops in clay soils.[6] Since the weevil that feeds on these plants, *B. ornatus*, is flightless and does not travel far, populations may be isolated from each other.

The bulbs are large, usually 15cm, but sometimes up to 40cm in isolated areas or as described in historical records (see below). The flower head typically spans half a metre. The leaves of *A. coranica* form an unusual horizontal spiral, with the large, dark green, strap-like leaves lying directly on the ground, while the leaves of *B. disticha* form a vertical fan with the erect blue-green leaves standing up from the bulb: disticha means 'two rows' (Cunliffe and Teicher 2005). Much of *B. disticha* lies above the ground and the bulbs are covered in thin, paper-like scales from the desiccated leaf bases forming the bulb's tunic. The flowers and inflorescence of many pink to mauve florets bloom directly from the bulb before the leaves appear fully in spring to mid-summer. In a veld environment where fire is

---

5   *Boophone disticha* (L.f.) Herb., Bot. Mag. 52: t. 2578 (1825). (Accepted name WCSP).

6   *WCSP (2012) World Checklist of Selected Plant Families.* Facilitated by the Royal Botanic Gardens, Kew. Available at: http://apps.kew.org/wcsp/ Retrieved 1 November 2012. http://apps.kew.org/wcsp/namedetail. do?name_id=300915

frequent the papery covering of the bulb chars, leaving a hard black covering on the above-ground bulb. The flowers are especially dramatic in the spring when the rest of the veld may be burnt black. The large desiccated flower heads detach from the stem in summer and roll across the veld with the wind, depositing already-sprouting seeds.

All southern African ethnic/linguistic groups have used several different genera and species of the amaryllis family of flowering plants for 'medicinal' purposes (Githens 1949; Mason, Puschett and Wildman 1955; Neuwinger 1996; Neuwinger and Mebs 1997; Sandager, Nielsen, Stafford, Van Staden and Jäger 2005; Sobiecki 2014; Watt and Breyer-Brandwijk 1962). 'Bushman' usage of what is probably *B. disticha* or *A. coranica* was recorded by Lucy Lloyd in January 1878, for instance:

> [6088] [The substance with which the pieces of glass are made into arrow heads] It is ǀkwae; it is ǀǀhuanni juice. It resembles a pumpkin; it is round. Its juice is white; it resembles water; its [6089] juice is not a little white; its whiteness resembles milk. It is poison. We cut it and set it down open, then we hold under it a tortoise shell [6090] because we wish its juice to be in the tortoise shell; that we may make ǀkwae of it. And we warming it, making it hot; and we heat it, when it feels hot. Then we [6091] beat cooling it. And we take it up like this with a driedoorn stick,[7] we do this to it with the driedoorn stick, [imitating meanwhile taking it up by rolling it upon a stick] as we make it round [?cool], because we think that we mean to make little springbok arrows.[8]

The bulb seems to have produced both mastic and a poison that were used throughout the region for different purposes. Robert Moffat (1846: 81), a

---

7   Driedoorn (?Driedoring [Afrikaans], 'three thorn') probably refers to the shrub *Rhigozum trichotomum*, of the *Bignoniaceae* family, a common dry land shrub in the Karoo, from which the originator of this text comes. The common name Driedoorn, in Dutch, refers to the Honey Locust, *Gleditsia triacanthos*, a European species.

8   Lucy Lloyd's Book VIII-1, catalogue BC 151 A2 1 076, 10–28 January 1878. Available at: http://lloydbleekcollection.cs.uct.ac.za/books/ BC_151_A2_1_076/A2_1_76_06088.html

missionary of the Scottish Congregational church and father-in-law of the explorer-missionary David Livingstone, was probably talking about the same bulb when he described its use in the Tswana funerary rites for a mature man:

> The grave, which is frequently made in the fence surrounding the cattle-fold, or in the fold itself, if for a man, is about three feet in diameter, and six feet deep. The interior is rubbed over with a large bulb. The body is not conveyed through the door of the fore-yard or court connected with each house, but an opening is made in the fence for the purpose. It is carried to the grave, having the head covered with a skin, and placed in a sitting posture ... [The grave is then filled with earth.] ... A large bowl of water, with an infusion of bulbs, is then brought, when the men and women wash their hands and the upper part of their feet, shouting 'Pula, Pula', rain, rain (Moffat 1846: 81).

In this case it appears that the bulb is rubbed on the walls of the grave to protect the buried corpse and to protect those who have participated in the funeral, who wash their hands with it.

In my research experience the bulbs are used in eastern Mpumalanga traditional medical practices as hallucinogens and for treating a range of other symptoms and complaints, but are also widely known to be poisonous in larger doses. *Boophone disticha*, also known as 'bushman poison' or '*bosiesman se gif*' (Afrikaans), and *incotho* (isiZulu) (Koorbanally, Mulholland and Crouch 2000), is widely grown in the small gardens often kept by healers of many sorts, including sangomas, herbalists and 'prophets' who use it to induce trance and trance-like states.

The bulb is sold in many herbalist and *muti* shops in the Johannesburg urban area. For instance, it was available for R80 in a herbalist shop called the 'Muti King and College' in Roodepoort, a western suburb of Johannesburg. The healer-in-training and shop assistant called it *isibhuko* (mirror in isiZulu) and said the bulb is used 'when the sangomas cannot tell you who the witch is, but can give you this *muti* that you can find out for yourself'. He said it was also called *inqumbu* (queen termite), because of its large size and glossy brown-white colour and its life at the boundary between underground and above ground. Its name, 'mirror', like *incotho* (book), implies visions that reveal the witch through dreams.

The plant has a number of other names, including *incwadi* ('book' in isiZulu), a name that might be derived from the paper-like texture and layering of the tunic around the bulb. It is more likely, however, that both the Setswana *leshoma* (tell, accuse) and the isiZulu *incwadi*, refer to the use of the plant as a kind of 'truth serum'. Venda people, who call it *zwitungulo*, use it, similarly, to find witches or those who have killed or caused harm. The plant is often planted in the corners of homesteads for protection against evil of all kinds. The isiZulu term is applied to both species, *Boophone disticha* and *Ammocharis coranica*.

These plants are often found in close association with the man-made features on the landscape that are often called 'stone circles'. This specimen was in Highveld grassland vegetation a few kilometres south of Machadodorp.

The large bulb growing naturally in the veld holds great potency. The specimen in Figure 9.9 is about 15cm in diameter and is located in uncultivated veld near many loose stone-built ancient structures that are typical of the area. Such plants are usually avoided by people walking in the veld unless they are specifically being sought for use in witch-finding procedures or to replant as protection on the margins of homesteads or in association with dwellings.

FIGURE 9.9: *Isibhuko*, 'mirror', from Muti King and College shop, Roodepoort, Johannesburg.

FIGURE 9.10: *Boophone disticha*, photographed in the field approximately 12.5km south-west of Machadodorp, Mpumalanga, 2012.

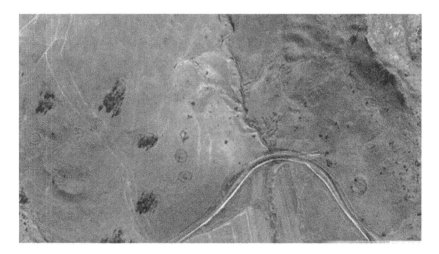

FIGURE 9.11: Site of *Boophone disticha* specimen in Figure 9.10. Note the presence of large stone circles – evidence of ritual use for this ground – in the vicinity. The arrow marks the location of one of the *B. disticha* specimens shown (Source: screen capture from Google Earth).

FIGURE 9.12: Inflorescence of *Boophone disticha* from the same ecological environment as the plant in Figure 9.10. The flowering head is nearly 0.5m across. The scale bar in the photograph is 30cm long.

The *B. disticha* inflorescence shown in Figure 9.12 is over 50cm. The flower heads break off and seem to 'walk' across the veld on their own, maturing seeds at the tips, that seem to plant themselves. Thus, the plant appears to have some agency, a power of its own.

In addition to being sourced in the wild, *B. disticha* is often planted by healers either inside the circle of their 'surgery' or 'spirit house' (*indumba*) or in a stone circle with other important herbs. Magodweni, planted *B. disticha* together with an *Erythrina caffra* (Thunb.) tree in the centre of a stone circle along with *Hypoxis hemerocallidea* (star flower, African potato [Eng], *gifbol* [Afr], *inkomfi* [isiZulu]) and a few maize plants (outer circle). *Erythrina caffra* ('lucky bean', Coast Coral Tree [Eng.], Kuskoraalboom, Kafferboom [Afr.], *umsinsi* [isiZulu]) is known throughout southern Africa as one of the most ritually significant of all plants. In Afrikaans, as in Linnaean Latin taxonomy, it is called Kafferboom ('Kaffer tree', 'African tree' or 'Caffra', in Latin), since this was the name by which the southern coast of South Africa was known in seventeenth-century Europe, where the

FIGURE 9.13: A sangoma's herbal medicine garden, Barberton, Extension 11. The garden was planted and tended by Magodweni.

species acquired its Latin name. It is the 'Spirit tree', where African ances-tors (*madlozi* [isiZulu], *madimo* [Sesotho-Setswana]) and spirits are known to sit. The English name, 'Luckybean tree', also points to its well-known role in ensuring health and protecting from misfortune. Like *B. disticha* and *Hypoxis* it is poisonous, but is nevertheless used cautiously in indige-nous medical applications. *Hypoxis hemerocallidea*, today known widely as 'African potato', and formerly as 'poison bulb' (*gifbol*), like *B. disticha*, has acquired a strong but undeserved reputation as a cure for HIV and AIDS.

Planting all these together within a stone circle creates powerful magic and echoes the form of many much larger stone circles – often believed to be 'cattle kraals' – that are found all over the southern African landscape. The garden in Figure 9.13 is formally identical to the earlier ritual circles in South Africa that are often sought out by people searching for medicinal herbs, since they host many such plants and are held to be especially pow-erful sites in the landscape.

Domsticated, *B. disticha* is planted in the establishments of many sangomas throughout eastern southern Africa, but in nature it prefers undisturbed, often quite remote locations such as the slopes of high mountains. This is possibly because it is heavily exploited when found closer to habitation, but its power is associated with its remoteness, too. The specimen in Figure 9.10 was photographed in a Highveld grassland environment (25°39'57" S 29°59'32" E at 1840.4m above sea level). It was locally fairly plentiful, but generally rare. I have not seen *A. coranica* planted domestically, but it is also widely used and gathered.

Both *A. coranica* and *B. disticha* contain a number of alkaloids that are poisonous, depending on dosage, including Acytylcaranine, Ambelline, Caranine, Crinamine, Lycorine, and many others (Bay-Smidt, Jäger, Krydsfeldt, Meerow, Stafford, Van Staden and Rønsted 2011; Hutchings 1996; Koorbanally, Mulholland and Crouch 2000; Mason, Puschett and Wildman 1955; Van Wyk and Gericke 2007: 156).

The plant is used to treat 'mentally ill patients', hysteria, and 'unspecified afflictions resulting from witchcraft' (Koorbanally, Mulholland and Crouch 2000: 93; Watt 1967). As mentioned above the same substance is also used by the ǀXam Bushmen (and probably others) as a mastic for fixing arrowheads to shafts (Koorbanally, Mulholland and Crouch 2000; Nortje 2011: 27, 73; Pole-Evans 1938). The bulb scales yield a plastic-like pitch when heated and are used to form the torus-shaped headring, *incotho* (or *incoco*) often worn by chiefs and indunas (headmen) among the Swazi and Zulu. Hilda Kuper (1947: 77) notes the use of such headrings, *incotho*, for instance, in the Swazi king's puberty ritual (*sibimbi sokutfomba*): 'In olden times the king and a small number of selected followers would have been crowned after this ceremony with the waxen head ring which marked the age of marriage.'

Although this custom was abandoned under the reign of Sobhuza II, the 'waxen headring' was most likely made of *Boophone disticha* or the *Ammocharis coranica* plant, also called *incotho* (like the headring) in isiZulu and siSwati. It is copied, however, in other materials and is still used today in ritual contexts.

Rather than simply signalling status or 'coming of age', the significance of the ring probably had a great deal to do with its power to protect against evil, witchcraft and misfortune. That is why chiefs and those with political power or status wore it.

FIGURE 9.14: The black headring (*incotho*) can be seen on the head of the senior representative of King Mswati of Swaziland (right front in photograph), in attendance at the Chief's *ummemo*, or annual community levy, October 2009. The Chief (*inkosi*), Prince Kenneth Dlamini of Emjindini 'Royal Swazi Tribal Trust', is in the centre with Julius Matsebula, Emjindini headman (*induna*) and Senior Curator, Barberton Museum, to the Chief's right. The author is in the second row, towards the far left of the photograph.

Since use against witchcraft is attested to in the literature on medicinal plants and since the headring is held to be an effective protection against witchcraft, it is likely, too, that the *Brachycerus ornatus* beetle was also held to be protective against witchcraft. Because the beetle consumes these amaryllids, which contain significant amounts of alkaloids and other poisons and psychotropic agents, it is likely that it also acquired some chemical protective effect against predators.

Brachycerus and the amaryllids in southern African history

The Swedish naturalist Carl Per Thunberg was probably the first to collect an amaryllis type specimen. In 1778 he described the specimen as: 'Poisonous bulbous plants (*giftbolles*), *Amaryllis disticha* [*Boophone*, in this locality *B. haemanthoides*] grow commonly in several places. Hottentots use the roots for poisoning their arrows' [Thunberg, C. P. 2: 163, 2 November 1778] (Koorbanally, Mulholland and Crouch 2000; Nortje 2011: 27, 73; Pole-Evans 1938).

Thunberg called the plant *Amaryllis disticha*, but the following years brought much disagreement among naturalists over the classification of the amaryllids of southern Africa. John B Ker-Gawler, however, is responsible for the relatively stable nomenclature of the plant for most of the nineteenth and early twentieth centuries. In 1816 he described a plant, which he called *Amaryllis coranica*, in the 'Botanical Register', tab 139, noting that 'This plant had been collected by Burchell in the "Corana" [Koranna] country...several days' journey beyond the Orange River.'

John Barrow (1802) may have been the next to describe the amaryllids in the Cape. Travelling in what is now the Northern Cape, near Kamieskroon (30°15'925" S 17°57'114" E), in April 1798, he described with equal disgust the pendulous breasts of an 'old Hottentot woman' and the 'want of points and uninterrupted rotundity' of a Dutch woman, suggesting that 'some principle...that sheds its influence on the animal and even on the vegetable part of creation' was responsible for the disproportion of both. The example he gave of 'vegetable creation' was the enormous bulbs and flowers of several of the amaryllids, including *B. disticha*:

> Another species of Amaryllis, called by the botanists the *disticha* [identified as *Boophone disticha* by Skead], common on all the mountainous part of the Colony, was now on the Khamies berg throwing out its long broad leaves in opposite pairs forming the shape of a fan. Both the bulb and the leaves of this plant have been ascertained to be, without any preparation, the most virulent poisons that act on the animal system whether taken into it by the stomach or by the blood. The farmers pull up the root and leaves wherever they find them growing. It was said that the juice of this bulb, mixed with the mangled body of certain species of spider, furnishes the Bosjiesmans [Bushmen] with poison for their arrows more deadly than any other they are acquainted with (Barrow 1802: 391; Skead 2009: 61).

The plant also came to the attention of another traveller, German zoologist Hinrich Lichtenstein, at a cattle kraal on the Kuruman River in June 1804.

> In the midst of the space lay an enormous bulb which must have measured nearly a foot [30cm] in diameter, probably *Haemanthus* or *Ornithogalum* species [most likely *Boophone disticha*][9] ... they were charms, he [Kok] said, by which cattle were preserved from enchanters and would not be parted with by the possessor at any price ... (Barrow 1802: v.1, 391; Skead 2009: 61).

The traveller, botanist and southern African explorer, William J Burchell, noted in 1812:

> Plants of *Amaryllis toxicaria* [*Boophone disticha*] were in many places very abundant, their bluish undulating leaves rising out of the ground and spreading in the form of a fan ... Well known to the Bushmen on account of the virulent poison contained in its bulb. It is also known to the colonists and Hottentots by the name of giftbol [Dutch, 'poison bulb'; entry dated 15 February 1812] (Lichtenstein and Plumtre 1815 [1928]: 395; Skead 2009: 260).

Burchell also provided a specimen of the *Amaryllis toxicaria* (classified now *Boophone disticha*) to the Royal Botanical Garden (now Kew), and several *Brachycerus* specimens that are now in the Oxford Museum collections.[10] Burchell's collections include what he called *Brachycerus imperialis, granosus*

---

9   Botanical identification in contemporary taxonomic nomenclature is by Cuthbert Skead (2009: 260), here and in subsequent quotes citing Skead (2009).

10   Filed as *Ammocharis coranica* Herb [family Amaryllidaceae], as a type specimen. Burchell #ex B-47 No. 2, collected 15–07-1821, Cape Province: Klipfontein. Identifications: *Amarillis coranica* Ker-Gawl; *Ammocharis coranica* Herb; *Ammocharis falcate* Herb. Information of JSTOR Plant Science, filed as *Ammocharis coranica* http://plants.jstor.org/specimen/k000 365397

and *apterus*.[11] There is no *B. ornataus* in his collection but it appears that he used different names for this beetle.[12]

David Livingstone (Burchell 1822: vol. 1: 541; Burchell 1953, cited in Skead 2009: 265), who noticed the flowers in the vicinity of the mission station at Kuruman in 1852, remarked on the plant, giving yet another use for it. He reported many genera, including:

> Ixias and large flowering bulbs, the *Amaryllis toxicaria* [*Boophone disticha*] and *A.* [*Amaryllis*] *brunsvigia multiflora* [either *Ammocharis coranica* or *Brunsvigia radulosa*] (the former a poisonous bulb) yields in the decayed lamellae [tunics] a soft silky down, a good material for stuffing mattresses.

According to some reports it was not the 'silky' quality of the material that made it useful for mattresses but rather the fact that Afrikaner farmers in the Karoo used mattresses filled with the material to calm hysteria and cure sleeplessness (Livingstone 1857: 112; Skead 2009: 278). Later in 1852, in north-eastern Botswana, Livingstone (1857: 171; Skead 2009: 311) revised and improved his description of *B. disticha*:

> The poison more generally employed [by 'Bushman'] is the milky juice of the tree *Euphorbia arborescens* [*Euphorbia cooperi* or *E. ingens*]. This is particularly obnoxious to the equine race. When a quantity is mixed with the water of a pond, a whole herd of zebras will fall dead from the effects of its poison before they have moved away 2 miles. It does not however kill men and oxen. On them it acts as a drastic

---

11 There is a specimen labelled '*Brachycerus apterus*' (Olivier 1790) in the Musee Zoologique de Strasbourg that looks identical to *B. ornatus* in online pictures: http://commons.wikimedia.org/wiki/File:Brachycerus_apterus-Musée_zoologique_de_Strasbourg.jpg, accessed 25 January 2012. There are also a number of other specimens labelled *B. apterus* that are very similar. *B. granosus* (Gyllenhal 1833) is also a currently accepted name. The image on GoogleImages appear to be nearly identical with *B. ornatus*. Burchell's *B. imperatus* is not a currently accepted name.

12 Pers. comm. Mr James E Hogan, Hope Entomological Collections, Oxford University Museum of Natural History, 23 January 2012.

purgative only. This substance is used all over the country, though in some places, the venom of serpents and a certain bulb, *Amaryllis toxicaria* [*Boophone disticha*], are added to increase the virulence.

Emil Holub was perhaps the first to discover the association of the weevil, *Brachycerus ornatus*, with these plants. He kept exceptionally detailed records of insects and plants, but seems not to have included *Brachycerus ornatus* in particular. However, he made significant observations about the weevils:

'In the course of the march during the afternoon, I found a good many weevils under the leaves of a liliaceous plant, as well as several kinds of locusts that were new to me'.

We lost no time in making a start the following morning, and, turning into a wide valley that ran northwards, we came in sight of a native village, consisting of about forty huts, the shape of which evidenced that they were the property of Koranna and Bechuana Barolongs (Holub 1881: 242).

The 'liliaceous plant' is *B. disticha* or *A. coranica*, probably the latter, since it was in the territory of the Koranna and Barolong sub-section of the Tswana, in the neighbourhood of today's Kuruman. Further north, after crossing eastern Botswana (then 'Bechuanaland') and passing to the east of the Makgadikgadi [Kalahari] salt pans, Holub (1881: 174) again noted the 'poisonous lily' on what he called a 'high sandy plateau' with numerous seasonal pans':[13]

I must call attention to the fact that it is dangerous to cross this plateau from October till December on account of the growth of a poisonous lily, which kills the cattle in a few hours. After the grass has grown up the cattle do not touch this poisonous plant.

---

13 From the map published with *Journey through central South Africa*; he travelled along the road between Nata in north-eastern Botswana and Pandamatenga on the Zambia-Botswana border, roughly 19° S 25° 30′ E. The road still exists.

Holub was not able to bring back to Europe any specimens from this segment of his exploration as the canoe containing all his material and his guns capsized on the Zambezi as he was en route to the western coast at Luanda and he was forced to turn back. It is very likely that his collection of insects would have contained instances of *B. ornatus*.

Henri-Alexandre Junod, one of the premier early ethnographers of southern African peoples, also collected the beetle and described episodes of 'play' among Tsonga children in southern Mozambique that appear to involve it, or one like it. Like Thunberg, Barrow, Burchell and Livingstone, Junod had extensive medical, botanical and zoological knowledge, especially in entomology. When he arrived in South Africa as part of the Swiss Romande Mission Society he pursued studies of indigenous insects and collected many specimens that are still in South African collections today (Holub 1881: 246; Michler 2003), including two *B. ornatus* specimens, now in the Transvaal Museum.

Junod was as passionate about beetles as he was about his evangelical mission, according to his son, Henri-Phillipe Junod (Michler 2003: 40), who recalled in a memoir about his father that:

> Evangelism journeys…are magnificent opportunities to observe, to take notes, to be instructed. School exams, sermons, collections of beetles and butterflies, study of herbs, etc. Enthusiasm grew in the heart of the young missionary who was beginning to understand the wonderful development Africa was offering to his scientific talents.

Junod worked for many years with the Tsonga peoples of southern Mozambique and, later, in South Africa (Harries 1981, 1989). He was particularly struck by the indigenous knowledge of plant and animal life in this environment:

> Having collected beetles and butterflies extensively for years, I have had the opportunity of recognizing the power of observation of these boys who were my best hunters! Of course they particularly appreciate things edible…especially the *shitambela*, a big Bupresta beetle that they roast and suck. Learning, as they do, the native names of all these creatures and their habits, they certainly acquire a great amount of knowledge during these years (Junod 1912: 65).

B. ornatus contains large fat reserves and may also have been eaten roasted by children, although it is possible that it would have been toxic to humans if the alkaloids were fat soluble. 'Bupresta' is a common name in French (and Latin) for a wide range of endophytic borer beetles (weevils), so the beetle in Junod's text might have been *B. ornatus*. Whatever the case, this illustrates how insects, like plants and animals (either whole or in part), were woven into daily practice.

Junod (1912: 67) also described a game called '*shifufunu*' which was played by children and imitated the behaviour of a beetle. The behaviour illustrated by the children's game closely resembles the behaviour of *B. ornatus*, which would have been especially prominent and noteworthy:

> The game of the beetle (*shifufunu*) is played as follows: one child is the beetle, and, as a distinguishing mark, he puts a handkerchief round his head. A hole is dug in the sand; he enters it, nestles in it as do some insects until quite covered with earth. He remains there perfectly still whilst his comrades sing to him the following song:
>> Beetle of mine...
>> I will marry thee...
>> Say 'yes' to your brother.
>> For the price of an ox ....

In the only detailed entomological study of *B. ornatus* in the Free State province, Louw (1990: 30) describes similar behaviour to that mimed by the Tsonga children in Junod's account. After copulation, the female *B. ornatus* beetles deposit eggs under the leaves of the *A. coranica* after digging a hole and crawling into it.

> After adopting a characteristic 'head-up' position four to eight eggs (N=7) are laid with a time lapse of up to 10 minutes between each egg. Fluid is released after each egg is laid, whereafter it is covered with a layer of soil. After ovipositing, the hind legs and pygidium are used to cover the hole firmly with soil. The female then remains for up to several hours in the depression.

The children's games seem to mimic this beetle's behaviour since it is large, flightless (and therefore cannot escape human attention easily), exhibits distinctive behaviour and is ritually important (making it worth the 'price of an ox'). Junod collected two specimens of the *B. ornatus* – one from 'Delagoa Bay' (not dated in collection records) and one from 'Lourenço Marques', now Maputo (collected in 1909). The specimens are now in the Transvaal Museum's entomological collection.

Contemporary usage

Boophone disticha is heavily exploited today by healers and herbalists, together with *Hypoxis hemerocallidea* and *Euphorbia clavaroides* (Junod 1912: 67), among others, that are found in the same grassland habitat. Russel Wagner (2012) reports that *Boophone disticha* 'currently' (2012) 'sells for $1.50 for a large bulb' in Johannesburg's herbal medicine/magic markets. By 2016 they cost about R500 to R1 000 ($30–$60) in similar shops.

    B. disticha, in particular, is used in several ways by sangomas in the SiSwati-speaking areas near Barberton. During my fieldwork there I have seen it in almost every healer's collection that I have had the chance to observe and I have seen it being collected and dried. According to healers in Barberton and the Sheba settlement near the Sheba Mine, Mpumalanga, clients who are afflicted by witchcraft and who have so far failed to prevent its influence or to find the witch use this method as a last resort.

    The patient consumes a part of the bulb by chewing it or drinking a water decoction and is then made to sit in front of a blank wall in a darkened room or hut. Hallucinations or visions begin to occur as a result of the herb and appear to be projected onto the blank wall in front of the patient. This gives the method its names. The patient is then expected to be able to 'see' the witch that is causing the problem. Both healers and lay people report, however, that the method is very dangerous. The patient may die of these poison-induced visions. In local belief, it is the witches and malefactors that are seen in the visions that kill, not the poison. In other words, the 'intangible persons' in the dream world kill, while the herbal concoction and the 'trance' state it induces only makes these encounters possible. Death is attributed to the witch, who, having been seen and thus found out, may take revenge by killing the patient before the patient can recover and kill the witch.

Personal accounts of this attest to a long recovery period from the use of this plant, during which the patient is comatose, sometimes for days. 'My cousin was not right for two years after doing it,' says one, and others attest to the death of many subjects. No healer wants to have to deal with a dead patient and resorts to such dangerous measures only as a last resort.

Generally, too, other herbs and remedies have been prescribed prior to and in conjunction with *B. disticha*-induced visions, or 'bioscope' (a South African term for cinema). The use of emetics and steaming are also common in such cases, resulting in dehydration as well as the consequences of whatever presenting illness or misfortune may already have weakened most patients. It is difficult, then, to assess the virulence of the alkaloids and other psychotropic chemicals the plant may possess.

The plant is used today in many other ways. It is reported to be used to calm 'hysterical' people and to stop bleeding from circumcisions and ear piercings.

Most of the related genera of the amaryllids, including *Clivia*, *Scadoxus*, *Haemanthus*, *Ammocharis* and others (Van Wyk and Gericke 2007: 156, 164, 198, 240), have similar uses, especially in relation to protection from witches or in the treatment of witchcraft or as 'charms' and 'amulets' against witches. All of them contain similar alkaloids, usually named after the plants from which they are obtained, such as lycorine and hyocine, haemanthamine, buphanimine and so on, and are said to be responsible for fatal poisonings (Hutchings 1996).

In the areas in which the plant grows (near Machadodorp and near Louws Creek, both in Mpumalanga), there is ample evidence that they are exploited. In late 2012 I found specimens on a derelict farm, now 'community'-owned as the result of land restitution and redistribution programmes. Although some Nguni cattle had been pastured in the large, unfenced area, there was no cattle dung in the places we walked, and only kudu spoor and reebok and duiker. The wild plant biodiversity was extraordinarily high, perhaps because the farm had been unused for some time. This had created an important ecological and economic contradiction: the farm was no longer economically productive, but it was therefore reverting to a wild(er) state with greater biodiversity that was increasingly exploited by medicinal plant market-gatherers and local healers (*dingaka/ligedla/ tangoma*). They were, however, not entirely careless with their harvesting: although they took whole plants, they did not exploit all the plants in any area, careful to leave some to reproduce.

These and other plants were dug up with single-use stone tools made opportunistically, by plant harvesters, from the ubiquitous dolerite (diabase) rock that originates in many dykes and ridges in the immediate area. The opportunistic use of stone tools helped the herb gatherers to avoid being caught on private lands with iron tools such as pangas, typically used to dig herbs in more secure locations. Instead they use an ancient human lithic technology – large, very sharp flakes from local rock. Percussion points and fracture surfaces were fresh, with dust still adhering to some.

This technology is probably both opportunistic and energy efficient. But it also illustrates the continuity with much earlier lithic technologies. What has been called the 'Iron Age' in the southern African archaeological context was also a 'Stone Age'. The two technologies are present in most

FIGURE 9.15: Dolerite (diabase) rock, recently chipped to obtain a stone tool used for digging medicinal herbs in the veld. Three strike points and a bulb of percussion are visible in the centre of the cusp between the two faces of this core.

archaeological sites of the past 1 500 years or so. Iron did not exclude stone, since, for most of the period in which iron was known and used in southern Africa it was used to make beads and/or amulets, not hoes or spears.

When *B. disticha* is collected in the bush, the hole from which it has been taken must be left open to allow it to continue to communicate with its origin and to convey this power to the patient. In sections of veld where this and other plants grow, then, it is common to see open holes that can be mistaken for holes made by animals such as porcupines or warthogs that forage for roots. The healer copies the animals that also dig for roots.

Similarly, a beetle on a string of beads connects the sufferer or the victim of sorcery to the earth by means of a magical connection. The red spotted weevil is not, itself, magical, it is an element of the set of relations among acts, objects, places, land(scape) and meaning that provides a way to manipulate the flows of 'power' or energies that can protect and heal, that can lead to trance and vision, or that can kill. Beads are often placed in the landscape as a reciprocal connection, and may be left in the holes

FIGURE 9.16: Characteristic holes (centre) and flat stone digging tools (bottom centre) are left by healers (herbalists and sangomas) digging for herbs in the veld. The holes are left open to maintain the potency of the herb.

from which powerful herbs are dug. In this way, beads are 'strung' onto the land just as beads (or beetles) on a string represent the bush and connect the person to the bush. Just as the healer goes to the land to find the herbs, landscapes are mapped onto persons – tangible and intangible. This can only be fully understood if we see the landscape and its parts as the southern African healer does: the parts of animals, plants and minerals, including beads, are agents in an active landscape that also includes humans.

Things good to string: Beads, natureculture and history

Strangely, the lived history of healing in southern Africa shows why practising healers in this tradition deny historical time itself. First, parts of plants and animals – 'natural' objects in the Western view – are as much a part of 'culture' as non-human agents. They are viewed as agents of healing because, by virtue of their direct connection to the non-human landscape, they protect humans from other humans and from the intangible persons usually called 'spirits' and 'witches'.

Second, objects of this sort are visible in the archaeological records of 40 000 years. This is also the period during which anatomically modern humans with identifiable symbolic cultures have existed, so change is not accountable in historical time. Some aspects of the regional material culture appear to have been extraordinarily stable. The natureculture nexus it embodies is powerful and – evidently – healing. This is especially true for what I have called 'magical bundles' – things that are good to string.

Since each healer's magical and medicinal materials are buried with him or her they do not survive in contemporary costumes or technical kit as material 'memory' or memorials. 'History' is erased, while culture endures. Each new healer must assemble his or her own costumes and magical regalia according to the unique direction of the 'ancestors' and the *gobela* (spiritual guide or teacher). Thus, although each element of the healer's kit has – in principle – a history, time and memory are irrelevant to the 'mapping' that links persons and landscape in the healing event. The historical account that I have constructed from textual resources in this account, have no analogue in *bungoma* philosophy.

We do not know who originally made the beaded beetle amulets, but evidence shows that they were used throughout the region as variations on a common theme. The bundles of beads, plants and animal parts are a universal feature of southern African healing and protective systems. They map flows of power or energy (*amandla* [isiZulu]; *mathlo* [Sesotho-Setswana] or *n/om* [!kung, and some other San/Bushman languages]) into other people, objects, places and environment or landscapes. These bundles of beads and objects of natureculture make this power visible and useful. The landscapes become 'healing scapes'.

Beads, and the other elements of protective magic – especially in archaeological contexts – are made of a large range of materials: plant, animal, mineral, and of manufactured substances such as metals and glass. Their significance for healing and protection is their connection to the landscape, especially to the powerful uninhabited 'bush' regions that are traversed (ideally) only by healers themselves and, of course, their enemies, the witches and other agents of misfortune. The beetle translates this power into the strings that contain it, while the plants, *B. disticha* and *A. coranica*, present their powers more directly as psychotropic agents that allow the healer and patients to inhabit a magical landscape where witches and spirits can be seen walking and can be identified.

This set of relationships involves the specialised exploitation of resources embedded in a landscape. These constitute an element of a larger ecology and are not simply 'ecological'. Whereas ecology and 'economy' entail flows of values, nutrients and energy, in this case, life worlds or *umwelts* (Hutchings 1996) of a particular set of people, plants and insects define a unique set of entangled life-ways. Beetle and plant have meanings enabled and engaged through specialised relationships involving spatial patterns, mutual dependencies (for example, domestication of the plant, parasitism of the beetle) and specialised needs. When these beetles were also used for divination their spatial relationships with each other and with other divination tokens point again to their place in the landscape of healing that divination reveals.

While the relationship between beetle and plant is parasitic, the plant provides an entire 'landscape' or environment for the life cycle of the beetle (Kirksey 2010), while the beetle indexes the potency for human healers and their patients of the plant in the veld. The beetle's colour references the symbolic black-red-white triad of colours that is central to the colour symbolism used throughout healing systems in southern Africa (Louw

1990) and is directly incorporated into material culture that is worn close to the body and protects the patient (or healer) from ill.

This is not, then, an 'ecology' – although it is that too – but rather a *landscape of natureculture* in which 'nature' and 'culture' merge in the most practical ways. What emerges for our analytic vision is a mostly-hidden landscape of persons, beetles and plants and the uses they make of each other in defining their lifeways. The natureculture landscape of beetle, plant and human crosses ecological and cultural boundaries with the many other cultural practices related to healing and protection. Practices and beliefs of this sort illustrate the network of relationships that span the southern African sub-continent, linking the many local or sub-regional healing regimes. As Landau (2010: 49) remarks: 'The whole of southern Africa was [in the past] an area of common learning and mutual experience', much as it is today.

CHAPTER 10

Magical empiricism and the 'exposed being' in public health and traditional healing

Healing in a time of public health

Reasoning incorrectly from empirical evidence, the magical logic of the traditional healer arrives at conclusions that cannot be scientifically demonstrated because it generalises too broadly from discrete ('accidental') instances of success. But this is not only a logical error it is also a strategy to recruit clientele or patients by claiming that some specific empirical success can be generalised to any patient.

Public health practitioners must also recruit both patients and experimental subjects. The ostensible object of public health, however, is not its 'public' (patients and experimental subjects) but rather the abstract biological notion of the 'population'. In order to reason from population to patient, public health must invert the magical logic of the healer: it must reason from the general to the specific. The randomised controlled trial (RCT), for example, seems to specify effectiveness for the single instance from the statistically general case and creates the impression for its audience, the public, that its findings are proportionally valid for any and all instances. Thus magic and RCTs exhibit invalid chains of reasoning based on sound empirical observations.

This is what I call 'magical empiricism', that is, a property of both the 'evidence-based' medical systems and interventions deriving from the

RCT, and the 'magical' medical systems of traditional healing and complementary and alternative medicine. But the difference lies in the fact that the traditional healer and his or her patient do not lose their social being like the subject of the modern medical and public health regime who can be characterised as having only 'bare life' (Agamben 1998: 10) as an element of the 'population'. This, in turn, allows us to understand the appeal of the healers' magic, their flawed logic and, often, their surprising efficacy.

The magic of the healers

Magic, as James George Frazer showed in *The Golden Bough* (1922) and other works, reasons incorrectly from empirical evidence, arriving at conclusions that cannot be scientifically demonstrated. But magic is much more than this. While Frazer backs up his argument with oceans of ethnographic data, my claim here is more limited. I argue that what I am calling 'magic', despite its error of logic, has real efficacy, if only because it recruits a clientele for the 'magician'. The magic of modern public health and biomedicine also has to recruit a clientele and it does so with a similar logical error. I am not contesting the efficacy of biomedicine and public health; they are effective, even if not in all cases. But I also assert that the 'magic' of traditional healing practices and complementary and alternative medicine (CAM) is also efficacious – sometimes. With very few exceptions, nothing works in all cases, every time, or forever. Some things work for some, sometimes, and often for reasons that we do not understand. Biomedical science, public health, traditional healing and CAM deal with these facts of uncertainty in different ways. This essential, inescapable indeterminacy keeps them all in the market for healing.

Here I will label as 'magic' what both the traditional healer and the CAM practitioner do. Just as ethnography is 'serious fiction' (Clifford 1988: 10), I take healing to be serious magic. Whether or not we call the efficacy of many forms of non-pharmacological and non-biomedical healing a 'placebo effect' there is no doubt about its occasional efficacy. I will assume this here without further justification.

In his 12 volumes of *The Golden Bough*, which he later reduced to one because of its vast popularity, Frazer was not shy about stating his own views about the efficacy of magic:

The reader may well be tempted to ask, How was it that intelligent men did not sooner detect the fallacy of magic? How could they continue to cherish expectation that were invariably doomed to disappointment? With what heart persist in playing venerable antics that led to nothing, and mumbling solemn balderdash that remained without effect? Why cling to beliefs that were so flatly contradicted by experience? (Frazer 1922: 35).

Magic persists as a mode of reasoning today as in the past, as many have attested (Childe 1949; Evans-Pritchard 1937; Krige 1944; Malinowski 1935; Rowlands and Warnier 1993; Schwemmer 2011; Tambiah 1968; Turner 1964, 1968). Frazer knew, too, that users of magic were not, in fact, 'doomed to disappointment'. Despite protestations to the contrary, Frazer (1922: 35) succeeded in showing that magic – or magical thinking and action – was a fundamental element of human life. He suggested,

But let an argument of precisely the same calibre be applied to matters which are still under debate, and it may be questioned whether a British audience would not applaud it as sound... If such reasonings could pass muster among ourselves, need we wonder that they long escaped detection by the savage?

So what is wrong with magic? And what is the difference between what a 'British audience' would applaud as sound and what it would not?

For one thing, magic generalises too broadly from discrete instances by means of several lines of logical process that are called 'sympathetic' or 'contagious' magic. But the methods of empirical public health research, specifically the RCT, work its magic from the other side. One 'magic' we applaud, the other we do not.

Statistical results that are only 'valid' within margins of error, and only over the population, not for specific individuals or acts, are nevertheless taken by medical clients to be effective in their own discrete case. Reporting of scientific findings, especially in popular media, often creates the impression that its findings are proportionally valid for all instances. Thus, if some intervention, drug or act is found to provide x% 'protection' or 'efficacy', most people act as if they believe that this means that its efficacy is distributed over each instance in the entire population. That is, that each individual will receive $x\%$ protection or efficacy in all instances. This is, of course, not the case, yet this magical generalisation is repeated in virtually every press release about medical results obtained through randomised controlled trials (RCT).

This represents an invalid chain of reasoning from the general, statistical results that apply over populations to the claims of specific efficacy for discrete individuals, acts or treatments. Thus magic and RCTs, relative to each other, and in practice, present invalid chains of reasoning based on sound empirical observations. Moreover, the errors of logic are inverses of each other. While the RCTs (more accurately, the audience's reception of the findings of RCTs) make invalid logical leaps from the general to the specific, magic makes invalid logical leaps from the specific to the general.

People we call 'scientists' are perfectly aware that the logic that appears in popular accounts of their results is not applicable in the vast majority of cases to all individuals, or even to any. Many results are only applicable, in fact, to very small numbers of persons, and the identity or circumstances of these persons cannot usually be predicted in advance, except as probabilities.

The logic of the science, however, necessarily assumes that all bodies are equal and that only 'confounding factors' separate them from one another. Moreover, it is assumed that randomisation can eliminate the effects of social structure, economic inequality or other differentiating factors, leaving only 'pure biology' behind.

The editors of the special issue of the journal *Culture, Medicine and Psychiatry*, Allison Schlosser and Kristi Ninnemann, noted, for instance, that:

> Whyte et al. (2002b: 33) stress that pharmaceutical treatments are 'based on the principle that medicines have the same action in all patients: dosages are standardized…and the effects are considered to be universal.' The underlying assumption is that biological bodies are the same in all settings, and that pharmacological action is located in the medical substance that is ingested (Schlosser and Ninnemann 2012: 2).

These are important assumptions since they imply that the aggregate of human beings constitutes something we call a population. A population is understood to be some subset of the biological species of the genus *Homo*, which has only one member, the species '*sapiens*'. But '*sapiens*' implies that this species is not simply biologically constituted: it has knowledge. This has implications. The confounding factors of the RCT are not merely 'confounding', they constitute the object of its knowledge, humankind as the knowing and knowledgeable beast. One of the primary fields of knowledge of this species is magic, that is, its own ability to deceive itself and to posit power in myriad forms. This allows humans to heal themselves in many ways, including by just believing themselves to be healed.

Included in the assumption that biological bodies exist, that there is, in all instances, a biological substrate to humanity, rather than a uniquely human character to its biology, are additional assumptions about how populations of such bodies are constituted. This is a bold assumption given all that we know about humans.

The problem that biomedicine faces, then, as do traditional healers or other alternative medical practitioners, is how the general character of humanness can be linked to a particular instance of the species, that is, a single person. Given human diversity, how is it possible to validate general knowledge in any specific instance? In this case, the problem becomes how to utilise personal experience – uniquely the property of the single person – to make valid generalisations about people and, ultimately, the human population as a whole. The biomedical practitioner and the 'magician'/sangoma share this problem. Contrary to Frazer's conclusion that it is merely an error of logic, this 'problem' creates the space in which magic operates. The specific magical act is taken to have general efficacy and the general principles of magic appear to be universal in human thinking while they are only ever seen or experienced in each individual instance.

People we call 'magicians', or traditional, complementary or alternative healers, are also generally aware that the results they may obtain in specific therapeutic instances are often 'lucky' – that is, they are unpredictable and are said to be controlled by non-empirical intangible entities called 'gods', 'God', 'spirits', 'wind', '*qi*', 'energy', 'forces' and so on. Nevertheless, based on individual successes, they do predict to their audiences (or clients) that their therapies will work in general, that is, on any and all unspecified future patients (including the client at hand). Magicians, traditional and CAM practitioners and public health scientists are acutely aware that they depend for their livelihoods on this magical logic.

Clients, too, are generally aware that any therapy or intervention may not work, and are willing to 'take their chances'. Despite claims to the contrary, then, 'evidence-based medicine', RCTs, traditional healers and CAM practitioners all rely on different kinds of specious logic.

The herbal therapies are not fixed by tradition, but are generally 'dreamed' and/or concocted in discussions with other sangomas who belong to the same 'root' (*mpandze*) or 'family' of practitioners. These are then tried out 'experimentally' on patients and the results are monitored for success or failure. Some sangomas even send patients to professional medical laboratories where CD4 counts and viral loads are tested and reported to the healers. This quasi-empirical process is driven by a 'magical' (non-scientific) logic, but frequently results in some effective strategies for treating opportunistic infections and other problems (thrush, diarrhoea, appetite loss and weight loss, for example).

It appears that some effective 'holistic' treatments, combined with ritual and other therapeutic interventions that appear to alleviate depression in some clients, are emerging from this 'magical-empirical' process. Thus, what sangomas are doing today in response to HIV/AIDS may provide an analogy with the emergence of scientific medicine in the West from previous folk remedies and magical treatments in earlier centuries.

Within this community of healers, the *gobela* and his/her group of trainees constantly discuss patients and therapies. Ivy Mlotshwa, a newly qualified traditional healer in Mpumalanga, noted in an interview on 10 June 2002, for instance, that '[t]here is a lot of referral from [other] traditional healers as we work together at all times; such as in the case when you know someone has some herbs you might not have'.

These practitioners constitute a coherent social and professional group whose members explicitly understand themselves to be traditional medical practitioners. They often style themselves 'Traditional Dr' or 'T Dr' in their written materials (such as advertising handbills, calling cards or certificates) and compare themselves explicitly to medical doctors. To a degree, they see medical doctors and other medical personnel such as nursing sisters as competitors, but also as colleagues in the same profession.

Thus, the sangoma can be compared usefully to the medical doctor and might be able to co-operate with medical doctors in a medical programme designed to extend and strengthen care for HIV/AIDS patients.

One traditional healer told the following story of how he sought information about HIV/AIDS. It demonstrates the relationship between a younger and a more senior traditional healer, in this case involving three countries – South Africa, Zimbabwe and Malawi. The way in which the healer attempts to think through the problem and to come up with a solution is typical of the logic used by most traditional healers.

> One day after that other girl died [of AIDS] I had to go to Zimbabwe to find out how to deal with this thing. As a sangoma I was sensing this thing even when I hear on TV because I had another nursing sister who is my friend. I asked her to tell me about this. Tell me everything about it, what is it? And why does it have to eat you up?
>
> Well she told me everything that she knows; that AIDS eats you up until to an extent that if you have a history of a certain disease it capitalises on that disease. So it seems as if you have been killed by that disease, but in actual fact you have been killed by it [AIDS]. So you no longer have a 'part' that would work to prevent illnesses such as flu. I asked her, 'What is this thing that eats you up?' I asked her.
>
> And she said the thing which eats you up is ...
>
> [RT (interviewer): A virus? (*ivirus? Igciwane?*)]
>
> Such things ... and she uses their medical terms.
>
> I said, 'All right but I think this thing of AIDS ... but it's just that I do not have courage (*khaliphile*). I can solve it but I do not have courage.'
>
> I then went to Zimbabwe, just to get some herbs. There is one sangoma who is my friend but he is a powerful sangoma there.
>
> And I told him, that old man, 'Here is a problem; we are suffering!'
>
> He said, 'We are also suffering!' But he comes from Malawi; but he stays in Zimbabwe. So he said, 'This is AIDS', because he speaks Ndebele [intelligible to Zulu speakers]; he said 'We can cure it. If you could just come back, we would search for a herb for AIDS.'
>
> I said, 'How?'
>
> He said, 'Let us sit down. What do they say this thing is like?'

I explained what I have been told by the nursing sister; and also based on what I have seen; because you would think that it's sores, and then later on it's a cough, rash and all those things.

And then he said, 'When you come back we must go to the bush; there is a certain white worm. That worm eats a tree even if that tree is as big as this house. It eats that tree until it falls down. That small worm eats a tree until it falls; which means it's that worm which eats a person until he falls down dead.'

[RT: He falls slowly? ...].

Yah he falls slowly because it also eats a tree slowly until it falls down. It does not matter after how many years, but that tree will eventually fall. So he said let us go and look for that tree and then [take the soil] because that worm eats and it takes out the soil and then it creates a [mountain] of soil. We will look for that tree and the soil; and then mix with the herbs ... we look for that worm and then mix it with herbs of those people who have slept with women who have had an abortion; and for those that have died. We mix that worm with those herbs because we are able to heal diseases that results from sleeping with a person who has had an abortion; or whose husband or wife has died. We mix them and then come up with medication; and then we try it on one person who has just been infected. Then from there he must go back to the hospital for testing.

He said, 'All right go and then you must come back. I will be leaving very soon; because the problem is that in winter we are unable to dig herbs because it's dry.'[14]

Clearly, the sangoma operates on a radically different basis from that of the medical doctor. In this story, Oupa Magosinyana explains the logic by which a traditional remedy is discovered. He consults with another sangoma in Zimbabwe who draws an analogy between the way a certain 'worm' kills a tree slowly and the way AIDS kills by 'eating up' certain parts of the body until the sufferer dies. He reasons that the *muti* that uses this worm will work against the same process that he sees in AIDS patients. Like many other healers in southern Africa, he assumes that AIDS

---

14 Oupa Magosinyana, Naledi, Gauteng.

is caused by proximity to death, either through an abortion or through a close personal relationship with someone who has died, for example, a spouse. The logic for devising a treatment is a form of 'sympathetic magic'. The treatment must then be tested.

The plan was to administer it to a patient 'who has just been infected' and the results of this 'experiment' monitored to see if it works. This is a mixture of magical and empirical reasoning – a syncretism of magical reasoning and what might be recognised as a simple scientific empiricism in that it sets up 'experiments' and observes the results. Since there are no controls on these experiments, however, and because most involve single cases, they do not yield scientifically valid results, but they do serve to validate the knowledge of the practitioners and their clients, and they constitute a style of reasoning from observation (induction) that is modern in outlook.

There are many other differences, of course. For instance, the sangoma's client does not declare symptoms from which the sangoma might diagnose an illness. Instead, both client and sangoma consult a divinatory set of objects – 'throwing the bones' (*kushaya ematsambo*, or *kupengula*) to determine the reason for the client's visit, or the nature of the disease. This seems, on the surface, entirely arbitrary and occult, but it is not. Each object in the set has a role or meaning. For instance, one piece represents each member of a family (grandparents, parents, youths, children), there is one for each sex, while others indicate good or evil, money or misfortune, talk or silence. Some function as 'modifiers' or 'adjectives', indicating degrees of seriousness or importance, largeness or smallness, closeness or distance. Still others have different meanings depending on their context. A line of three dots on a dice cube or domino might represent a snake or a pathway, depending on its position and the choices of its interpreter – it can even represent the number three.

In any case, these treatments and practices exist in parallel with biomedical practices and with many other forms of healing and medicine from all over the world. South Africans typically use many different types of medical interventions, concurrently or serially. For instance, herbal treatments are used after biomedical treatments in order to cleanse the body of the 'chemicals' and toxins that the pharmacological agents are believed to have left. People often 'try out' traditional cures before they 'try out' medicine. Very often neither herbs nor medicine is given particular priority. While trying out herbs before biomedical treatment seems to privilege herbs and alternative therapies, this is often just a process of trial. Traditional and biomedical treatments are exploited serially in such cases. Often, too, people take 'herbal supplements' together with antibiotics in order, as they understand it, to 'balance' the effects. The notion of balance provides a rationale for concurrent use of both medical pharmacology and herbal or other 'magical' agents. Efficacy can then be ascribed to neither, or both – and failure can be excused, or just explained.

By a similar logic, South Africans often medicalise their highly pluralistic environments. Foreign people, especially other Africans are believed to be the source of witchcraft. Traditional healers from Malawi, northern Mozambique and Zimbabwe, in particular, are held to have more powerful medicines than South African herbalists. South African herbalists also frequently travel north in order to obtain more powerful herbs for the home market. The history of South Africa and of apartheid, of course, is replete with beliefs about the dangers posed to whites by black people; less remarked are beliefs among black South Africans that white people pose dangers to them, especially to children. In these and many other ways, South Africans medicalise their diversity.

Inverse magics

Is this magic simply a logical error? The public health 'magician' erroneously specifies the instance from a statistical generalisation, while the 'traditional healer' seeks to generalise from the specific without statistical validation. This 'magical relation' between the general and the specific is present in all forms of healing, including biomedicine.

The 'general', for the modern biosciences, is identified here with the 'population' and 'the public'. Foucault further links this to systems of state power he calls 'biopower' and its disciplinary control through 'biopolitics' (Agamben 1998: 11–13, 66; Dreyfus and Rabinow 1982: 133–142; Foucault 1978: 147). This kind of generalisation is valid, however, primarily for the biomedical and public health intellectual regimes of twentieth-century Euro-American states. The public in this case is ambiguously identified with the 'population' and the population is an entity to which can be attributed 'health' or illness. It is not, in other words, simply a statistical number called 'N' (the population 'size').

The notion of the 'public health', the public, and the population is as fundamental to biomedical practice and understanding as it is to the modern state. For alternative healers, however, the constitution of their public and the way in which they generalise from patient to population is as different as their concept of the body and the way it works. Moreover, the body is not all that is at stake, nor is the imagination of the body's physiology all that differentiates biomedicine from its competitors in the 'medical rainbow' that we see throughout southern Africa. The way in which concepts like 'society', 'public' and population differ is also significant.

In this sense, 'public health' points to the core of the difference. First, 'public health' is a misnomer because 'health' is not a property of anything that could be called a public; it is a property of the individual. Second, it is not about 'health', since this state is virtually undefinable. Rather, it is about disease and its distribution across populations, and about interventions meant to control disease that are ultimately political, not therapeutic. But the notion of 'the public' defines its most critical feature: the concept and practice necessarily relies on the presence of an undifferentiated biological population of the species *Homo* (although its principles are now extended to virtually all species) of which any 'random' instance is a proxy for the whole, and the whole a model of any specific instance. Each instance, or person, is regarded as fully independent of any other. The real connection between them, that is, all that makes life human, 'confounds' this truth.

This involves a kind of magical metaphor that is at the heart of public health and biomedicine. This public-as-population is the idealised client of biomedicine, but, since the individual is the actual client, there is implicitly an unwarranted leap to the specific. This is the magic. Sometimes it works, and sometimes it doesn't. But the magic itself is never in question, nor is the magician doubted.

The client of the healer, however, is radically different. The healer addresses a clientele, rather than a population. Each element of this clientele has nothing – or everything – in common with any other client. They all suffer, but the nature of their suffering is endlessly different. Each suffering is unique, but is also uniquely shared by the healer, who feels the pain. Dreams, *liphupho*, and ancestors, *emadloti*, guide the process, as does virtually everyone else who may be in the social networks and context of healer and client. In other words, there is no definable public, but the clientele is also not limited. The client of the healer is always individuated by the unique constellation of persons and influences that constitute both his health and his illness.

However, to attract new clients the healer must generalise beyond the uniqueness of the case. This is the unwarranted leap of logic from the specific. Sometimes the magic works and sometimes it doesn't. But the magic automatically generates the next client.

In short, we might characterise the clientele of the healer, as opposed to the public of 'public health' or of biomedicine, as being like a crystal. The population, by contrast, is more like a liquid in which each molecule is like every other. The clientele of the healer is constituted not by the set of patients, clients or sufferers but by the set of social relations that links them together.

In this way, the 'client' of the healer is not the patient at all, but rather the relations – some broken, some dangerous, some healthy, some ambiguous – that tie healer, patient and many others together in a complex universe that includes living persons, but also many other person-like entities – the so-called spirits, or ancestors – that have influence over these persons.

The magical empiricism of the healer assumes that the patient is a whole person, that is, a person who is part of a social whole but is, above all, a complex and competent social being: namely, a person. By contrast, the magical empiricism of the RCT assumes no such thing. In fact, the notion of a whole, complex and competent person is voided by the statistical method and by the methodology that seeks to remove all but the natural species-being of the human animal *qua* animal. This is done, as we all know very well, in order to control extraneous variables and other 'confounding factors'. What confounds the statistics is the person, not the person as biological or animal being, but as cultural being. The RCT necessarily removes the 'human factors' in order to accomplish its goal, which is, of course, the improvement of human health. But the health with which it is concerned is the health of the 'citizen' of the 'republic' of therapy, whose role in the experiment is simply to lend his or her body without the confounding factors of personhood (Nguyen 2010). Of course, this does not remove personhood or anything else from the participants since the removal is conceptual and mathematical, but it is nonetheless true that the person *as person* is not what is of interest.

The healer, however, must assume that the patient is already and fully a part of the symbolic, cultural and social universe. The fundamental and fully explicable and comprehensible magical act of healing entails a subject who knows what it is to be ill, who is able to act on that knowledge and who may or may not believe that healing has been accomplished by means of the procedures that have been conducted.

These assessments require, further, that the patient has learned what illness is and how to treat it in any number of ways, and has made a choice of one therapy over others. Even if the 'traditional healer' of any culture and social situation is the only choice, that choice is still a choice, since the patient may also choose to suffer, or to die. Suffering and death are legitimate choices that may or may not be significantly affected by the choice of other therapies.

Thus, there is always a choice of meaningful action – whether this is 'therapy' or 'suffering', or both. Therapy in any form always, at the very least, gives meaning to suffering. To the extent that a non-pharmacological therapeutic intervention is simply 'meaningful', the minimum action of any therapy has been achieved. This minimum criterion of therapy does not depend on efficacy at all.

Similarly, to the extent that death or suffering is meaningful, something akin to therapy has also already been achieved. This is 'life threatened by death', that is more than 'meaning' and more than 'bare life' (Agamben 1998). It is an existential condition.

Logical errors and public relations

To return to Frazer's question: How can we understand the persistence of 'solemn balderdash' and 'venerable antics'?

The key is in how we ask the question, and in whether it needs to be answered at all. In other words, it may not be a valid question.

The logic of the magic may be less important relative to healing and human being than the complex of symbolic and social relations that it enables. The over-specification characteristic of the claims made for RCTs and other public health interventions is less significant than the use that is made of this 'error'. Scientifically, the error can be and is usually specified with statistical measures of the distribution (standard deviation, skewness/kurtosis and so on), the probability that the variable's value is valid ('p values'), or other measures (such as odds ratios).

These measures rarely figure in drug company promotions and figure even less in the public's assessments of the value of a drug or treatment. The value is determined largely by the public relations campaigns, communication strategies, doctor-patient relations, popular culture, concepts of the body, the Internet, Facebook and Twitter, among many other factors. Even the best possible evidence-based medicine must have an audience of doctors and patients, the infrastructure to implement delivery and compliance, finance, technicians and cultural acceptance involving an implicit and shared model of the body that 'explains' its efficacy.

Similarly, the logical error of the healer's magic is less important than the relationship it helps to build between the healer and his or her audience. The success of the over-generalisation of the case depends critically on cultural models of the body that allow it to make sense. Even the simplest herbal remedy implies a complex taxonomy of nature, and a cultural model of 'natural' processes. Working though social networks that also spread gossip, social knowledge and cultural values, the healer reaches an audience through such 'errors', and whether or not any particular instance of healing is effective, a patient is recruited. 'Magical' knowledge is deployed and empirically tested.

If we assume, with Frazer, that magic is or can be 'efficacious' and that a failure of magic results in doomed expectations, then we must also conclude that its failure is rooted in faulty logic. Nevertheless, magic endures, not through ignorance of its errors, but because it is congruent with cultural models and the health needs of its clientele and allows them to act within their own implicit health-seeking processes and models of the body.

I argue, then, that it is not logic that is at issue, but rather the place of magic in making meaning. This allows a better understanding of the appeal of multiple forms of healing as being involved in the project of making persons, making meaning and making the best outcome meaningfully *possible*. The creation of persons whose meaning is affirmed, whether well or ill, is the ultimate good.

Traditional healing practices in southern Africa, together with most other forms of healing, are ethical projects aimed at achieving 'the good', especially insofar as the good is embodied in the person. The good generally includes health and well-being, but need not. People who are healed still die. Thus, the ethical project is, paradoxically, independent of practical efficacy. Nevertheless, patients and clients intensively evaluate the efficacy of healing in achieving a desired good state.

Any project seeking to understand how and why this may be true should not, therefore, be about logic and context, but rather about discovering and describing the ways in which healing entails and creates the social forms, bodily states and relations that most embody the good.

The 'exposed being'

In order to comprehend fully the difference between the sangoma's concepts of generalising or specifying clients/patients with respect to their populations, we need to consider more closely the sangoma's understanding of two notions. These are 'person' and 'population'.

Here, Foucault's notion of 'biopower' (Foucault 1978, 2008: 147) founded on his analysis of the public health discourse (Foucault 1975) and the social 'disciplining' of sex, is of little use, since the healer's magic does not refer to a population, or to such large-scale aggregates. The primary reference point in any episode of healing – divination, cleansing rituals, witch smelling-out (*kufemba*), or protection magic or amulets for 'good luck' (*inhlanhla*) – is the person and his or her relationships with other people.

This set of relations, however, does not imply a 'population' in the terms of biomedicine, statistics or public health, but rather networks of people who are linked in some way. Their linkage may concern the illness or disease they share, or the gossip and cellphone networks that pass knowledge between people. Links may consist of people of the 'same kind', however this may be constituted – such as people of the same gender or sexuality, co-workers, kin or people who share a taxi. What is important is not the generic nature of the kind of relationship, but rather the relationships themselves. Above all, the sangomas believe themselves to be working on and through these relationships.

This has implications for the way in which sangomas understand their patients. Patients do not suffer alone, and they do not suffer as aggregates. Academic concepts such as 'social violence', or nations suffering as a whole, seem to make sense within a system that focuses on the uniqueness of the patient's own suffering. I have tried to explain these widely used sociological concepts to sangoma friends and failed. It is not that they do not understand the concept but that they object to its attribution of suffering to a mass of people, or to one person alone. The sangoma suffers with the patient and, through his or her relationship with the patient, is caused to experience the patient's pain. Since the patient's pain is also the result of his or her relationships with other people, the network of pain and suffering links both healer and patient to a ramifying network of suffering people. This is not a population and it is not 'society' that suffers, but rather suffering that is propagated through people in relation to one another.

The focus on the relations between people makes this mode of healing seem 'traditional'. Although the healers themselves insist that their knowledge comes 'through the ancestors', in fact it comes through intensive regimes of teaching and of the disciplines of dance, music, ritual practice and travel. Healers today travel far and often and, indeed, seem to have done so in the past. Most early travellers' accounts, missionary and government reports, among other documents, say that healers come from some place other than where they are encountered by those who write about them. In their own terms, they come from 'underwater' – a metaphor for deep knowledge and trance induction – that signifies travel from other forms of consciousness; but they also travel physically. They travel to attend each other's rituals, 'graduations' of new sangomas, funerals and to attend to patients. Sangomas also survey other forms of healing and are usually syncretic and accommodating in their practice. In response to questions from two local visitors at another healer's house in October 2005 Magodweni presented one standard political-historical account of this that is widely shared.

> I was a person who hated sangomas...I was born to church goers, I was born in people who believe in God, Jesus, and they were not believing in, ahh...sangomas.

> [But] the Bible says that there were sangomas before, who were working with the ancestors...and under them, and who were the witches, and the sangomas...and you know what? I want to tell you something that happened before the white people came. They [white people] ignored our culture. They ignored our culture. The doctors, and the other things, and the Christianity, they were not here in Africa. The Christians came with the white people. And the inyangas and the traditional healers were the people who were healing the people who were living here in AFRICA. Not in South Africa...in AFRICA! In Africa they were using herbs.

In other words, sangomas are not particularly 'traditional', but neither are they modern, especially with respect to the way they understand that most modern concept, the 'social mass'. Instead, they see their patients as embedded in webs of potentially harmful relations with others, who are similarly embedded. They seek to treat these webs.

By contrast, the biomedical practitioner understands a patient as an isolated organism who is part of a population, or of the human species, but not as a set of relations. This is specifically what the randomisation of trials of medical interventions is meant to exclude. Insofar as medicine is 'evidence based' at all, social relations must be excluded. For the biomedical practitioner the patient is part of a social mass; an 'organism' possessing 'bare life', to use Agamben's terminology – life in the face of systems of power and knowledge that reduce people to the biology of their being, especially including the possibility of their death. Death defines them.

For the southern African healer death is always a possibility but it never defines a life. A life is defined by the relations in which it comes into being, is made known and in which it continues after death as an 'ancestral' spirit if it is lucky, and if that life has relations that may continue to define it after death. Life is never 'naked', to use Agamben's term, in the face of death. This gives the healer considerable scope to experiment, since death is not the failure of the cure.

Healers in the southern African context are not public health practitioners, even though they have consistently been portrayed as such by government and often by well-meaning consultants who see them as a cheap way to augment failing or weak health systems. They cannot, quite simply, do this job.

But nor are they simply more 'holistic' medical practitioners either. They are not 'holistic' because their understanding of the patient is as limited as that of the strictly biomedical practitioner. Neither sees the patient as a whole socio-biological entity, comprising a physiological and bio-mechanical part, or as a 'socially constructed' culturally imbued whole human being.

Conclusion

While writing this book I became increasingly sceptical about the received categories that framed this discourse in anthropology and, more generally, in African Studies and the popular literature on 'traditional healing'. Throughout this text, then, I challenge the many misconceptions held in the worlds of government, public health and medicine, in popular literature and in much of the scholarly literature, including anthropology, my own discipline. Most importantly, I argue that *bungoma* is not, as is often supposed, about witchcraft or '*muti* killings'. It is also not primarily concerned with curing physical disease. It is not a makeshift psychology and does not provide either 'barefoot doctor' services on the cheap, or bush psychotherapy. It stands on its own, as I have tried to show.

Critique would be sterile if I could not offer an alternative way of seeing – that is theorising – the practices, knowledge and beliefs in the context and time that concern me here. I have tried, then, to present a more-or-less coherent set of terms and concepts that might allow us to re-imagine this rich fund of African knowledge and give it its due.

Much of what I say about the little corner of South Africa in which I worked can be generalised. *Ngoma*, as practiced in Barberton and Umjindi, is but one facet of a vast set of flexible yet sturdy concepts and practices – all designated by the root word – '*ngoma*' – that are pervasive throughout the southern half of Africa. *Ngoma* in its many forms has been understood as 'cults of affliction', as 'deep knowledge', as 'tradition' itself. Its simplest, referential meaning is 'drum' and 'dance'. But it is all of these and more. I have tried to show ways in which it is, or can be understood as political, economic, ritual, ecological, philosophical, medical and even empirical.

Whatever else it is, however, it is not religion and it is not tribal. Thus, I argue that it cannot be usefully comprehended as, for instance, 'Zulu religion'.

Above all, I have been especially concerned to show that *bungoma* is not 'superstition' or 'witchcraft', just as much as it is not deficient science, flawed medicine or primitive religion. I have portrayed the sangoma as being situated in networks of relations that entangle healers and those they would heal. These webs are enmeshed with a larger web of human and ecological relations. *Bungoma* in this context is best understood as both an intellectual tradition and a technical practice.

Umjindi Local Municipality, with its central town, Barberton, is an area on the border. It lies just north of Swaziland and west of Mozambique, squeezed to the north by the Kruger National Park, and still a long way (300km) from the metropoles of Pretoria and Johannesburg. Yet it is, in its way, a cosmopolitan city with great ethnic and cultural diversity. The canonical (that is government-defined) races of South Africa are represented in Umjindi in roughly the same proportions they are in the rest of South Africa. The settlement of Barberton dates back 120 years, and that of the earlier predominately siSwati speaking population no more that 160 years. It is old in South African terms, and exceptionally young on any global scale. It contains a diversity of people struggling with one of the highest HIV prevalences in the world and with rates of TB and multi-drug resistant TB also extremely high. All these factors, and many others besides, threaten the life and livelihoods of these people and make *bungoma* especially salient in most people's lives.

Nevertheless, I have shown that people are often sceptical about the efficacy of traditional healing, just as they are sceptical about biomedicine and the many other therapies offered in what I have called a 'market' for healing. Their approach to health is fluid and uncertain and healing options are conditional and circumstantial. Patients and clients of healers must be adaptable and selective.

I have described this situation as constituting a market in which those who suffer seek relief, but also the meaning of their suffering. Suffering – as much as it is truly suffering and often horrible suffering unto death – has its own value in this system since the sangoma healer also suffers. Suffering is, in this sense, communication among exposed beings, as it is both the unbearable suffering of illness, disease and misfortune and the shared suffering of the human condition, ubuntu. It is the condition for the possibility of being healed. And suffering is also a protection against jealousy, the jealousy of others that might, in turn, and under certain conditions, be the very cause of suffering.

The practice of the sangoma in this part of eastern Mpumalanga would be more or less incomprehensible without understanding the 'politics' of suffering and of interpersonal distress. Above all, the sangoma seeks to heal relationships among people since it is these that cause illness, disease, misfortune and suffering. I present this in terms of a collection of four concepts, or fundamental premises that bond and fracture the body politic. I argue, however, that these should not be understood as principles of 'structural violence', conflict arising from 'social change' or social 'stress'. The principles – the equivalence of persons (especially men of similar age), jealousy, suffering, and respect – characterise the social links of the interpersonal network.

Bungoma places much emphasis on the person as individuated subject in a way that leaves little room for the imagination of 'society'. Relations and their mutuality, contexts and interdependence constitute the network in which the sangoma works. As exposed beings, persons are not 'subject' to society as Durkheim (and the bulk of social theory today) would have it, but are rather subject to each other, that is, exposed. Shared suffering, from which some people escape; feared jealousy that is despised but 'always there'; demands and expectations that one's fellows are just like oneself, even as they rarely are; the expectation of respect and the fear that it will not be accorded: these are the political terms of social discord that shape the 'structure of feeling' in which the sangoma operates.

Bungoma is taught and learned. It is a field of knowledge as much as a practice of ritual, healing, song and dance. I have explained how *bungoma* is learned and taught and how knowledge is packaged and received. Sangomas are embedded in the landscape. They dig plants, hunt or scavenge animals to obtain healing fats and other parts like bones, claws and teeth; they collect clays, stones and minerals such as ochre. They also buy beads, cloth, ritual regalia, shells and shell beads, among many other things. All of this presents a complex materiality, or material culture that is central to *bungoma* in this part of the world. Even drums – the core meaning of *ngoma* – are made of wood, metals, animal skins and fats and are treated with fire, water and herbs. Accordingly, I have situated the sangoma in the landscape. In one chapter I discuss a small element of this embeddedness, that of the vision-inducing or poisonous plant called *Boophone disticha* and a large ostentatious beetle called *Brachycerus ornatus*. This provides a glimpse into the ways in which *bungoma* interacts with its environment. It is part of a human ecology that links the 'bush' and 'homestead' through a complex of metaphors and metonymies.

The use of the term 'magic' as a useful label for how sangomas work, and how what they do works might be surprising. I do not use this term in the pejorative sense as mere trickery, conducted in bad faith, in order to accomplish what cannot in fact be accomplished. Rather, I use it in its deeper original sense. The Ancient Greeks borrowed the term 'magos' (μαγος) directly from the Persians, with whom they were often at war, and who they believed had powerful 'magic'. But the Persian magicians were also despised because they were obviously impious with respect to the Greek gods, and on the wrong side of the wars.

From the Persian perspective, the magi were specialists in religious and intellectual matters and in technologies. In the Christian gospels of Luke and Matthew, for instance, the Magi are portrayed as three wise men who came 'from the East' (Persia). They came bearing ritual herbs and metals, that is, frankincense, myrrh and gold. They were said to have 'observed [the Christ child's] star at its rising', meaning that they were astrologers, or ancient astronomers. They were respected enough by King Herod, according to the tale, that he instructed them to return to him with the news of the child they sought, but they were clever enough to 'return to their own country by a different path'. It is in this sense that I use the term 'magic' – sangomas as 'magi' (μαγι) – or at least to provide the intellectual context in which the term should be read. More specifically, I agree with Daniel Schwemmer (2011: 419), who, in writing about 'magic' in Akkadian and Babylonian cuneiform texts during three millennia of Mesopotamian history describes it as 'the wayward child of science and religion, combining the latter's credulous engagement with the supernatural with the former's belief in the unlimited power of human actions'. This more or less captures the sense of the sangoma's magic.

Bungoma

I have used the term *bungoma* to refer in general to the overall ideas, beliefs and practices that inform sangoma practitioners in the siSwati-speaking areas of Barberton and Umjindi, South Africa. By introducing this term into English I have tried to isolate from the wider literature what I offer here by way of anthropological explanation and description. This has some costs, of course, since many will not have found in this book the familiar tropes of primitive religion, African healing, witchcraft and witchdoctoring, among other things that they might have expected. Instead, I have sought to destabilise terms such as 'tradition', 'religion', 'healing', 'health', 'magic' and others in order to present *bungoma* in its own terms.

Implicit in this is the statement 'as I see it', for, as I stated at the beginning of this book, I present *bungoma* as an indigenous anthropology rather than as African religion or African healing. I have tried to present this as a professional anthropologist would present the work of other anthropologists, that is, I explain it in my own terms where I feel this is necessary, adumbrate particular points that I feel are most significant and present in detail its fundamental assumptions, findings, approaches and 'methodologies' and knowledge practices.

This work falls short in a number of respects. Detailed description of rituals, dance, songs, rhythms, dress and material culture is largely absent. I have erred in the direction of context and theory. For me, this period of thought and work is also filled with the smells, music, rhythms and tastes experienced during the many events in which I participated, through which I lived and loved, and from which I drew much wisdom. I regret that my readers are not able to experience this fully, however vicariously, through my text. All I can say at this point is that whatever else it is, *bungoma* is a total life experience that plunges all the senses into deep vats of liquid consciousness and awareness. I experienced trance almost involuntarily. After hours of intense drumming, the closeness of other bodies, the smell of sweat, meat, blood, herbs and smoke, dancing and song, trance become almost inevitable. When one reaches for it then, it is there. This is one of the mysteries of *bungoma*. There are, of course, other mysteries that I cannot recount. But I believe these are minor compared to what I have tried to recount here.

The fundamental premise of *bungoma*

The fundamental cultural premise on which *bungoma* is predicated is that all people are 'exposed', that is, vulnerable, to each other's presence (*isithunzi*) and 'power,' 'energy' or 'capacity' (*emandla*). This principle is what makes healing in the cultural framework of *bungoma* possible, since both the client and the healer are exposed to each other. As many authors writing on *ngoma* in Africa have remarked, the rhythm of drums, dancing and song has a direct physiological effect on consciousness. It is not too far a stretch to say that *ngoma* directly embodies knowledge in those who hear the beat and songs that convey this knowledge. This is also what makes possible the assimilation of knowledge and knowledge production in *bungoma* to be understood also as 'being under water', that is, part of a universal flow of embodied wisdom, just as rain, rivers and oceans recreate water through flow and fluidity. Blood, semen, milk, foam, smoke and water are symbols of this flow in *bungoma* and represent ways in which bodies flow into each other, across time and space, and thus become exposed.

The focus of *bungoma* practice is the person. This involves a particular theory of the person, and of life. The basic concept of the person with which *bungoma* operates is, as I have written, that people are exposed to each other, but that they can also be augmented in ways that protect them and that protect life.

The healer counters exposure by augmenting the person. Augmentation has many forms, and most of what a sangoma does is to provide one form of personal augmentation or another. Knowledge is just as much an augmentation of the patients' being as other forms of therapy, or of ritual acts and objects that serve to protect by means of enacted performance ('ritual' or 'work'), or physical objects ('amulets'). In this way, divination using magical tokens thrown on a mat ('throwing the bones') provides knowledge of the client's environment. This is not merely 'diagnosis', as one often hears, but is itself therapeutic in a direct way since it protects the person from real or imagined harm.

I have used the term 'exposed' rather than 'vulnerable' since the exposure of each to the other is more than simply vulnerability. Vulnerability is also an exposure, but the term implies a differential of social power in which the vulnerable is the real or potential victim of the other. By 'exposure' I mean to emphasise the mutuality of the relationship. While there may be a social power of domination or victimisation in any relationship of this type, the relationship between the healer and the client (or patient) is not necessarily unequal. In fact, the equality of the healer and the patient is paradigmatic, and allows the direct interaction of the two bodies in the healing space.

The term 'beings' in the title of this book refers to people, of course, but also to the more generalised concept of the person. I have used the idea of 'the person' here to integrate a number of phenomena and beliefs that have been treated quite separately in some other works, specifically witches, zombies, ancestors, spirits, and other apparently 'transcendent', 'occult' or immaterial entities. I have argued that the beliefs and practices involving these and other similar entities rest on the notion that they are all persons in that they all have intentions and the power to act on their 'intentions', and that they therefore have – or are believed to have – what we call 'agency'. Their agency is seen in the effects they have. That is to say, if illness, disease, bad luck, failure and assorted misfortune are attributable to other people's intentions, and to the effects of witchcraft, ancestors and other non-material agents, these latter entities must also be accorded the status of persons. This, again, is one of the fundamental premises on which *bungoma*, in this context, is based.

Witchcraft, among other characteristics of the southern African cultural understanding of illness and healing, is a logical consequence of these fundamental premises. The intellectual system, of which witchcraft – taken seriously – is a part, is a version of what Christian theologians and philosophers have called 'theodicy', that is, a theory of evil.

Given the pervasive influence of all types of persons and objects – including plant-, mineral- and animal-derived substances – what can a sangoma do? Within this logic, the body itself is necessarily healthy and whole until its natural quality is impinged upon by external influence. Since external influences are everywhere, unpredictable and not necessarily visible, the sangoma aims to protect the body of the patient. Each healer does this in a different way, using a wide range of bathing (in water or smoke), cleansing (vomiting, emetic-induced diarrhoea, sweating, washing), ingestion of medicine/*muti* by mouth or anus, rubbing of substances into the skin or into small cuts on the surface of the skin at points of juncture or flexion (neck, elbow, wrist, knees, ankles, waist or brow), or through use of amulets that are worn on the body, usually also at points of juncture. The focus on joints, that is points of flexure and juncture, is meant to control the 'weakness' of these points where exposure is greatest. Not surprisingly, these are points where most people feel some pain, at least occasionally, and often chronically. This accounts for the importance of beads and strings of other kinds of powerful substances – marine shells such as cowries, conus and whelks, glass and metal beads, seeds, pieces of wood and other herbs, among other things that can be strung on a cord. All of these serve to protect the body, and therefore to augment the person.

Sangomas, therefore, try above all to protect the exposed being, and this is the most significant part of their practice. It is also one of the most varied and one that involves a large range of material items. All these can be understood as constituting parts of a material logic that when constructed, and placed in relation to vulnerable parts of the body, achieve the protection that the sangoma's patient desires and the sangoma attempts to provide. These guarantee the wholeness, and therefore the health, of the patient. This is what I have called here apotropaic magic, that is, the technology of a material logic of protection that wards off untoward influence, or even reflects it back whence it came.

As I have shown throughout this study, these methods also connect persons with other persons and with the larger environment, especially with the power of the bush. The bush is pure because it is free from humans, according to the sangoma's understanding and practice. The spatial category of 'the bush' is simply any uninhabited space. In urban areas, often the only 'bush' available is waste ground between settlements, on or near mine dumps (in Johannesburg) or in any area that is not built up. At best, it should have running water (even if it is laden with mine wastes and acid or sewerage) and perennial vegetation (even if they are just 'weeds'). All southern African towns and cities have 'bush' of this sort within their boundaries and all have more natural bush immediately on their outskirts. It is 'naturally' best to gather *muti* of all kinds from the bush, even though today it can also be farmed or purchased.

Bungoma does not aim to achieve a cure, but rather is content with making pain meaningful as valid, human suffering. In a very real sense, meaning becomes medicine.

Magic

I have presented the 'magic' of the South African healer's art as a meta-practice, that is, as a set of materials (*'muti'*) and acts ('ritual') that index the patient's plight as serious and as a legitimate concern of the healer, the patient and the people who constitute their social networks. Whatever else this magic does – including its 'placebo effect' as a real physiological intervention – the processes of divination, talk about the condition, the narratives that are constructed by healer and patient, all, together, constitute a metapragmatic discourse (Silverstein 1993) about the evil, ill luck or illness the patient suffers. In this way it individualises the suffering and gives it special meaning.

This individualisation makes the meaning of the magic the unique property of the person/patient who requests it. No two patients share an identical network of forces and persons to which they are vulnerable; no therapy is routine or regularised. This signals that the illness is serious and must be taken seriously by all who are aware of it. Through the agency of ancestors, spirits and sorcery, even those who are not aware of this particular suffering become aware of it. In a social context where a high value is placed on the equivalence of persons and their connectivity, the uniqueness of the therapy gives it a high emotional value. The patient becomes not just an exposed being but a unique person. The sangoma's intervention, like the uniqueness of the treatment and of the sangoma him or herself, makes this individuality clear. This is essential to the efficacy of magic.

Equally, the established expertise of the healer gives his or her magic substance and credibility. The patient is able to believe and, through this, the 'placebo effect', if we call it that, is multiplied, and the patient and his or her problem are individuated.

The 'meta' status of the magical is what makes the magical and the empirical compatible. Magic is not a failed instrumentality, a primitive precursor of science or a deficient medicine, it is a set of practices, including knowledge practices, that envelop and situate pragmatic and empirically-grounded acts in an appropriate emotional – or 'spiritual' – context. This is the metapragmatic function of magic. Ultimately, both biomedicine and 'traditional' healing require magic. If some forms of healing seem 'magical' in relation to the empirical science of other therapies, it is not because one precedes the other but because this is the way in which parallel medical systems define one another in the South African Lowveld, and also, probably, elsewhere.

The difference between the practices and medical strategies of the sangoma and of biomedicine may be better comprehended, finally, by examining the way in which each conceives of the specific patient and of the population: x_i in relation to N, on the one hand, or the suffering of the exposed being in relation to fields and networks of power and mutual exposure. The usual contrast between 'traditional' healers and 'modern' doctors frames this distinction with reference to the active therapeutic agents as providers of a service: the one 'magical', the other 'scientific'.

The contrast I have sought to develop here, however, relates to the patient as 'exposed being' and to a different construction of the patient's personhood. For biomedicine, especially in epidemiology and the RCT, the individual specificity of the patient is neglected in favour of seeing the patient as an instance of a general class of phenomena (a diagnostic category, a 'population'), or as a single instance of a biological life form, *Homo sapiens*, or even just 'bare life'. The inverse logic with respect to the relationship between the general and the specific, the universal and the particular, the population and the patient, defines the relation between biomedicine and healing.

The anthropology of healing

Finally, anthropology is a study of the human condition in context with a definite intellectual tradition. Not all its fundamental theoretical premises are accepted by everyone, but they make the practice of anthropology possible. I have presented *bungoma* here as a kind of anthropology of a particular context, and as an intellectual tradition that has its own set of fundamental concepts that guide its practice. Many are sceptical, even within the tradition. This, too, is similar to the academic version of our quest for human understanding. I have attempted to present *bungoma* in its own terms as far as possible. Ultimately, this is not entirely feasible since a translation between languages, practices, beliefs and their expression is required at every turn. But this is precisely what both anthropology and *bungoma* do: they translate the terms in which each person lives his or her own life into other terms, presenting narratives and 'understanding' to both an external audience and to the closest participants. If suffering is part of the human condition, so is translation. Sangomas ultimately provide narratives and description of other people's lifeways, their distress, their illnesses and pain. Anthropology does much the same thing. Some of this is healing. Some of it simply provides meaning. But dance, music, drumming, the play of minds, metaphors, magic and mysteries that lie at the heart of *ngoma* are also fundamental forms of knowledge, and are among the greatest pleasures we can experience.

References

Agamben, G. 1998. *Homo sacer: Sovereign power and bare life*. Stanford: Stanford University Press.

Amanzio, M., Corazzini, L. L., Vase, L. and Benedetti, F. 2009. A systematic review of adverse events in placebo groups of anti-migraine clinical trials. *Pain*, 146, 261–269.

Andrews, J. R., Shah, N. S., Gandhi, N., Moll, T., Friedland, G. and Tugela Ferry Care and Research Collaboration. 2007. Multidrug-resistant and extensively drug-resistant tuberculosis: Implications for the HIV epidemic and antiretroviral therapy rollout in South Africa. *Journal of Infectious Diseases*, 196 Suppl 3, S482–490.

Arnold, M. 1869. *Culture and anarchy: An essay in political and social criticism*. London: Smith.

Árnason, A., Ellison, N., Vergunst, J. and Whitehouse, W. (eds). 2012. *Landscapes beyond land*. New York: Berghahn.

Ashforth, A. 2005. *Witchcraft, violence and democracy in South Africa*. Chicago: University of Chicago Press.

Askew, K. 2003. As Plato duly warned: Music, politics and social change in coastal East Africa. *Anthropological Quarterly*, 76, 609–637.

Augustine, Bishop of Hippo. 1890 [ca. 410 CE]. *St Augustine's city of God and Christian doctrine*. New York: The Christian Literature Publishing Co.

Augustine, Bishop of Hippo. 1961 [ca. 398 CE]. *The confessions*. London: Penguin Books.

Bähre, E. 2007. *Money and violence: Financial self-help groups in a South African township*. Leiden: Brill.

Bähre, E. 2012. The Janus face of insurance in South Africa: From costs to risk, from networks to bureaucracies. *Africa*, 82, 150–167.

Bank, A. and Bank, L. (eds). 2013. *Inside African anthropology: Monica Wilson and her interpreters*. Cambridge: Cambridge University Press.

Bank, L. 2013. Witchcraft and the academy: Livingstone Mqotsi, Monica Wilson and the Middledrift healers, 1945–1957. In: A. Bank and L. Bank (eds), *Inside*

African anthropology: Monica Wilson and her interpreters. Cambridge: Cambridge University Press.

Banks, E. C. 2014. *The realistic empiricism of Mach, James, and Russell: Neutral monism reconceived*. Cambridge: Cambridge University Press.

Barrow, J. 1802. *A narrative of travels in the interior of southern Africa: From the Cape of Good Hope to Graaff Reynet, and the countries of the Kaffers, Bosjesmans, Namaaquas, etc. Performed in the years 1797 and 1798*. London: J. Lee.

Basu, H. 2008. Music and the formation of Sidi identity in western India. *History Workshop Journal*, 65, 161–178.

Bay-Smidt, M. G. K., Jäger, A. K., Krydsfeldt, K., Meerow, A. W., Stafford, G. I., Van Staden, J. and Rønsted, N. 2011. Phylogenetic selection of target species in Amaryllidaceae tribe Haemantheae for acetylcholinesterase inhibition and affinity to the serotonin reuptake transport protein. *South African Journal of Botany*, 77, 175–183.

Bishop, F. L., Jacobson, E. E., Shaw, J. R. and Kaptchuk, T. J. 2012. Scientific tools, fake treatments, or triggers for psychological healing: How clinical trial participants conceptualise placebos. *Social Science & Medicine*, 74, 767–774.

Blacking, J. 1985. The context of Venda possession music: Reflections on the effectiveness of symbols. *Yearbook for Traditional Music*, 17, 64–87.

Bleek, W. H. I. 1864. *Reynard the fox in South Africa, or, Hottentot fables and tales*. London: Trübner & Co.

Bleek, W. H. I. 1875. *A brief account of Bushman folk-lore and other texts*. London: Trübner & Co.

Bleek, W. H. I., Lloyd, L. and Bleek, D. F. 1923. *The mantis and his friends: Bushman folklore*. Cape Town: Maskew Miller.

Bleek, W. H. I., Lloyd, L. and Theal, G. M. 1911. *Specimens of Bushman folklore*. London: G. Allen & Co.

Bornman, H. 2006. Pioneers of the Lowveld. *SA Country Life*.

Bourdieu, P. 1984. *Distinction*. London: Routledge, Kegan & Paul.

Bryant, A. T. 1929. *Olden times in Zululand and Natal: Containing earlier political history of the eastern-Nguni clans*. London: Longmans, Green.

Burchell, W. J. 1822. *Travels in the interior of southern Africa, Volume 1. With an entirely new map, and numerous engravings*. London: Longman, Hurst, Rees, Orme, and Brown.

Burchell, W. J. 1953. *Travels in the interior of southern Africa*. London: Batchworth Press.

Callaway, H. A. 1868. *The religious system of the Amazulu in their own words*. London: Trübner & Co.

Callon, M. 1998. Introduction: The embeddedness of economic markets in economics. *The Sociological Review*. Special Issue: The laws of the markets, 46, 1–57.

Campbell, C. A. and Eastman, C. M. 1984. *Ngoma*: Swahili song performance in context. *Ethnomusicology*, 28, 467–493.

Cant, S. and Sharma, U. (eds). 1999. *A new medical pluralism? Alternative medicine, doctors, patients and the state.* London: Routledge.

Carrithers, M., Collins, S. and Lukes, S. (eds). 1985. *The category of the person: Anthropology, philosophy, history.* Cambridge: Cambridge University Press.

Caton, S. 2006. Coetzee, Agamben and the passion of Abu Ghraib. *American Anthropologist*, 108, 114–123.

Chavanduka, G. 1978. *Traditional healers and the Shona patient.* Gwelo: Mambo Press.

Chidester, D. 1996. *Savage systems: Colonialism and comparative religion in southern Africa.* Charlottesville: University of Virginia Press.

Chidester, D., Kwenda, C., Petty, R., Tobler, J. and Wratten, D. 1997. *African traditional religion in South Africa: An annotated bibliography.* Westport: Greenwood.

Childe, V. G. 1949. *Magic, craftsmanship, and science, The Frazer Lecture, Liverpool University.* Liverpool: Liverpool University Press.

Clifford, J. 1988. *The predicament of culture.* Cambridge MA: Harvard University Press.

Clottes, J. and Lewis-Williams, J. D. 1996. *Les chamanes de la préhistoire: Transe et magie dans les grottes ornées, Collection 'Arts Rupestres'.* Paris: Seuil.

Cocks, M. and Dold, A. 2000. The role of 'African chemists' in the health care systems of the Eastern Cape province of South Africa. *Social Science & Medicine*, 51, 1505–1515.

Cocks, P. 2001. Max Gluckman and the critique of segregation in South African anthropology 1920–1940. *Journal of Southern African Studies*, 27, 739–756.

Comaroff, J. 1981. Healing and cultural transformation: The Tswana of southern Africa. *Social Science & Medicine*, Special Issue: Causality and Classification in African Medicine and Health, 15, 367–378.

Comaroff, J. 1985. *Body of power, spirit of resistance: The culture and history of a South African people.* Chicago: University of Chicago Press.

Comaroff, J. and Comaroff, J. L. 1990. Goodly beast, beastly goods: Cattle and commodities in a South African context. *American Ethnologist*, 17, 195–216.

Comaroff, J. and Comaroff, J. L. 1991. *Of revelation and revolution.* Chicago: University of Chicago Press.

Comaroff, J. and Comaroff, J. L. 1992. *Ethnography and the historical imagination.* Boulder: Westview Press.

Comaroff, J. and Comaroff, J. L. 1993. *Modernity and its malcontents: Ritual and power in postcolonial Africa.* Chicago: University of Chicago Press.

Comaroff, J. and Comaroff, J. L. 1999. Occult economies and the violence of abstraction: Notes for the South African postcolony. *American Ethnologist*, 26, 279–303.

Comaroff, J. and Comaroff, J. L. 2006. *Law and disorder in the postcolony.* Chicago: University of Chicago Press.

Crandon, L. 1987. Medical dialogue and the political economy of medical pluralism: A case from rural highland Bolivia. *American Ethnologist*, 13, 463–476.

Cumes, D. 2004. *Africa in my bones: A surgeon's odyssey into the spirit world of African healing*. Cape Town: Spearhead.

Cunliffe, J. and Teicher, U. 2005. *Botanical names and their meaning*. https://www.Yumpu.Com/en/document/view/17614303/botanical-names-and-their-meanings-bioscience-communications/17, Internet, BioScience Communications, Yumpu. https://www.yumpu.com/user/biosciencecommunications.dk.

Dapper, O., Ten Rhyne, W. and de Grevenbroek, J. G. 1933 [1688]. In: I. Schapera (ed), *The early Cape Hottentots [from texts by] Olfert Dapper, Willem Ten Rhyne en Johannes Gulielmus de Grevenbroek*. Cape Town: Van Riebeeck Society.

Davison, P. and Mahashe, G. 2012. Visualizing the realm of a rain-queen: The production and circulation of Eileen and Jack Krige's Lobedu fieldwork photographs from the 1930s. *Kronos*, 38, 47–81.

Dawkins, R. 2006. *The god delusion*. Boston: Houghton Mifflin.

De Prada-Samper, J. M. 2007. The plant lore of the /Xam San: //kabbo and =/kasing's identification of 'Bushman medicines'. *Culturas Populares, Revista Electronica* 4.

D'Errico, F., Backwell, L., Villa, P., Degano, I., Lucejko, J. J., Bamford, M. K.,…Beaumont, P. B. 2012. Early evidence of San material culture represented by organic artifacts from Border Cave, South Africa. *Proceedings of the National Academy of Sciences*, USA, 109, 13214–13219.

D'Errico, F., Vanhaeren, M., Barton, N., Bouzouggar, A., Mienis, H., Richter, D.,…Lozouet, P. 2009. Out of Africa: Modern human origins, Special Feature: Additional evidence on the use of personal ornaments in the Middle Paleolithic of North Africa. *Proc Natl Acad Sci USA*, 106, 16051–16056.

Dilger, H., Kane, A. and Langewick, S. (eds). 2012. *Medicine, mobility, and power in global Africa*. Bloomington: Indiana University Press.

Doke, C. M., Vilakazi, V. D., Malcolm, M. and Sikakana, J. M. A. 1990. *English–Zulu, Zulu–English dictionary*. Johannesburg: Wits University Press.

Dovey, K. and Mjingwana, R. 1985. Psychology, religion and healing: The *amagqira* in traditional Xhosa society. *Theoria*, 64, 77–83.

Dowson, T. A., Lewis-Williams, J. D. and Annegarn, H. J. 1994. *Contested images: Diversity in southern African rock art research*. Johannesburg: Wits University Press.

Dreyfus, H. L. and Rabinow, P. 1982. *Michel Foucault: Beyond structuralism and hermeneutics*. Chicago: University of Chicago Press.

Durkheim, É. 1995 [1912]. *The elementary forms of the religious life*. New York: The Free Press.

Du Toit, B. 1980. Religion, ritual and healing among urban black South Africans. *Urban Anthropology* 9, 21–49.

Eliade, M. 1961. *The sacred and the profane.* New York: Harper Torchbooks.

Eliade, M. 1963. *Myth and reality.* New York: Harper and Row.

Engelke, M. 2001. The idiom of spirit: Possession and *ngoma* in Africa. *African Affairs,* 100, 143–150.

Evans-Pritchard, E. E. 1937. *Witchcraft, oracles and magic among the Azande.* Oxford: Clarendon Press.

Fabian, J. 2014. Time and the other: *How anthropology makes its object.* New York: Columbia University Press.

Fadlon, J. 2004. Meridians, chakras and psycho-neuro-immunology: The dematerialising body and the domestication of alternative medicine. *Body and Society,* 10(4), 69–86.

Fafchamps, M. 2004. *Market institutions and sub-Saharan Africa: Theory and evidence,* Cambridge MA: Massachusetts Institute for Technology Press.

Farmer, P. 2006. *AIDS and accusation: Haiti and geography of blame.* Berkeley: University of California Press.

Feierman, S. 1981. Therapy as a system-in-action in northeastern Tanzania. *Social Science & Medicine,* 15, 353–360.

Finniss, D. G., Kaptchuk, T., Franklin Miller, J. and Benedetti, F. 2010. Biological, clinical, and ethical advances of placebo effects. *Lancet,* 375, 686–695.

Flint, K. E. 2008. *Healing traditions: African medicine, cultural exchange, and competition in South Africa, 1820–1948.* Pietermaritzburg: University of KwaZulu-Natal Press.

Fortes, M. and Evans-Pritchard, E. E. (eds). 1940. *African political systems.* Oxford: Oxford University Press.

Foucault, M. 1972. *The archaeology of knowledge.* New York: Harper Colophon.

Foucault, M. 1975. *The birth of the clinic: An archaeology of medical perception.* New York: Vintage, Random House.

Foucault, M. 1978. *The history of sexuality, Volume 1: Introduction.* Trans. M. Hurley. New York: Vintage Books, Random House.

Foucault, M. 2008. *The birth of biopolitics: Lectures at the Collège de France, 1978–1979.* New York: Palgrave Macmillan.

Frazer, J. G. 1922. *The golden bough: A study of magic and religion* (abridged edition). London: Macmillan.

Geertz, C. 1983. *Local knowledge: Further essays in interpretive anthropology.* New York: Basic Books.

Geschiere, P. 1997. *The modernity of witchcraft: Politics and the occult in postcolonial Africa.* Charlottesville: University of Virginia Press.

Githens, T. S. 1949. *Drug plants of Africa.* Philadelphia: University of Pennsylvania Press.

Glaser, B. G. and Strauss, A. 1999 [1967]. *The discovery of grounded theory: Strategies for qualitative research.* Chicago: Aldine.

Gleick, J. 2003. *Isaac Newton.* New York: Pantheon.

Gluckman, M. 1940. Analysis of a social situation in modern Zululand. *Bantu Studies*, 14, 1–30.

Gluckman, M. 1942. Some processes of social change illustrated from Zululand. *African Studies*, 1, 243–260.

Gluckman, M. 1960. *Custom and conflict in Africa*. Oxford: Blackwell.

Good, B. 1994. Medical anthropology and the problem of belief. In: B. Good (ed), *Medicine, rationality and experience: An anthropological perspective*. Cambridge: Cambridge University Press.

Gordon, C. (ed). 1980. *Power/knowledge: Selected interviews and other writing by Michel Foucault*. New York: Pantheon Books.

Gordon, R. J. 1988. *Robert Jacob Gordon: Cape travels, 1777 to 1786*, Brenthurst Second Series. Johannesburg: Brenthurst Press.

Government of the Republic of South Africa. 1957. Witchcraft Suppression Act 3 of 1957 as amended by Witchcraft Suppression Act 50 of 1970 and Abolition of Corporal Punishment Act 33 of 1997. *Government Gazette*.

Green, E. C. 1999. *Indigenous theory of contagious disease*. Walnut Creek: AltaMira/Sage.

Green, E. C., Thornton, R. J. and Sliep, Y. 2003. *Traditional healers and the bio-medical health system in South Africa*. Washington, DC: Medical Care Development International (MCDI) and the Margaret Sanger Center International, South Africa.

Green, E. C., Zokwe, B. and Dupree, J. D. 2000. The experience of an AIDS prevention program focused on South African traditional healers. *Social Science & Medicine*, 40, 503–515.

Grimaldo, E. R., Tupasi, T. E., Rivera, A. B., Quelapio, M. I., Cardaño, R. C., Derilo, J. O. and Belen, V. A. 2001. Increased resistance to ciprofloxacin and ofloxacin in multidrug-resistant mycobacterium tuberculosis isolates from patients seen at a tertiary hospital in the Philippines. *International Journal of Tuberculosis and Lung Disease*, 5, 546–550.

Hall, K. T., Loscalzo, J. and Kaptchuk, T. J. 2015. Genetics and the placebo effect: The placebome. *Trends in Molecular Medicine*, 21, 285–294.

Hamilton, A. 1971. The equivalence of siblings. *Anthropological Forum: A Journal of Social Anthropology and Comparative Sociology*, 3, 13–20.

Hammond-Tooke, W. D. 1975. The symbolic structure of Cape Nguni cosmology. In: M. G. Whisson and M. E. West (eds), *Religion and social change in southern Africa*. Cape Town: David Philip.

Hammond-Tooke, W. D. 1978. Do south eastern Bantu worship their ancestors? In: J. Argyle and E. Preston-Whyte (eds), *Social system and tradition in southern Africa*. Cape Town: Oxford University Press.

Hammond-Tooke, W. D. 1985. Who worships whom: Agnates and ancestors among Nguni. *African Studies*, 44, 47–64.

Hammond-Tooke, W. D. 1986. The aetiology of spirit in southern Africa. *African Studies*, 45, 157–170.

Hammond-Tooke, W. D. 1989. *Rituals and medicines: Indigenous healing in South Africa*. Johannesburg: Ad Donker.

Hammond-Tooke, W. D. 1994. *Creed and confession in South African ancestor religion, Margaret Shaw lecture*, Cape Town, South African Museum.

Hammond-Tooke, W. D. and Schapera, I. 1974. *The Bantu-speaking peoples of southern Africa*. London: Routledge & Kegan Paul.

Harries, P. 1981. The anthropologist as historian and liberal: H-A Junod and the Thonga. *Journal of Southern African Studies*, 8, 37–50.

Harries, P. 1989. Exclusion, classification and internal colonialism: The emergence of ethnicity among the Tsonga-speakers of South Africa. In: L. Vail (ed), *The creation of tribalism in southern Africa*. Oxford: James Currey.

Hirst, M. 1997. A river of metaphors: Interpreting the Xhosa diviner's myth In: P. McAllister (ed), *Culture and the commonplace: Anthropological essays in honour of David Hammond-Tooke*. Johannesburg: Wits University Press.

Hodder, I. and Mol, A. 2015. Network analysis and entanglement. *Journal of Archaeological Method and Theory*, 1–29.

Holub, E. 1881. *Seven years in South Africa: Travels, researches, and hunting adventures, between the diamond-fields and the Zambesi (1872–1879)*. London: S. Low, Marston, Searle & Rivington.

Huffman, T. 2007. Leokwe and K2: Ethnic stratification during the Middle Iron Age in southern Africa. *Journal of African Archaeology*, 5(2), 163–188.

Hutchings, A. 1996. *Zulu medicinal plants: An inventory*. Pietermaritzburg: University of KwaZulu-Natal Press and South African National Botanical Institute.

Ingold, T. 2011. *The perception of the environment: Essays on livelihood, dwelling and skill*. London: Routledge.

Ingold, T. 2012. The shape of the land. In: A. Árnason, N. Ellison, J. Vergunst and A. Whitehouse (eds), *Landscapes beyond land: Routes, aesthetics, narratives*. New York: Berghahn.

James, D. 2014a. 'Deeper into a hole?' Borrowing and lending in South Africa. *Current Anthropology*, 55, S17-S29.

James, D. 2014b. *Money from nothing: Indebtedness and aspiration in South Africa*, Stanford: Stanford University Press.

Janzen, J. M. 1978. *The quest for therapy: Medical pluralism in lower Zaire: Comparative studies in health systems and medical care*. Berkeley: University of California Press.

Janzen, J. M. 1987. Therapy management: Concept, reality, process. *Medical Anthropology Quarterly, New Series*, 1, 68–84.

Janzen, J. M. 1991. Doing *ngoma*: A dominant trope in African religion and healing. *Journal of Religion in Africa*, 21, 290–308.

Janzen, J. M. 1992. *Ngoma: Discourses of healing in central and southern Africa, Comparative studies of health systems and medical care*. Berkeley: University of California Press.

Janzen, J. M. and Feierman, S. (eds). 1992. *The social basis of health and healing in Africa*. Berkeley: University of California Press.

Jevons, W. S. 1876. *Money and the mechanism of exchange*. http://www.Econlib.Org/library/ypdbooks/jevons/jvnmme2.html.

Jevons, W. S. 1888 [1871]. *The theory of political economy*. http://www.Econlib.Org/library/ypdbooks/jevons/jvnpe3.html.

Jiroušková, J., Kandert, J., Mlíkovský, J. and Šámal, M. 2011. *Emil Holub's collection in the national museum, Editio Monographica Musei Nationalis Pragae*. Prague: National Museum.

Jung, C. G. 1972 [1956]. On the psychology of the trickster figure (A commentary). In: P. Radin, *The trickster: A study in American Indian mythology*. New York: Schocken.

Jung, C. G. 1981 [1959]. *Archetypes and the collective unconscious. The collected works of C. G. Jung*. Princeton: Princeton University Press.

Junod, H-A. 1912. *The life of a South African tribe*. Neuchatel: Attinger Frères.

Kirksey, S. E. 2010. The *umwelt* of an uncommon ant, *Estatomma ruidum*, through multispecies commodities and spectacles, Session: Natureculture. Annual Conference of the Society for Cultural Anthropology. La Fonda Hotel, Santa Fe, New Mexico, 7–11 May 2010.

Kirksey, S. E. 2015. *Emergent ecologies*. Durham NC: Duke University Press.

Kirksey, S. E. and Helmreich, S. 2010. The emergence of multispecies ethnography. *Cultural Anthropology*, 25, 545–576.

Kirsch, I. 2011. The placebo effect has come of age. *Journal of Mind–Body Regulation*, 1, 106–109.

Kleinman, A. 1973a. Some issues for a comparative study of medical healing. *International Journal of Social Psychiatry*, 19, 159–165.

Kleinman, A. 1973b. Toward a comparative study of medical systems: An integrated approach to the study of the relational between medicine and culture. *Science, Medicine and Man*, 1, 55–65.

Kleinman, A. 2010. The art of medicine: Four social theories for global health. *The Lancet*, 374, 1518–1519.

Kleinman, A., Das, V. and Lock, M. (eds). 1997. *Social suffering*. Berkeley: University of California Press.

Kleinman, A., Eisenberg, L. and Good, B. 2006 [1978]. Culture, illness, and care: Clinical lessons from anthropologic and cross-cultural research. *Focus: The Journal of Lifelong Learning in Psychiatry*, 4, 140–149.

Knight, C. 2008. Early human kinship was matrilineal. In: N. J. Allen, H. Callan, R. Dunbar and W. James (eds), *Early human kinship*. Oxford: Wiley-Blackwell.

Koorbanally, N., Mulholland, D. A. and Crouch, N. 2000. Alkaloids and triterpenoids from *Ammocharis coranica* (Amaryllidaceae). *Phytochemistry*, 54, 93–97.

Kresse, K. 2007. *Philosophising in Mombasa: Knowledge, Islam and intellectual practice on the Swahili coast*. Edinburgh: Edinburgh University Press.

Krige, E. J. 1950. *The social systems of the Zulus.* Pietermaritzburg: Shuter & Shooter.

Krige, E. J. and Krige, J. D. 1943. *The realm of a rain queen: A study of the pattern of Lovedu society.* Oxford: Oxford University Press.

Krige, J. D. 1944. The magical thought-pattern of the Bantu in relation to health services. *African Studies,* 3, 1–13.

Kruger, J. S. 1995. *Along edges: Religion in South Africa: Bushmen, Christian, Buddhist.* Pretoria: University of South Africa Press.

Kuper, H. 1947. *An African aristocracy: Rank among the Swazi.* Oxford: Oxford University Press.

Landau, P. S. 1993. When rain falls: Rainmaking and community in a Tswana village, ca. 1870 to recent times. *The International Journal of African Historical Studies,* 26, 1–30.

Landau, P. S. 2010. *Popular politics in the history of South Africa, 1400–1948.* Cambridge: Cambridge University Press.

Langdon, E. J. 2007a. Shamans and shamanism: Reflections on anthropological dilemmas of modernity. *Vibrant: Virtual Brazilian Anthropology,* 4, 27–48.

Langdon, E. J. 2007b. The symbolic efficacy of rituals: From ritual to performance. *Antropologia em Primeira Mao,* 95, 1–39.

Langlitz, N, 2011. Alien forms of life. *BioSocieties,* 6, 324–365.

Langwick, S. A. 2011. *Bodies, politics, and African healing: The matter of maladies in Tanzania.* Bloomington: Indiana University Press.

Langwick, S. A. 2015. Partial publics: The political promise of traditional medicine in Africa. *Current Anthropology,* 56, 493–514.

Last, M. 1986. The professionalisation of African medicine: Ambiguities and definitions. In: M. Last and G. Chavanduka (eds), *The professionalisation of African medicine.* Manchester: Manchester University Press.

Last, M. and Chavanduka, G. (eds). 1986. *The professionalisation of African medicine.* Manchester: Manchester University Press.

Latour, B. 2014. From ontology to deontology: General anthropology division distinguished lecture 2013. *General Anthropology,* 21, 1–4.

Legg, C. 2010. *An ethnography of adults living with aphasia in Khayelitsha.* Unpublished PhD thesis, University of the Witwatersrand.

Leibniz, G. W. 1951 [1710]. *Theodicity: Essays on the goodness of God, the freedom of Man and the origin of evil.* Trans. E. M. Huggard. London: Routledge and Kegan Paul.

Lévi-Strauss, C. 1966. *The Savage Mind.* Chicago: University of Chicago Press.

Lévi-Strauss, C. 1978. *Myth and meaning.* Abingdon: Routledge & Kegan Paul.

Lewis-Williams, J. D. 1981. *Believing and seeing: Symbolic meanings in southern San rock paintings, Studies in anthropology.* London: Academic Press.

Lewis-Williams, J. D. 1996. *Discovering African rock art.* Cape Town: David Philip.

Lewis-Williams, J. D. 2002. *The mind in the cave: Consciousness and the origins of art.* London: Thames & Hudson.

Lewis-Williams, J. D. and Challis, S. 2011. *Deciphering ancient minds: The mystery of San Bushman rock art.* London: Thames & Hudson.

Lewis-Williams, J. D. and Pearce, D. G. 2012. The southern San and the trance dance: A pivotal debate in the interpretation of San rock paintings. *Antiquity*, 86, 696–706.

Lichtenstein, H. and Plumtre, A. 1812 [1928]. *Travels in southern Africa in the years 1803, 1804, 1805 and 1806.* Cape Town: Van Riebeeck Society.

Lindenbaum, S. and Lock, M. 1993. *Knowledge, power and practice: The anthropology of medicine in everyday life.* Berkeley: University of California Press.

Livingstone, D. 1857. *Missionary travels and researches in South Africa.* London: J. Murray.

Livingstone, J. 2012. *Improvising medicine: An African oncology ward in an emerging cancer epidemic.* Durham NC: Duke University Press.

Louw, S. 1990. The life history and immature stages of *Brachycerus ornatus drury* (Coleoptera: Curculionidae). *Journal of the Entomological Society of Southern Africa*, 53, 27–40.

Low, C. 2004. *Khoisan healing: Understandings, ideas and practices.* Unpublished D. Phil thesis, Oxford University.

MacGaffey, W. 2002. Ethnographic notes on Kongo musical instruments. *African Arts*, 35, 12–19+90.

Machiavelli, N. 1998 [1513]. *The prince.* Chicago: University of Chicago Press.

Maclean, U. 1982. The WHO programme for the integration of traditional medicine. In: C. Fyfe and U. Maclean (eds), *African medicine in the modern world.* Edinburgh: Edinburgh University Press.

Malinowski, B. 1935. *Coral gardens and their magic: A study of the methods of tilling the soil and of agricultural rites in the Trobriand islands.* London: Allen & Unwin.

Malinowski, B. 1993 [1915]. A fundamental question of religious sociology. In: R. J. Thornton and P. Skalník (eds), *The early writings of Bronislaw Malinowski.* Cambridge: Cambridge University Press, 243–246.

Mason, L. H., Puschett, E. R. and Wildman, W. C. 1955. Alkaloids of the Amaryllidaceae. Iv. Crystalline alkaloids of *Ammocharis coranica* (ker-gawl.) herb., *Brunsvigia rosea* (lam.) Hannibal and two crinum species. *Journal of the American Chemical Society*, 77, 1253–1256.

Mauss, M. 1985 [1938]. A category of the human mind: The notion of person, the notion of self. In: M. Carrithers, S. Collins and S. Lukes (eds), *The category of the person: Anthropology, philosophy, history.* Cambridge: Cambridge University Press.

Mbiti, J. 1975. *Introduction of African religion.* London: Heinemann.

Mbiti, J. 1990. *African religions and philosophy.* Oxford: Heinemann Educational Publishers.

Meintjes, E. 2004. Shoot the sergeant, shatter the mountain: The production of masculinity in Zulu *Ngoma* song and dance in post-apartheid South Africa. *Ethnomusicology Forum*, 13, 173–201.

Michler, B. J. 2003. *Biographical study of H-A. Junod: The fictional dimension.* Unpublished MA dissertation, University of Pretoria.

Milne-Redhead, E. and Schweickerdt, H. G. 1939. A new conception of the genus *Ammocharis* herb. *Journal of the Linnaean Society of London, Botany,* 52, 159–197.

Mkhwanazi, N. 2015. Medical anthropology in Africa: The trouble with a single story. *Medical Anthropology* 35(2): 193–202

Moatshe, R. 2015. Incensed healers in aromatic protest. *IOL News,* 11 December. http://www.iol.co.za/news/south-africa/gauteng/incensed-healers-in-aromatic-protest-1959143.

Moffat, R. 1846 [1842]. *Missionary labours and scenes in southern Africa.* London: John Snow.

Mönnig, H. O. 1967. *The Pedi.* Pretoria: Van Schaik.

Morris, D. R. N. M. 2002. *Driekopseiland and 'the rain's magic power': History and landscape in a new interpretation of a Northern Cape rock engraving site.* Unpublished MA dissertation, University of the Western Cape.

Mthethwa, B. 2015. Sangomas reject health minister's 'un-African' prescription. *Sunday Times,* 13 December.

Muller, M. 1866. *Lectures on the science of language delivered at the Royal Institution of Great Britain in April, May, June of 1861.* London: Longmans, Green & Co.

Myburgh, A. C. 1949. *The tribes of Barberton district.* Pretoria: Government Printer, Department of Native Affairs.

Neuwinger, H. D. 1996. *African ethnobotany: Poisons and drugs.* London: Chapman & Hill.

Neuwinger, H. D. and Mebs, D. 1997. *Boophane disticha.* Eine halluzinogene pflanze Afrikas. *Deutsch Apoteker-Zeitung,* 137, 1127–1132.

Newton, I. 2004 [ca. 1670s–1680s]. Untitled treatise on revelation (Section 1.1). http://www.Newtonproject.Sussex.Ac.Uk/view/texts/normalized/them00135. *The Newton Project:* http://www.newtonproject.sussex.ac.uk/prism.php?id=1.

Ngubane, H. 1977. *Body and mind in Zulu medicine: An ethnography of health and disease in Nyuswa-Zulu thought and practice.* London: Academic Press.

Ngubane, H. 1981. Aspects of clinical practice and traditional organization of indigenous healers in South Africa. *Social Science & Medicine, Part B,* 15, 361–365.

Nguyen, V-K. 2010. *The republic of therapy: Triage and sovereignty in West Africa's time of AIDS.* Durham NC: Duke University Press.

Niehaus, I. A. 1998. The ANC's dilemma: The symbolic politics of three witch-hunts in the south African Lowveld, 1990–1995. *African Studies Review,* 41, 93–118.

Niehaus, I. A. 2005. Witches and zombies of the South African Lowveld: Discourse, accusations and subjective reality. *Journal of the Royal Anthropological Institute,* 11, 191–210.

Niehaus, I. A. 2013. *Witchcraft and a life in the new South Africa.* Cambridge: Cambridge University Press.

Niehaus, I. A., Mohlala, E. and Shokane, K. 2001. *Witchcraft, power, and politics: Exploring the occult in the South African Lowveld*. London: Pluto Press.

Nordal, I. 1982. Amaryllidaceae. In: R. M. Polhill (ed), *Flora of tropical East Africa*. Rotterdam: Balkema.

Nortje, J. M. 2011. *Medical ethnobotany of the Kamiesberg, Namaqualand, Northern Cape province, South Africa*. Unpublished MSc dissertation, University of Johannesburg.

Nyamongo, I. K. 2002. Health care switching behaviour of malaria patients in a Kenyan rural community. *Social Science & Medicine*, 54, 377–386.

Orwell, G. 1945. *Animal farm: A fairy story*. London: Secker & Warburg.

Özden-Schilling, C. 2016. The infrastructure of markets: From electric power to electronic data. *Economic Anthropology*, 3, 68–80.

Pascoe, F. P. 1887. Description for some new species of *Brachycerus*. *Transactions of the Royal Entomological Society of London*, 35, 7–18.

Pedersen, I. K. and Baarts, C. 2010. 'Fantastic hands' – but no evidence: The construction of expertise by users of CAM. *Social Science & Medicine*, 71, 1068–1075.

Pels, P. 1996. Kizungu rhythms: Luguru Christianity as *ngoma*. *Journal of Religion in Africa*, 26, 163–201.

Picker, M., Griffiths, C. J. and Weaving, J. 2004. *Field guide to insects of South Africa*. Cape Town: Struik/Random House.

Pole-Evans, I. B. 1938. *Ammocharis coranica. Flowering Plants of South Africa*, 18, 712.

Pool, R. 1994. On the creation and dissolution of ethnomedical systems in the medical ethnography of Africa. *Africa*, 64, 1–20.

Porter, N. 2013. Bird flu biopower: Strategies for multispecies coexistence in Vietnam. *American Anthropologist*, 40, 132–148.

Pratt, J. P. 2004. Daniel's prophecy foretells date of crucifixion. *Meridian Magazine*, September 15. http://www.johnpratt.com/items/docs/lds/meridian/2004/daniel.html.

Radcliffe-Brown, A. R. 1952. *Structure and function in primitive society*. London: Cohen & West.

Radin, P. 1972 [1956]. *The trickster: A study in American Indian mythology*. New York: Schocken.

Reis, R. 2002. Medical pluralism and the bounding of traditional healing in Swaziland. In: W. Ernst (ed), *Plural medicine, tradition and modernity, 1800–2000*. London: Routledge.

Richter, M. 2003. *Traditional medicines and traditional healers in South Africa*. Johannesburg: AIDS Law Project and Treatment Action Campaign.

Robertson-Smith, W. 1927 [1894]. *Lectures on the religion of the Semites: The fundamental institutions*. New York: Macmillan.

Rock Art Research Unit. 2012. The South African rock art digital archive: www.sarda.co.za

Rodima-Taylor, D. and Bähre, E. 2014. Introduction: Mutual help in an era of uncertainty. *Africa*, 84, 507–509.

Rowlands, M. J. and Warnier, J-P. 1993. The magical production of iron in the Cameroon grasslands. In: T. Shaw, P. Sinclair, B. Andah and A. Okpoko (eds), *The archaeology of Africa: Food metals and towns*. London: Routledge.

Rycroft, D. K. 1981. *Concise siSwati dictionary*. Pretoria: Van Schaik.

Sahlins, M. D. 1972. *Stone age economics*. Chicago: Aldine-Atherton.

Sandager, M., Nielsen, N. D., Stafford, G. I., Van Staden, J. and Jäger, A. K. 2005. Alkaloids from *Boophane disticha* with affinity to the serotonin transporter in rat brain. *Journal of Ethnopharmacology*, 98, 367–370.

Schapera, I. 1957. *Married life in an African tribe*. London: Faber.

Schlosser, A. V. and Ninnemann, K. 2012. Introduction to the special section: The anthropology of psychopharmaceuticals: Cultural and pharmacological efficacies in context. *Culture, Medicine and Psychiatry*, 36, 2–9.

Schwemmer, D. 2011. Magic ritual: Conceptualisation and performance. In: K. Radner and E. Robson (eds), *The Oxford handbook of cuneiform culture*. Oxford: Oxford University Press.

Setiloane, G. M. 1973. Modimo: God among the Sotho-Tswana. *Journal of Theology for Southern Africa*, 4, 6–17.

Setiloane, G. M. 1976. *The image of God among the Sotho-Tswana*. Rotterdam: A. A. Balkema.

Setiloane, G. M. 1986. *African theology*. Johannesburg: Skotaville Press.

Silverstein, M. 1993. Metapragmatic discourse and metapragmatic function. In: J. Lucy (ed), *Reflexive language: Reported speech and metapragmatics*. Cambridge: Cambridge University Press.

Statistics South Africa (Stats SA). 2017. Umjindi. http://www.statssa.gov.za/?page_id=993&id=umjindi-municipality.

Skead, C. J. 2009. Historical plant incidence in southern Africa, *Strelitzia 24*. Pretoria: South African National Biodiversity Institute.

Smith, A. 1904 [1776–1789]. *An inquiry into the nature and causes of the wealth of nations*. London: Methuen.

Smith, A. 1984 [1759]. *The theory of moral sentiments*. Indianapolis: Liberty Fund.

Smith, B. W. and Ouzman, S. 2004. Taking stock: Identifying Khoekhoen herder rock art in southern Africa. *Current Anthropology*, 45, 499–526.

Smith, E. W. 1929. *The secret of the African: Lectures on African religion*. London: United Society for Christian Literature.

Sobiecki, J-F. 2014. Psychoactive plants: A neglected area of ethnobotanical research in southern Africa. *Ethno Medicine*, 8, 65–172.

Stow, G. W. and Theal, G. M. 1905. *The native races of south Africa: A history of the intrusion of the Hottentots and Bantu into the hunting grounds of the Bushmen, the aborigines of the country*. London: Macmillan.

Strathern, M. 1988. *Gender of the gift*. Cambridge: Cambridge University Press.

Sujatha, V. and Abraham, L. (eds). 2012. *Medical pluralism in contemporary India.* Hyderabad: Orient BlackSwan.

Sundkler, B. G. M. 1948. *Bantu prophets in South Africa.* London: Lutterworth Press.

Tambiah, S. J. 1968. The magical power of words (the Malinowski memorial lecture delivered at the London School of Economics on 20 February 1968). *Man,* 3, 175–208.

Thornton, R. J. 1987. Culture: A contemporary definition. In: E. Boonzaier and J. Sharp (eds), *South African keywords.* Cape Town: David Philip.

Thornton, R. J. 1994. South Africa: Countries, boundaries, enemies and friends. *Anthropology Today,* 10, 7–15.

Thornton, R. J. 1995. The colonial, the imperial, and the creation of the 'European' in southern Africa. In: J. Carrier (ed), *Occidentalism: Images of the West.* Oxford: Clarendon Press.

Thornton, R. J. 1996a. Malinowski and the birth of functionalism or, Zarathustra in the London School of Economics. *The Study of Time,* 8, 251.

Thornton, R. J. 1996b. The potentials of boundaries in South Africa: Steps towards a theory of the social edge. *Postcolonial Identities in Africa,* 136–161.

Thornton, R. J. 2000a. Ethnicity and the geometry of power: The aesthetics of ethnicity in the imagination of the polity. *Critical Arts,* 14, 16–43.

Thornton, R. J. 2000b. The landscape: Land and landscapes in contemporary South Africa. In: P. Skalnik (ed), *Sociocultural anthropology at the turn of the century: Voices from the periphery.* Prague: Set Out.

Thornton, R. J. 2001. South Africa: Sociocultural aspects. *International Encyclopedia of the Behavioural and Social Sciences.* Amsterdam: Elsevier.

Thornton, R. J. 2002. Environment and land in Bushbuckridge, South Africa. In: L. Zarsky (ed), *Human rights and the environment: Conflicts and norms in a globalizing world.* London: Earthscan Publications.

Thornton, R. J. 2003. Traditional healers and bio-medical practice: Prospects and barriers to co-operation. *Adler Museum Bulletin,* 29, 8–16.

Thornton, R. J. 2008. *Unimagined community: Sex, networks, and AIDS in Uganda and South Africa.* Berkeley: University of California Press.

Thornton, R. J. 2010. The market for healing and the elasticity of belief: Medical pluralism in Mpumalanga, South Africa. In: M. Dekker and R. van Dijk (eds), *Markets of well-being: Navigating health and healing in Africa.* Leiden: E. J. Brill.

Thornton, R. J. 2012a. Magical empiricism and the 'exposed being' in public health and traditional healing. Workshop: 'The (un)healthy body in southern Africa'. Wits Reproductive Health and HIV Institute. Johannesburg: Unpublished.

Thornton, R. J. 2012b. Traditional authority and governance in the Emjindini Royal Swazi chiefdom, Barberton, Mpumalanga. In: D. I. Ray, T. Quinlan, K. Sharma and T. O. Clarke (eds), *Reinventing African chieftaincy in the age of AIDS, gender, governance and development.* Calgary: University of Calgary Press.

Thornton, R. J. and Skalník, P. 1993. *The early writings of Bronislaw Malinowski*. Cambridge: Cambridge University Press.

Turner, V. W. 1964. An Ndembu doctor in practice. In: A. Kiev (ed), *Magic, faith and healing*. Glencoe IL: The Free Press.

Turner, V. W. 1968. *The drums of affliction: A study of religious processes among the Ndembu of Zambia*. Oxford: Clarendon.

Turner, V. W. 1969. *The ritual process: Structure and anti-structure, The Lewis Henry Morgan Lectures*. Chicago: Aldine.

Turner, V. W. 1995. *The ritual process: Structure and anti-structure, The Lewis Henry Morgan Lectures*. New York: Aldine de Gruyter.

Tutu, D. 1999. *No future without forgiveness*. New York: Doubleday.

Van Binsbergen, W. 1991. Becoming a sangoma: Religious anthropological fieldwork in Francistown, Botswana. *Journal of Religion in Africa*, 21(4), 309–344.

Van Binsbergen, W. 2005. We are in it for the money: Commodification and the sangoma cult in southern Africa. In: W. van Binsbergen and P. Geschiere (eds), *Commodification: Things, agency, and identities: 'The social life of things' revisited*. Berlin: Münster Lit Verlag.

Van Dijk, R., Reis, R. and Spierenburg, M. (eds). 2000. *The quest for fruition through Ngoma: Political aspects of healing in southern Africa*. Athens OH: Ohio University Press.

Van Wyk, B-E. and Gericke, N. 2007. *People's plants: A useful guide to plants of southern Africa*. Pretoria: Briza.

Van Wyk, I. 2014. *The Universal Church of the Kingdom of God in South Africa: A church of strangers*. Cambridge: Cambridge University Press.

Wagner, D. R. 2012. Not just pretty: *Euphorbia clavarioides in Johannesburg's muti market*. Cactus and Succulent Journal, 84(1), 4–7.

Wainaina, B. 2005. How to write about Africa. *Granta*, 92, 92–94.

Waldram, J. B. 2000. The efficacy of traditional medicine: Current theoretical and methodological issues. *Medical Anthropology Quarterly*, 14, 603–625.

Watt, J. M. 1967. African plants potentially useful in mental health. *Lloydia*, 30, 1–22.

Watt, J. M. and Breyer-Brandwijk, M. G. 1962. *The medicinal and poisonous plants of southern and eastern Africa, being an account of their medicinal and other uses, chemical composition, pharmacological effects and toxicology in man and animal*. Edinburgh: E. & S. Livingstone.

Weber, M. 1952. [1917–1919]. *Ancient Judaism*. Glencoe IL: The Free Press.

Weber, M. 1978. *Economy and society: An outline of interpretive sociology*. Berkeley: University of California Press.

Werbner, R. 2015. *Divination's grasp: African encounters with the almost said*, Bloomington: Indiana University Press.

West, M. E. 1975. *Bishops and prophets in a black city: African independent churches in Soweto*. Cape Town: David Philip.

White, H. 2016. The materiality of marriage payments. *Anthropology Southern Africa*, 39, 297–308.

Wiley, A. S. and Allen, J. S. 2013. *Medical anthropology: A biocultural approach*. Oxford: Oxford University Press.

Willerslev, R. 2007. *Soul hunters: Hunting, animism, and personhood among the Siberian Yukaghirs*. Berkeley: University of California Press.

Williams, R. 1977. *Marxism and literature*. Oxford: Oxford University Press.

Wilson, M. H. 1936. *Reaction to conquest: Effects of contact with Europeans on the Pondo of South Africa*. Oxford: Oxford University Press.

Wilson, M. H. 1951. Witch beliefs and social structure. *American Journal of Sociology*, 56, 307–313.

Wittgenstein, L. 1952. *Philosophical investigations*. Oxford: Blackwell.

Wolf, E. 1982. *Europe and the people without history*. Berkeley: University of California Press.

Wood, K and Lambert, H. 2008. Coded talk, scripted omissions: The micropolitics of AIDS talk in an affected community in South Africa. *Medical Anthropology Quarterly*, 22, 213–233.

Wood, M. 2000. Making connections: Relationships between international trade and glass beads from the Shashe–Limpopo area. *Goodwin Series*, 8, 78–90.

World Health Organization. 2002. *WHO traditional medicine strategy, 2002–2005*. Geneva: World Health Organization, United Nations.

Wreford, J. 2005. Negotiating relationships between biomedicine and sangoma: Fundamental misunderstandings, avoidable mistakes. CSSR Working Paper No. 138. Cape Town: Centre for Social Science Research, University of Cape Town.

Wreford, J. 2008. *Working with spirit: Experiencing izangoma healing in contemporary South Africa, Epistemologies of healing*. Oxford: Berghahn.

Yoder, P. S. 1982. Issues in the study of ethnomedical systems in Africa. In: P. S. Yoder (ed), *African health and healing systems*. Los Angeles: Crossroads Press.

Index

Printed and bound by CPI Group (UK) Ltd, Croydon, CR0 4YY

09/06/2025

14685802-0001